IMMORTALITY, INC.

ALSO BY THIS AUTHOR

IMMORTALITY, INC.

RENEGADE SCIENCE,
SILICON VALLEY BILLIONS,
AND THE QUEST TO LIVE FOREVER

CHIP WALTER

NATIONAL
GEOGRAPHIC

WASHINGTON, D.C.

Published by National Geographic Partners, LLC
1145 17th Street NW, Washington, DC 20036

Library of Congress Cataloging-in-Publication Data
Names: Walter, Chip, author.
Title: Immortality, Inc. : renegade science, silicon valley billions and the quest
        to live forever / Chip Walter.
Description: Washington, D.C. : National Geographic, [2020] | Includes
        bibliographical references and index.
Identifiers: LCCN 2019012360 (print) | LCCN 2019013535 (ebook) | ISBN
        9781426219801 (trade hardback)
Subjects: LCSH: Immortality. | Longevity. | Life spans (Biology)--Research. |
        Medical technology--Research.
Classification: LCC QP85 .W318 2020 (print) | LCC QP85 (ebook) | DDC
    612.6/8--dc23
LC record available at https://lccn.loc.gov/2019012360
LC ebook record available at https://lccn.loc.gov/2019013535

Since 1888, the National Geographic Society has funded more than 13,000 research, exploration, and preservation projects around the world. National Geographic Partners distributes a portion of the funds it receives from your purchase to National Geographic Society to support programs including the conservation of animals and their habitats.

Get closer to National Geographic explorers and photographers, and connect with our global community. Join us today at nationalgeographic.com/join

For information about special discounts for bulk purchases, please contact National Geographic Books Special Sales: specialsales@natgeo.com

For rights or permissions inquiries, please contact National Geographic Books Subsidiary Rights: bookrights@natgeo.com

Interior design: Nicole Miller

Printed in the United States of America

19/BVG-CG/1

To the FamSquad:
My north, my south,
my east, my west . . . forever

In Memoriam:
Tom Wolfe, the wizard of words

CONTENTS

Death be not proud, though some have called thee

Mighty and dreadfull, for, thou art not soe,

. . . .

One short sleepe past, wee wake eternally,

And death shall be no more, death thou shalt die.

—JOHN DONNE, HOLY SONNET X

CAST OF CHARACTERS

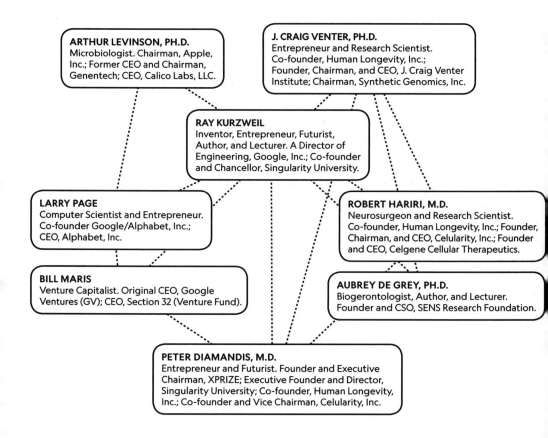

ARTHUR LEVINSON, PH.D.
Microbiologist. Chairman, Apple, Inc.; Former CEO and Chairman, Genentech; CEO, Calico Labs, LLC.

J. CRAIG VENTER, PH.D.
Entrepreneur and Research Scientist. Co-founder, Human Longevity, Inc.; Founder, Chairman, and CEO, J. Craig Venter Institute; Chairman, Synthetic Genomics, Inc.

RAY KURZWEIL
Inventor, Entrepreneur, Futurist, Author, and Lecturer. A Director of Engineering, Google, Inc.; Co-founder and Chancellor, Singularity University.

LARRY PAGE
Computer Scientist and Entrepreneur. Co-founder Google/Alphabet, Inc.; CEO, Alphabet, Inc.

ROBERT HARIRI, M.D.
Neurosurgeon and Research Scientist. Co-founder, Human Longevity, Inc.; Founder, Chairman, and CEO, Celularity, Inc.; Founder and CEO, Celgene Cellular Therapeutics.

BILL MARIS
Venture Capitalist. Original CEO, Google Ventures (GV); CEO, Section 32 (Venture Fund).

AUBREY DE GREY, PH.D.
Biogerontologist, Author, and Lecturer. Founder and CSO, SENS Research Foundation.

PETER DIAMANDIS, M.D.
Entrepreneur and Futurist. Founder and Executive Chairman, XPRIZE; Executive Founder and Director, Singularity University; Co-founder, Human Longevity, Inc.; Co-founder and Vice Chairman, Celularity, Inc.

PROLOGUE: NEVER SAY DIE

The idea that people like you and me might manage to live outrageously long lives first struck me several years ago, when Ralph Merkle and I were having lunch and he mentioned he planned to be frozen when he died. I looked across the table, put my fork down, and folded my hands.

"Really," I said.

"Yeah," said Merkle, cheerily.

Merkle was a witty and affable polymath who was not only one of the world's experts in nanotechnology, but also the co-inventor of the key encryption technology used for credit card transactions over the internet. His plan was that he would be slipped into one of several stainless steel canisters at the Alcor Life Extension Foundation in Scottsdale, Arizona, so that, sometime in the future, he could be brought back to life.

Alcor is one of three places in the world that specialize in freezing the faithfully departed. The process requires a series of complex medical procedures that result in its denizens being slowly cooled to a temperature of minus 310°F. That, said Merkle, was where he, and the rest of Alcor's clients, would remain—until science divined how to bring them all, entirely whole, back to the future.

"You know how in lab experiments you have the 'experimental' animal and the 'control' animal?" Merkle asked me.

"Yes," I said.

"The control is left alone, and the experimental animal is the subject of the test, right?"

I nodded.

"Well," said Merkle, "in this case I'm obviously the experimental animal. Maybe I'll be reanimated. Maybe not. But I already *know* what happens to the controls."

Long and pregnant pause.

"They *all* die."

I EVENTUALLY VISITED ALCOR, and I confess it made me wonder. Maybe science *could* find a way to pull off some sort of end run on death. But I also sensed a problem, and it had to do with the Big Wait. The rejuvenation of Alcor's occupants required that their animation be suspended. Their hearts had to stop before they could be slipped into their chilly thermoses. That was the law. Even if they could be safely frozen, reviving them would still require, at some unknown point, not only resuscitating their damaged bodies but also rewinding their biological clocks. Otherwise they would return no better off than they had been when they first departed. And what good was that?

This, it seemed to me, made Alcor's approach what you might call plan B, but not plan A. Plan A was to avoid death in the first place, solve what killed you *before* you passed through the veil. Who wanted the Big Wait? Put another way, Alcor didn't really solve *the* fundamental problem of curing the one thing that got us all (assuming something else didn't get us first): aging.

Where was the solution to that?

So I began digging deeper. I can get to the bottom of this as well as anyone, I thought. Wasn't I a science author and documentary filmmaker, a National Geographic grantee who had also been a CNN bureau chief? All I had to do was formulate the right questions, hunt down the best people to ask, and then come up with a scintillating way to unfold the story.

Simple.

Except it wasn't.

I pillaged the internet and rifled through armloads of books. I explored the fields of geriatrics and gerontology (there is a difference) and reviewed research being done at the National Institutes of Health, including the National Institute on Aging. I investigated Earth's so-called Blue Zones, the places where people live unusually long. Blearily, I scoured actuarial tables and found that Americans, even though nearly 70 percent were overweight, had, during the past 120 years, somehow been doing an otherwise exemplary job of extending their life spans. As of 2015 the average American lived 78.7 years; in 1900 the number was 48. And yet, although we might be living longer, it didn't seem we were necessarily living better; the last years of life were often costly, long on suffering, and short on quality.

Despite this news, the mainstream media said still longer lives lie ahead. Books, magazines, and the internet were swimming in hype about diets, fitness regimens, and cosmetic procedures that could make one live longer, look better, stay stronger. Between 2013 and 2015, *Time, National Geographic, Scientific American,* and the *Atlantic* published cover stories proclaiming that living well past 100 years was just around the bend.

About the same time, I came across a Pew Research Center study entitled *Living to 120 and Beyond*. I tracked down the authors and found that baby boomers were especially fond of the idea of longer lives. Boomers made up the generation of humans bookended between the ages of 50 and 68. I was familiar with those people. I was a boomer myself. It turned out they were busy spending billions of dollars annually not only to extend their lives but to extend the quality of their extended lives. Name the drug, diet, supplement, exercise, or scientific breakthrough that might broaden the distance between boomers and the grim reaper, and they were buying it by the boatload. Not that they were the only ones. Everyone, even millennials, it seemed, loved the idea of remaining indefinitely youthful.

DESPITE OUR FASCINATION WITH YOUTH, the very idea that we can live forever strikes the brain as fundamentally silly, even wrong. When I would bring the subject up with friends or relatives, there was always a knowing rolling of the eyes: "Oh, pulleeeze, when I get old, just shoot me!" Or sometimes, "I've told my kids that when I can't remember their names, it's time for the Lethal Cocktail."

"Right," I would answer. "But what if you didn't *have* to grow old? What if science somehow found a way to roll back the clock and restore you to your best physical and mental self?"

Well, *that* was a different story.

But then, didn't other trouble await if everyone lived hundreds of years? Surely we would all be facing some Soylent

Green, dystopian world, stacked in urban silos living hollow-eyed, cheek by jowl. If that happened, wasn't it also inevitable that we soon would burn the planet to a cinder? And by the way, isn't this living super-long stuff for the rich only? A bunch of selfish, well-heeled, white, male, baby boomers who are looking down the barrel of their own mortality and not caring much for the view? Besides, who wanted to live in a future they might not understand—one bereft of family and friends who had failed to make everlasting muster? Death is a blessing! It gives life meaning! One *New York Times* opinion writer even called the drive for an extended life fundamentally "inhuman."

Others, however, saw the end of aging as a great blessing. Let's be honest, they said, getting old isn't the warm and fuzzy fairy tale we make it out to be. It grinds people down. Bit by bit we are robbed of our strength and spirit. We grow up, dream, work, slow down, and then watch the cells in our bodies clatter and fall apart like a battered car. Who enjoyed watching the people they loved grow weak and weary until one day they blipped out? And who wanted to *be* that person, someday?

Wouldn't a youthful life—five, even 10 times longer—be an upgrade? Wouldn't we grow wiser, build on our mistakes and knowledge, and become better friends, parents, workers—just better people? And wouldn't that collective wisdom enable us to learn from the wars and mayhem we seem to constantly repeat? How much more would Leonardo da Vinci, William Shakespeare, or Marie Curie have changed the world with a few additional centuries under their belts?

But more than anything, I wondered who among us—if we were truly handed the opportunity for a longer, healthier life—would say, "No, thanks. Today, I'm done. Take me now."

In the end, you could argue that the debates were all useless anyhow—because when I looked up from all my research, so far as I could tell 100 percent of the human race was still headed to the grave. Not one of my investigations and ruminations had revealed even a single major scientific breakthrough that might fundamentally change the long and mortal landscape of aging and death. Maybe, I thought, science didn't have a clue after all, and we were all doomed to spend the final stages of our existence blathering around the assisted living facility checking our name tags to recall who we were, and not a thing to be done about it.

Then came news. The announcement on September 18, 2013, of a corporation called Calico, funded largely by Google. "We're tackling aging," was the way the company put it, "one of life's great mysteries." Google? Now *that* was worth looking into. And just as intriguing was the news that Arthur D. Levinson had been asked to lead the company. Most people wouldn't have known Levinson if they tripped over him, but he was a force in Silicon Valley. He was the chairman of Apple, and just a year earlier had chaired Genentech, two of Silicon Valley's most storied early start-ups. When news of Calico hit the wires, the media snapped to. "Google vs. Death"—that was how *Time* magazine put it.

There is always a watershed moment that precedes any truly fundamental change in the human story. Calico's founding, I felt, might mark that moment. The very idea that a company with pockets as deep as Google's, and a leader with Levinson's pedigree, had chosen to undertake something that for so long seemed crazy, made it instantly *not*. This wasn't snake oil or mumbo jumbo; it wasn't even a few million federal or foundation dollars being thrown at a handful of scientists hoping against hope for some staggering breakthrough. This was hundreds of millions of dollars stoking the engines of a team capable of tackling really big, complex biological problems.

Then, just a few months after news of Calico emerged, another company rose up determined to take on aging: Human Longevity, Inc. (HLI). With a first-round investment of $70 million in March 2014, this venture didn't have Google in its financial pocket, but it was seeded by an impressive list of Silicon Valley investors. And at the helm it had J. Craig Venter, a scientist who, in the late 1990s, had found a quicker and better way to sequence the human genome, an approach that goosed the federal government's slower effort (and ruffled no end of feathers in the process). Today, the completion of the Human Genome Project remains one of the most important scientific advancements in human history. With Human Longevity, Inc., Venter said he wanted to focus his genomic expertise on extending a "high-performance" human life span.

Central to HLI's creation was one of the company's co-founders, a surgeon, researcher, and serial entrepreneur named Robert Hariri. Over the previous 15 years, Hariri had quietly become among the world's leading experts in cellular therapeutics, and the first to realize that stem cells supplied by the human placenta might deliver an entirely new way to safely extend life.

The sudden emergence of these two companies made me wonder. Why them? Why now? And that brought me to Raymond Kurzweil. Kurzweil isn't a microbiologist or expert in genomics or even a biologist: He is an engineer, inventor, and futurist, one of the world's best known. I had interviewed him several times over the years, and watched his prognostications about the exponential advance of artificial intelligence and human longevity bend mainstream culture to his often outrageous ways of thinking. Could his views and books and unrelenting talks have anything to do with Silicon Valley's emerging belief that technology could alter death as profoundly as it was already transforming brick-and-mortar stores, cars, and phones? As it turned out, the answer was yes.

THERE IS NOTHING RUN-OF-THE-MILL about these scientists. They are all troublemakers at heart. As I looked more deeply into them, I found each had his own plan for taking on death and dying. But together they all shared one common view: The conventional approaches most researchers and practitioners of the medical arts were applying to disease were, at the very least, misguided. Why squander billions of dollars trying to bring cancer to heel—or diabetes, heart disease, or Alzheimer's—when the *real* answer was to go for the truly big game: aging itself. Solve *that* problem, and all the rest would disappear.

Now as you ponder this, the same questions might be crossing your mind that crossed mine. Were these men crazy, or actually on to something? Was this hubris or genius, altruism or ego? Were they the Galileos, Newtons, and Einsteins of their time, or just a handful of deluded baby boomers whose wallets happened to be as outsize as their own talents? Why should these scientists succeed, when over the past 3.8 billion years, *every living thing on Earth had died!*

The world has witnessed big plays before, but what was bigger than death? Billions of dollars were now on the line, and movers and shakers were at the table. But would it really lead to anything? Could Venter truly revolutionize the practice of modern medicine? Could Hariri's stem cells rejuvenate the body? Was Kurzweil right that the exponential advance of computing would be our salvation? And could Levinson's team someday truly shift the biological paradigms of life and death? Given the rapid advances in genomics, genetics, and molecular biology, big data, nanotechnology, and machine learning, who could say? Maybe death *could* be cheated. Not with a lot of hand-wringing and mythical quests, not with religious and philosophical meditations—and certainly not with ellipticals, StairMasters, tinctures, or alchemic jars of snake oil. But with real and serious science.

Every great endeavor requires four forces to make it a reality. First, there has to be a need: a desire, a market. The second is the will and drive to fulfill the need. The third, resources: tools, money, expertise. And finally, people talented enough to succeed and achieve the dream. The human race—baby boomers, especially—had already provided plenty of need. But was all the rest in place too?

That was the ringing and elemental question. Because this was big. Nothing could possibly change the world more profoundly than the end of The End. Accomplishing that would represent the greatest scientific achievement in all of humankind.

But where to begin the quest? I couldn't think of a better place to start than the one place where absolutely no one wants to die.

PART ONE

NEED

———

Have you not a moist eye, a dry hand, a yellow cheek,

a white beard, a decreasing leg, an increasing belly?

Is not your voice broken, your wind short, your chin double,

your wit single, and every part about you blasted with

antiquity, and will you yet call yourself young?

—WILLIAM SHAKESPEARE,
Henry IV, **Part 2**

1 | THE BIG WAIT

I n the end, it did not go well for Dr. Laurence Pilgeram, Alcor Life Extension member A-1245. He was dead.

The best anyone could tell, it happened when he had been strolling outside his Goleta, California, home on a chilly April evening in 2015. The sky was clear that night, with a brisk breeze coming off the sea. Down on the beaches—beyond the Biltmore Hotel, beyond the adobe houses that still lined many of the otherwise prosperous streets of nearby Santa Barbara—the black, foam-ridged waves of the Pacific crashed beneath a starry sky. And then, Laurence Pilgeram's heart gave out. There may have been a moment, a split second, when the final, horrible revelation struck home: This was it. His time had come.

Santa Barbara's first responders arrived soon afterward, but promptly proceeded to make a mess of things. They never called in the Alcor Field Cryoprotection Team (FCP). Had they somehow missed the bracelet, right there on Pilgeram's wrist? The one dangling in plain sight with an engraved message: *"Call Now for Instructions! NO EMBALMING/NO AUTOPSY!"*

If they had, the Alcor team could have arrived within hours—maybe sooner—to chill his body close to freezing and undertake the Final Protocols: the ones designed to return Pilgeram among the living. But now, all that time had been lost. Santa Barbara's medical personnel had consigned the 90-year-old biochemist to the dark, refrigerated confines of the medical examiner's morgue, just like any other poor stiff. This was not a good thing—because when it comes to cryopreservation, cool is not cold. And cold is very important once a heart has thumped its last.

To make matters worse, the good doctor had passed away late on a Friday evening, which meant that once Alcor finally *did* get the call, it didn't come until Monday morning. By that time, the trillions of cells that the doctor's mortal remains comprised were already imperceptibly moldering, becoming chemically separated from their living versions—incalculably complicating not only Pilgeram's freezing, but his chances for future revival. Had everything gone according to plan, his body would already be in Scottsdale, Arizona, where Alcor could place him in the canisters that would preserve him, precisely as he wished. Because Laurence Pilgeram did not want to die. Not on that April night, not on any night. He wanted to live forever.

SCOTTSDALE, ARIZONA, sits on a skillet-flat mesa so parched it could turn an oyster to dust. There are no weeds, no kudzu or ivy—anything that green would just dry up and blow away. Back before Julius Caesar was conquering Gaul, the Hohokam people lived and farmed the land here. Then, 500 years ago, they mysteriously disappeared. Sometime later, the

Pima and O'odham, probably Hohokam descendants, returned. They were still living there when, in the early 1880s, an enterprising army chaplain named Winfield Scott came upon the sun-drenched, cactus-littered land and thought it might make a good place to grow oranges, figs, potatoes, and almonds. A few years later he founded the settlement of Orangedale, which in 1894 was duly renamed after him.

Nowadays, Scottsdale's network of roads and highways looks like the diagram of a silicon chip cut into the dirt and stone: a sharp grid filled in with car dealerships, office parks, and strip malls, punctuated here and there with a resort hotel and the occasional gated community.

Scottsdale's slogan is "The West's Most Western Town." That makes some sense. The sprawl hasn't yet entirely obliterated the ancient landscape. Just beyond Frank Lloyd Wright's famous Taliesin West, a visitor can still glimpse a bit of the old, primal lands that existed out there when the Hohokam ruled the roost. Just below, housing developments with names like Eagle Ridge and Paradise lay on the rocky landscape: house after tan-and-stucco house constructed for the 20 percent of Scottsdalians over age 65 who have sought to retire in the land of hot sun and antiarthritic air.

A desert might seem an odd place to deposit frigid canisters filled with frozen bodies, but that was where the Alcor Life Extension Foundation had located itself. There were good reasons, actually—the main one being that this sector of Arizona was one of the least cataclysmic places on Earth. When it comes to seismographs and Richter scales, it's an absolute flatline of geologic serenity. Never had an earthquake killed a single Arizonan, at least not as long as any records had been kept. And if any volcanoes ever were here, they had gone silent eons ago. No blizzards, tornadoes, or hurricanes either—because, truthfully, Scottsdale *has* no weather to speak of, except for the occasional torrential rainfall in late summer.

These traits make Sky Harbor International Airport, in nearby Phoenix, one of the nation's least likely to ever suffer a flight delay—and for Alcor, that was important. Even the airport's name seemed to fit Alcor's mission: Sky Harbor. What could be more fitting when making a pilgrimage to the foundation's frigid dewars than a harbor in the sky, a safe haven from earthly cares? Yes, when it came to transporting and lodging the temporarily deceased, everyone agreed, you couldn't ask for a better place than Scottsdale.

And so that was where all Alcorites found themselves immediately after being pronounced clinically dead: all 150 of them (with another thousand signed on), ice-bound in the hope that once science someday divined how to unfreeze and cure them, they might be free to go on living healthfully, forever. Housewives and science fiction writers stood chilled in Alcor's canisters; infants and centenarians, professors, doctors, scientists, dreamers, and hardheaded businesspeople. Kim Suozzi, a 23-year-old suffering from terminal brain cancer, is among them. She had learned about cryonics when she came across the writings of Ray Kurzweil, then raised some of the money needed for her preservation through the website Reddit. She became Alcor member A-2643. Ted Williams, probably the greatest pure hitter baseball has ever seen, is also there, along with his son John Henry Williams (who, before his own death from leukemia in 2004 at age 35, fought to have his father frozen at Alcor). Marvin Minsky, the great MIT computer scientist whom many called "the father of artificial intelligence," also joined the Alcor experiment when he passed in 2016.

Each of these people had giggled as children, struggled as teens, laughed and cried with their friends and lovers, raised families, built a life on their talents and hopes and dreams. And then one day Death came calling. A doctor or nurse made the "pronouncement," and Alcor's Final Protocols began.

That was the big, common experience that all of Alcor's denizens shared. Unlike those of us still living, each had stared into the abyss, had looked the Specter square in the eye, and, at the last yawning moment, known they were about to . . . blink . . . out. Or had they? Now, each occupied separate canisters, not very far from one another—proof that they also shared another thing, an overwhelming yearning to keep on living. Maybe they couldn't escape the thing that had stopped their hearts—not just yet. But wasn't this a helluva lot better than certain death? Assuming, that is, that someday they would reawaken.

LAURENCE PILGERAM first entered my life not long after he had departed his own: just a couple of days before I made my pilgrimage to Scottsdale by way of Sky Harbor. Serendipity brought us together and gave me an opportunity to learn how Alcor went about freezing its clients. Max More, Alcor's CEO, is a man who knows all there is to know about the Final Protocols. He approved of Ralph Merkle's lab rat analogy: the one in which the control groups all die, but the experimental one might not. There was a certain compelling weight to that argument. *Absolute death versus a shot at resurrection?* Which would *you* choose? More thought it made perfect sense. "You mean to tell me they used to *burn* all of those slightly damaged people, or put their bodies into holes in the ground, when they could have frozen and saved them?"

Not that More hadn't seen the raised eyebrows and dismissive smirks or heard the harrumphs and snickers. He had. *Why, for god sakes, would anyone want to freeze themselves like some halibut when they kicked off? That's just nuts! They have signed up how many people in this place?* And what if you *could* be frozen and resurrected? Would that mean that legions of the temporarily suspended would someday return like Lazarus from the dead? Don't we have enough people on this planet? How would we handle the glut? And what would God have to say about this? It's just not right!

But, asked More, has anyone noticed that the definition of death has been changing for some time now? Maybe a process like freezing yourself wasn't as crazy as some might think. There was a time, for example, when, if Joe had a heart attack, he would drop like a sack of cement and that was that. Then CPR came along. And Joe could be revived! His heart might falter, but this time, it could be restarted and life could go on—maybe for a long time, because eventually statins and defibrillators and beta-blockers and pacemakers arrived to keep him up and running much longer than his years, habits, and genes may have once allowed. These days, people were living into their 90s with 14 or 15 stents spread all over their vascular systems. And what about organ transplantation? How crazy is that?

No, better to think of cryonics as a new form of resuscitation. This made Alcor's denizens not deceased, but voyagers, temporarily suspended in time. "Cryonauts" was a term that More liked to use.

ALCOR'S FINAL PROTOCOLS always begin at the end. That's what makes them final. It's an ironic fact that only in death can there be any chance of coming back among the living. That's because, under the law, Alcor cannot begin to freeze a patient until a doctor or nurse declares the person to have officially passed.

In a perfect world, when an Alcor patient is "pronounced," the Field Cryoprotection Team is right there to begin the procedures designed to slowly cool the body and halt the deterioration of its cells. This is critical. Otherwise, four minutes after a patient's heart gives out, the first of the body's 100 billion neurons begin to die from lack of oxygen. And shortly after that, the remaining 99,900,000,000,000 cells start to degrade: heart, liver, pancreas, muscle, all of them gasping for oxygen, and not getting it, a process known as ischemia.

To reduce ischemic damage, Alcor's cryopreservation team cools the body in a bath of ice and begins circulating water to accelerate its refrigeration. Once the patient has arrived at Alcor itself, the medical team then fits the cryonaut with an automatic LUCAS Chest Compression System that ventilates and rhythmically thumps the chest to keep blood flowing while the FCP injects 16 different medications into the patient. These include drugs like propofol, the same anesthetic that ultimately killed Michael Jackson, and antacids and anticoagulants, membrane stabilizers, and antibiotics—a postmortem cocktail designed to keep the cellular apparatus preserved in the best possible condition before the really Big Chill is administered later. The idea is to neither revive nor allow patients to deteriorate—just keep them in a perfectly undamaged, steady state: suspended.

This idea isn't as crazy as it might sound. True, no human organs have ever been successfully frozen and thawed (a human heart can't even survive five hours of refrigeration). But human eggs, embryos, semen, and stem cells are routinely frozen and then revived. Jacob Lavee, director of the Heart Transplantation Unit at Sheba Medical Center in Israel, preserved the heart of a 220-pound pig for 19 hours at 30°F, then transplanted it into another pig. After some warming, the heart started chugging away, no problem.

In March 2015, a 22-month-old Pennsylvania toddler, little Gardell Martin, slipped into a creek, where the current carried him a quarter mile downstream. After a frantic half-hour search, a neighbor found the boy facedown in 34-degree water, no pulse. His temperature had dropped 20 degrees below normal, and it looked hopeless. First responders and doctors performed CPR on the boy for 101 minutes, and amazingly he woke up, his brain function completely normal! Every neuronal marble in place. Doctors said it was a miracle, and that the profound hypothermia was what had saved him.

The most startling example of cryopreservation might be the "Zombie Dog" story recounted in the *New York Times Magazine,* about canines at the University of Pittsburgh Medical Center (UPMC). One day in 2005, scientists replaced the dogs' blood with a chilled saline solution laced with oxygen and glucose that dropped their temperatures to 50°F. Clinical death quickly followed. The dogs remained that way for three full hours. Then the researchers gently replaced their blood, shocked the dogs' hearts, and lo! They returned to the living! So maybe, the researchers thought, doctors could do something similar for human patients suffering from traumatic injuries where the loss of blood was so rapid it couldn't be replaced. Rather than die, maybe they, too, could be chilled and later revived.[1]

Cooling the body is just the beginning of Alcor's Final Protocols. By the time a patient has been chilled and brought to the foundation's medical suite, the place is filled with technicians, a surgeon, and all manner of machinery burbling away. What happens next is not pretty—but then, anything that happens after you're pronounced dead rarely is. The chest is parted and the heart is linked to an assortment of tubes, while a corps of computers dutifully oversee the slow drainage of the very fluids that until now have been keeping the patient up and running—blood, water, hormones, neurotransmitters. All the while, these are being simultaneously replaced with a cryoprotectant: basically, high-grade antifreeze. This is called perfusion, and takes four to five hours until all of the microscopic nooks and crannies of one's clinically dead self are as saturated as a beach at high tide.

While this is going on, three holes are drilled into the patient's skull to provide windows on how the cryonic business is going. The brain, after all, is the seat of the self—the neuronal-synaptic repository of all memory, knowledge, and experience—and no one ever wants to mess with that.

The whole idea of perfusion is to ensure that Alcor's patients aren't, strictly speaking, frozen at all. Instead, they undergo something called vitrification, from the Latin word *vitrum,* meaning "glass." That's the goal: Make the body as solid as a Plexiglas paperweight, with every iota of the recently departed—every molecule, wandering atom, and orbiting electron—stopped cold, or at least slowed to an imperceptible crawl.

True vitrification, however, doesn't set in until the Big Chill itself gets under way. That requires four to five more days of refrigeration that slowly reduces the body's temperature to minus 148°F at about one to two degrees an hour. In the end, Alcor's patients find themselves 400 degrees colder than they were when up and about.

By the time Laurence Pilgeram arrived at Alcor, the FCP team had carefully separated the man's head from his body. That was the way Pilgeram had wanted it when he signed up with Alcor 24 years earlier. The procedure made him a "neuro"— shorthand for patients who didn't want their bodies preserved, only their brains. It's a personal choice. The day Pilgeram arrived, 92 of Alcor's patients, more than half the cryonaut population, were neuros. The thinking is that the day when science can bring an Alcor patient youthfully back among the living, fabricating a new body will be, relatively speaking, child's play. The key thing is to preserve the memories and knowledge encoded in all of that cerebral architecture—the stuff in your brain that really makes you *you*.

In the case of Pilgeram, after he was "separated," no other protocols were applied. His body had deteriorated too much, thanks to his sojourn in the Santa Barbara morgue. He was instead submitted to what Alcor calls a Straight Freeze, which is to say he was rapidly frozen and submersed in liquid nitrogen to better reduce as much of the ischemic damage as possible. Either way—straight freeze or not, neuro or not—all of Alcor's cryonauts eventually find themselves headed to the Chill Chamber (officially known as the Patient Care Bay), and the resolute attentions of Hugh Hixon.

HUGH HIXON EXHIBITS only some of the wear and tear of his 78 years. His skin is smooth as a baby's, but his hair—what remains—is white and wispy. He's slightly bent, stick-thin, and carries large, 1970s-style black glasses on the bridge of his straight nose. There's less spring in his step than there used to be. It turns out he's had a few of his own run-ins with the grim reaper. There was the quadruple bypass in 1996, the two stents implanted 10 years later, plus the two heart revascularization treatments. Those had worked particularly well. His parents also suffered from heart disease. He says it's in the DNA.

Hixon is Alcor's constant gardener. He trolls the arboretum's frozen canisters, regularly topping them off with liquid nitrogen to ensure the rigid bodies and brains of those within remain neither dead nor alive, but securely somewhere in between. "Time is our enemy," Hixon says. "I can't stop it, but I sure as hell can slow it down."

The Patient Care Bay is big, a good-size warehouse with high, corrugated walls, exposed beams, and smooth cement floors. Alcor's 18 canisters are 11 feet tall, stainless steel thermoses, slim, silvery, and upright. A doorway sits above the chamber like a large sunroof. Usually it's closed, but with the click of a button, Hixon can open it to the heavenly blue Arizona sky. This allows a crane, and its 2,000 pounds of chain, to reach below and carefully haul up and then deposit Alcor's patients into their appointed canister: a necessary piece of throwback machinery in the service of an unknown and mysterious future. One canister can house six full bodies, or 10 neuros, or some combination of both. It's tight quarters, but in the vitrified world, people don't seem to much complain about the crowding.

In 2016, of the 149 patients housed at Alcor, 37 were women; the other 112 were men. Another 1,116 had already signed on to join the current tenants at some future date, including people like Ray Kurzweil, PayPal co-founder Peter Thiel, biogerontologist Aubrey de Grey, nanotechnology pioneer Eric Drexler, and, of course, Ralph Merkle. The average age of the currently vitrified is 65.

Hixon is also Alcor's chief depositor. When a new patient arrives, he is the man who sees them to their next, but hopefully not final, resting place. Their bodies are swaddled in a chilled sleeping bag and slipped into a metal pod of Hixon's design. (Neuros are packed around with Dacron wool, and then placed in a "neuro can," a kind of metal helmet filled with liquid nitrogen.) Everything is painstakingly labeled and logged. (One wouldn't want to be misidentified when one awakens to a new future.)

After days of slow cooling, the patient is finally ready to head home. Hixon pushes the appointed thermos into position on the upright wheels that carry it. Then he shuffles back to the end of the long warehouse, where the other silvery canisters await at silent attention. There, he hits the white button, and a ritual unfolds. The gears crunch and clank. The chamber's roof opens again to the Arizona sky. Hixon cranks the chains down to the empodded cryonauts and attaches both ends before the machine heaves them horizontally, like Frankenstein's monster in the 1931 Boris Karloff movie. Then, one end of the pod is disconnected, leaving the patient dangling upside down before the rigid body or brain at last slips into its cryonic resting place. Once again Hixon hits the big white button, and the clanking eye of the roof disappears. There is a distant and solitary thud, and the job is done, for now. One more soul in limbo.

Events like this can make a man think. Some days Hixon wonders if the whole business isn't just a waste of time, all these people hovering between the eternal present and their someday futures. He figures the first cryonaut will be resuscitated within 50 years. But then, he's been saying that for 30 years, so who knows. Sometimes he feels like he's living in a science fiction novel, except he can't page forward to find out what the ending will be. Maybe people really will wait years in a metabolic coma, frozen in time, until science delivers the breakthroughs that will repair and revive the ragged versions of their former selves. Who could say? That is the thing about Alcor: Every story is unresolved—every life ... suspended.

Hixon knows the routine better than anyone. Just as he knows that someday, someone else will be pushing the button for *him*, and on that day the roof will again open to the heavenly blue Arizona sky, and the crane will hoist him to *his* glistening dewar, where he too will slip into his appointed slot for a very long nap.

2 | BOOMERS, BREAKTHROUGHS, AND FOUNTAINS OF YOUTH

For as long as *Homo sapiens* have existed, we have been trying to snip the gnarly snares of mortality: myth, religion, cults— heaven, Elysium, Valhalla, Nirvana, Heaven's Gate.[2] Alcor is just the latest example. Everyone knows Alcor's Final Protocols are a last-ditch effort to avoid death: a hedged bet, plan B. Even Max More admitted he didn't long to join in Alcor's Final Protocols. Better to enjoy a life where aging and death didn't exist: plan A.

No one yearned for plan A more than baby boomers. Just as they began hitting their 60s, the idea of super-longevity began rising up like some collectively unconscious Greek chorus. That was just around the time the Pew Research Center poll came out, and all those magazine covers began showing up on newsstands. *National Geographic*'s cover read, "This Baby Will Live to Be 120." The *Atlantic* asked, "What Happens When We All Live to Be 100?" *Time* proclaimed: "This Baby Could Live to Be 142 Years Old."

Truthfully, the *Time* article didn't reveal anything terribly new about how one might live 142 years. It rehashed information about telomeres, dispensed advice on the best places to live in your later years, nodded to the ways diets low in red meat and sugar and high in good fat seemed to slow heart disease, and revealed how rapamycin, a drug developed to reduce organ rejection in transplant patients, helped a lab mouse named UT2598 live eight months longer than normal. That sort of thing. All good and useful information, but certainly nothing that warranted the proclamations on the magazine's cover.

Why all the hoopla? Because the articles, books, and studies were tapping into the deepest fears of baby boomers. Boomers were a peculiar generation. They had emerged as the result of a massive case of pent-up, postwar lovemaking. For decades, child rearing had taken a weary backseat to the scarcity and menace of the Great Depression and World War II. But then, years of coitus interruptus gave way to a great blossoming of *coitus semper.*

In 1945, for the first time in nearly 20 years, the future looked like one lovely bed of roses, at least in America. The U.S. economy boomed, jobs soared, money flowed, and newborns arrived in great cherubic waves. By 1957, an American baby was being born every seven minutes, and by 1964, the statisticians had counted 76.4 million new children in the United States since the end of the war. Boomers soon made up almost 40 percent of the nation's population—and not one of them had yet reached age 20! In 1966, *Time* magazine made boomers its "Persons of the Year." Fifty years later, they were still plowing their immense demographic girth through the world's markets and culture like a pig through a python.

But now, boomers were growing—how could one put it delicately?—old. Between 2020 and 2035, the population of Americans age 55 to 64 was projected to grow a whopping 73 percent. The ruddy, glowing complexions and slim bodies of their Woodstock days had deserted them. And being a group that associated itself with making (or breaking) the rules and discarding the status quo, they did not much care for that. The very idea that they were actually mortal collided with their self-image as game changers: a generation whose youth and energy and power had always allowed them to accomplish just about anything.

What boomers didn't invent, they popularized to the point of transforming the very idea of youth into an immense and ever growing industry. In 2012 when Arianna Huffington, president of Huffington Post, hosted a roundtable on aging with celebrated authors like Gail Sheehy, she called boomers the wealthiest, most active generation ever. All their lives, they grew up genuinely expecting the world to improve as time passed. And obstacles like aging and dying just didn't fit in with the picture.

A fierce fusion began bubbling up, a boundless, generational desire for an all-out assault on the most hated enemy of humankind: aging. There was the vague but palpable hope that death and decrepitude didn't have to be inevitable, that living not simply longer (like their parents), but better, stronger, wiser, and happier could somehow be in the cards.

And every day, more attempts surfaced. You only had to look at the World Congress on Anti-Aging Medicine for proof. In the early 1990s, the convention amounted to nothing more than a trickle in the domain of medical purveyors. These days visitors arrive at the Congress by the thousands, and the marketeers make it clear that nothing is beyond the reach of modern medicine as it marches forward to advance "scientific and medical technologies for the early detection, prevention, treatment, and reversal of age-related dysfunction, disorders, and diseases." In 2014, the convention was such a big deal that J. Craig Venter, the master of genomics himself and winner of the 2008 National Medal of Science, delivered the keynote.

By the end of 2015, the once tiny trickle of the global anti-aging market had risen to $292 billion. Americans were turning 50 every seven seconds—12,500 people a day—and they wanted rejuvenation! Three out of every five consumers were taking supplements on a regular basis, with global sales topping $132 billion and growing at an 8 percent clip every year. Botox, the number one cosmetic procedure, was performed 2.8 million times in 2014, up 157 percent since 2002. And more Botox was in the pipeline. The same year, 54 million exercisers were zipping around the strip malls of America to sweat over row after row of ellipticals and bodybuilding machines.

Boomers themselves were not alone. Forty-five percent of all cosmetic procedures in 2014 were performed on people between ages 35 and 50—gen Xers and gen-Ys. Could gen-Zs be far behind?

But the real headline was that people over 50 now controlled 70 percent of America's financial assets, and 50 percent of its discretionary income. Even the financial analysts over at Merrill Lynch couldn't quite believe that the U.S. longevity investment sector would top seven trillion dollars in 2017, making it the world's third largest economy. It was like a great and ever inflating balloon.

Except that no one had yet found a way to truly stop time's clock. Alcor, after all, was clearly *not* delivering a solution for life everlasting. It wasn't as if millions were lining up for inclusion in the Chill Chamber over on East Acoma Drive. People wanted something more: They longed for the Big Breakthroughs.

But to be blunt, no such breakthroughs existed. Boomers and their descendants may have *wanted* them, and the media certainly wanted to see them delivered, but desire—no matter how ardent—hadn't yet provided anything that said, "Ah-ah! There is the path! The cure!" It wasn't even clear such a thing was biologically possible. As recently as 2015, articles in magazines like *Science* were still quoting researchers like Derrick Rossi at Harvard saying, "We age so completely and in so many ways. We are programmed to die." Well, who wanted to hear *that?*

3 | THE DRIVE TO SURVIVE

None of us can comprehend how the human race might manage living 300 or 400 years, or any other outrageously long time, without first understanding the social and scientific forces that have made the idea of it possible in the first place. That begins with explaining why we die.

In 1899, tuberculosis exterminated more people in the United States than anything else. Its killing was hideous, and easy to spread: a bacterial infection that essentially shredded the lungs and ravaged the body. The white plague, they called it. After tuberculosis came the next biggest killers: pneumonia, diarrhea, and gastroenteritis.

This was one reason the average white American lived only 48 years, the average black American 34 at most—just 15 years longer than our ancestors had survived during their days wandering the plains of Africa. Three hundred millennia of evolution, 10,000 years of civilization, and all the human race had to show for it was a meager 15 years of additional longevity!

By the time Henry Ford rolled out his first Model Ts and the fox-trot was all the rage, the average U.S. citizen was lucky to make it past his fifth birthday. One out of four children died of typhus, pneumonia, or scarlet or rheumatic fever, vanishing at the rate of 10 to 35 percent a year. The simplest accident could snatch a person's life. A worker might gash his hand at the factory, and die not long afterward of blood poisoning. In 1900, even the most advanced members of the medical arts would never in their wildest imaginations have considered that the average human could live 80 years.

And why would they? When archaeologists pored over the writings of healers from Mesopotamia, Egypt, India, and Israel, they found plenty about migraines, seizures, smallpox, cholera, dropsy, and leprosy, but precious little about cancer, diabetes, heart disease, stroke, or dementia. Why? Because aging never had time enough to get a toehold. There were far too many other ways to die.

But then, as the 20th century marched on, the statisticians who charted the nation's actuarial tables began to notice people were living longer. Significantly longer. At first, this was mostly thanks to simple advances in sanitation. Water was cleaner. And milk, a major source of infectious bacteria, was pasteurized.

In 1890, the first American sewage treatment plant using chemical precipitation was built in Worcester, Massachusetts. Large sanitation projects in big cities throughout Europe and America followed in the early 20th century, and chlorination was adopted in many cities after it was used to stem a typhoid fever epidemic in England in 1905.

Medical care improved too. Whereas surgeons as recently as the early 20th century didn't think twice about eating a sandwich while performing an amputation in the operating theaters of the day, they had learned by World War I that there was a connection between medical sanitation and the appalling number of deaths they had personally created. In fact, throughout society, the role that germs played in disease became better understood. The modern world grew cleaner, if not perfectly safe, from hospitals to restaurants to the workplace. Even the white plague began to vanish. By 1940, cases of tuberculosis in the United States plummeted by half.

The next big life extender was antibiotics. Even after improvements in sanitation, the really ugly killers were still infectious diseases. Often, the only barrier between life and a horrible death was the strength of whatever a person's DNA and immune system had the good fortune to bestow. Then, in 1928, a British biologist named Alexander Fleming noticed something odd as he gazed through the microscope in his lab at St. Mary's Hospital in London: The bacteria he was studying had stopped growing in their petri dishes. The reason: A few spores of a green mold called *Penicillium notatum* had accidentally gotten into the same dish.

Scientists already knew that certain molds and bacteria didn't get along. They had been waging predatory war with one another at the cellular level far longer than the human race had been around—probably billions of years. But thanks to this new bit of information, Fleming suspected the green mold could be used to kill bacteria outright—maybe whole battalions of bacteria. "When I woke up just after dawn on September 28, 1928, I certainly didn't plan to revolutionize all medicine by discovering the world's first antibiotic," Fleming later said. "But I guess that was exactly what I did." He called the substance "mold juice," but later named it penicillin.

Now all Fleming needed to do was create a vaccine or drug of some kind. But not being a chemist, his repeated efforts floundered. It took 12 more years—and the insights of an

Australian pharmacologist named Howard Florey and a German-British biochemist named Ernst Chain—to manage that. In 1941, they purified enough penicillin to treat their first patient. It took three more years before the drug could be produced in bulk and applied the way doctors use antibiotics today.

Scientific techniques now snowballed, and waves of more vaccines and antibacterial drugs followed: chloramphenicol in 1947, tetracycline in 1948, the first safe vaccine for polio in 1952. Between 1940 and 1950, the number of medicines that doctors commonly used more than doubled, and nefarious diseases that had been killing human beings since time immemorial fell like dominoes. Life expectancy leaped forward. Between 1900 and World War II, the average American's life span increased 26 years, nearly twice more than it had in the previous 300,000 years.

Nevertheless, people still died. But now they were dying later, and from different diseases. In 1899, cancer was not even listed among the top five killers in the United States.[3] It was so rare that when a respected surgeon named Roswell Park argued that cancer would someday become the nation's leading cause of death, the medical community thought he had lost touch with reality. And yet by 1950, cancer took its place as the nation's second leading killer. In the space of a single generation, the number of people surviving beyond 60 had nearly doubled. Good news—except now formerly rare diseases like heart attacks, cancer, and stroke were increasing. Longer life had created a new class of killers.

This situation gave rise to something entirely new: gerontology. Élie Metchnikoff, a Russian Nobel laureate and pioneer in immunology, had coined the term (literally the "study of old men") in 1903—but in those days, there really wasn't much need for the field, because so few people actually grew old.

Now, all of that was changing. Organizations like the Geronto-logical Society of America were formed, and pioneers like James Birren began to study how the body and brain aged.

The field quickly branched into examining anything at all related to advancing age: pharmacology, public health, and the psychological effects, economics, and sociology of aging. Yet not one of its practitioners—not even the biological branch—con-cerned itself with what actually *caused* aging, or what could be done to prevent it. Even the sister field of geriatrics focused only on treating and reacting to the inevitable deterioration of aging: problems like loss of memory, mobility, and strength, and dis-eases like osteoporosis, arthritis, heart disease, diabetes—what-ever began to break down the body. But no one seemed in any way concerned with what could actually *stop* aging.

To gerontologists, the reasons for this were obvious, because everyone knew that aging was simply something the body did. No respectable doctor gave any real thought to how one might arrest it. After all, everything, everywhere broke down, given enough time. Bridges, roads, machines, dogs, cats. Even mountains and valleys. It was entropy at work. The great circle of life. Why should we humans be any different?

Of course, it was true that some people lived longer than others. And there was the vague and accepted understanding that genes and personal habits—either good (exercise and proper diet), or bad (overeating, too much alcohol)—had an effect on how quickly one's biology would bite the dust. But there was never any doubt that bite it would. Aging was simply what happened to anyone who survived long enough to *have* it happen. The best you could hope to do was treat the inevitable symptoms. If you were really fortunate, your obituary might read: "Died from natural causes." Which was to say, you wore out. But the idea of slowing aging, or reversing it? That was the stuff of science fiction, not serious research.

Nevertheless, the trends set in motion in the postwar medical world continued. Life *was* lengthening. Life expectancy in the 1960s now began to approach 70. But again, of those who lived longer, cancer took increasingly more lives, and heart disease was skyrocketing. By 1968, death from damaged hearts peaked at more than 350 per 100,000 people. Because so many had for so long died of infectious diseases, the connection between heart attacks, smoking (everybody smoked), high cholesterol, or high blood pressure had gone right over the heads of the medical experts—they had never been major killers.

Now they were, and researchers in the life sciences began to glimpse the ways high blood pressure and atherosclerosis damaged the vascular system and heart. Not that they had it all figured out. In the 1950s and '60s, doctors still used a term called "essential hypertension" to explain that people actually *needed* higher blood pressure to get blood to patients' brains. That was what made it "essential." But when researchers began to develop beta-blockers and other drugs that reduced blood pressure, they realized "essential hypertension" wasn't essential at all. It was just hypertension, and it was blowing people's vascular systems apart like bad tires. Men (more than women) dropped over in their 60s, or even 50s, from acute coronary thrombosis or myocardial infarction with the random, but inevitable, destruction of a sudden thunderstorm. President Eisenhower had had two heart attacks while in office and finally passed through the veil in 1969. Louis Armstrong died in 1971. J. Edgar Hoover in 1972. President Lyndon Johnson in 1973. All from heart attacks.

Now, suddenly, saving hearts became imperative. On December 15, 1967, *Time* hailed Dr. Christiaan Neethling Barnard on its cover as the man who performed the first successful heart transplant. The surgery, the magazine said, was "epochal." The feat seemed both the most outrageous and, at the same time, perfectly sensible way to defeat the new scourge. Nevertheless, it wasn't a panacea. For most, heart disease, stroke, diabetes, and cancer simply became the new ways to die. It was sad, but what else could one do?

Researchers *did* have some ideas. Building on the breakthroughs in antibiotics and postwar molecular drug development, they began to connect new dots and develop pharmaceuticals that, if they couldn't cure the emerging diseases with the same lethal efficiency vaccines and antibiotics had, could perhaps treat the symptoms and slow the damage. The first beta-blockers became available in 1958. They included diuretics designed to slow damage from congestive heart failure and hypertension. Then came calcium channel blockers, and ACE (angiotensin-converting enzyme) inhibitors: more medications for treating high blood pressure, heart failure, and diabetic neuropathy. A long, long list of other "vasoconstriction" drugs flowed as the pipelines of the pharmaceutical industry continued to widen.

Yet, despite these incremental advances, none represented the sorts of breakthroughs that had been made with infectious disease, nothing like a single vaccine or drug, some silver bullet that could wipe out whole classes of killers. That was because these disorders were far more complex. By definition, infectious diseases came in the form of viral or bacterial attacks from *outside* the body. If you killed the bug, you killed the disease. But the newest top killers were different. They were the result of the body's *own* complex and inscrutable biology. Yes, smoking and poor diet and other outside factors could be, and often were, contributing factors. But diabetes, cancer, heart, and vascular disease were largely killing people because they were simply getting older, and the sources of the deterioration were tough to unmask.

Medicine had hit a new kind of wall. There were no knockout punches for these diseases. When it came to aging, the best that Medicine—the kind with a capital M—could manage was to nibble at the edges.

None of this, of course, was immediately obvious. When President Richard Nixon launched the war on cancer in 1971 with the passage of the National Cancer Act, it had the scent of John Kennedy's race to the moon. Throw enough money, brainpower, and technology at a problem and the next thing you know, you're bounding around the lunar surface hitting golf balls.

The problem was, going to the moon was largely about engineering and physics. Diseases were about biology, and biology was a far more unpredictable demon than engineering. In those days, the scientists spearheading the research thought cancer was a single disease. Forty years later, they had learned the hard way that it was 100 different diseases, at least, and each one required different treatments.

Not that progress wasn't made. By 2008, heart disease had been halved, strokes decreased by two-thirds, and new drugs joined with increasingly ingenious treatments and early cancer detection to reduce the disease 21 percent over the previous 13 years.[4] At Genentech, in the 1980s and '90s, Herb Boyer, Art Levinson, and the rest of their teams were snipping DNA with recombinant technology to create pharmaceuticals that attacked diabetes, heart failure, and colon, ovarian, and rectal cancers at the virological/molecular level. Under Levinson's leadership, Genentech developed some of the first monoclonal drugs, like trastuzumab (trade name Herceptin), which could seek out and destroy specific cancer cells—in this case, an ugly and lethal form of breast cancer. That, in turn, reduced the debilitating damage that radiation and chemotherapy did to the whole body. All of these were postponing death for millions of people. But there was still the dark side: People were living longer, yes, but too often they weren't living better.

4 | DROOL CUPS AND NAME TAGS

I n 1900, the number of Americans who lived past the age of 65 amounted to a mere 3.1 million people. By 2010, more than 40 million graced the nation. Baby boomers were watching more and more of their parents being kept alive by statins, beta-blockers, blood thinners, and diabetes medications, but still they watched them slowly deteriorate, shuttling in and out of hospitals, joining the ever expanding ranks of assisted living facilities. If living longer only meant passing your last years doddering around nursing homes with a drool cup awaiting the arrival of the Great Beyond, who wanted that?

Meanwhile, the cost of keeping the elderly alive was rising by the day. A generation earlier, these souls would have long ago passed away. Yet here they were, collecting Social Security and Medicare, enriching the pharmaceutical industry, and creating more patients for the world's hospitals than ever. In 2010 the National Institutes of Health (NIH) projected that by 2020, the cost of cancer care in the United States would top $157 billion a year—and the disease struck down the elderly far more than anyone else. The same went for treatments of old standbys like heart disease and arthritis, plus the latest new killer: dementia. Bodies were lasting longer, but brains were blinking out. Thirty-five million people had been diagnosed with some form of dementia around the world, and if the situation didn't change, the experts at the World Health Organization projected the caseload would triple to 115 million by 2050. The bill? Six hundred four billion dollars a year: one percent of the entire world's GDP. [5]

Not that anyone for a moment preferred a quick death over these treatments. But how long could this go on? Many experts simply assumed this was the tattered world in which most of the aged would live. Gerontologists meditated on how the thinning ranks of the young could possibly handle the economic sinkholes boomers would create as they became the next generation to fall to pieces—not just in the United States, but also throughout western Europe and Japan, and the other so-called advanced nations. In Japan, businesses were now delivering more diapers to the elderly than to infants and toddlers!

Policymakers perceived a supreme irony: Long life was creating an epidemic of new diseases. And baby boomers were not pleased with the results. They knew all too well how the body breaks down, and gerontologists could run the numbers for them in excruciating detail. Maximum lung capacity drops 40 percent between the ages of 20 and 80. At age 40, the eyes have difficulty seeing up close; heart rate drops 25 percent by age 75; half of a 30-year-old man's muscle mass disappears by the time he is 60; spinal disks are habitually crunched, bulged, or ruptured; bones weaken and veins twist. Arthritis and osteoporosis set in like some biological cat burglar. At 70, memory and reaction time begin to sputter. And this happens in people who are in reasonably good shape!

Yet—and this was the strange thing—this only seemed to add to the boomer mentality. All things were possible, right? So maybe there was some way to stop aging and maintain youth. Hadn't all the medical advances of the past century proved just that again and again? In the baby boomer's mind, if you were sick, you simply went to the doctor and were taken care of. It had always been that way. A shot, an antibiotic, a pill, a knee replacement, an MRI—some drug or treatment; there was always a solution, or at least that was the expectation. For boomers, invincibility was a birthright, and under no circumstances was the status quo acceptable.

Nevertheless, aging itself—the true molecular underpinnings of it—refused to knuckle under. Only now were some mainstream researchers beginning to grapple with its complexities. Truthfully, no one really knew what aging was. A disease? A series of diseases? Just the natural order of things, impossible to change, like it was impossible to travel faster than the speed of light?

Back in 1961, American anatomist Leonard Hayflick had found that if you put fresh human fetal cells into a petri dish and let them divide, they would hit their limit at 40 to 60 divisions, then give up the ghost. It was called the Hayflick limit, and it reinforced the idea that dying was a natural—and unstoppable—process.

In 2013, scientists from 10 top universities and institutes around the world published a paper entitled "The Hallmarks of Aging" in the scientific journal *Cell*. It outlined in yet more detail the many captivating ways the body deteriorates: genomic instability and mitochondrial dysfunction, stem cell exhaustion, and cellular aging. The free radical theory of aging explained how rogue oxygen cells insistently damage DNA like little bombs; the telomere theory held that each time a cell divides, its life span grows shorter until it can no longer be replicated; and the DNA repair theory said we simply lose our ability to effectively restore our cells as we age. Some scientists thought maybe marauding retrotransposons—scoundrel snippets of replicating genes—bogged down our DNA, or the cross talk between each of our own cells and the mitochondria within them became increasingly garbled. Any, or all, of these could be the source of our collective and inevitable doom.

Nor did researchers think aging was simply a matter of a body's cells breaking down like an old machine. Yes, the brutal hammering that life inflicts on DNA in every body every second—upwards of 10,000 insults a day, per cell (that's ten thousand hundred trillion hits a day)—takes its toll at the hands of common culprits like radiation from sunlight, chemicals in food and water, mental and emotional stress, and the work of dealing with rogue oxygen molecules (those itinerant free radicals). But that was only the half of it. Usually evolution's marvelously maximized molecular systems repaired this damage, and the human body continued to function just fine. But with age, the repair mechanisms themselves start to break down—and that accelerates the sabotage.

You could think of the whole arrangement as a recipe. Researchers had known for a long time that DNA doesn't simply hold the instructions for replicating a cell; it also acts as the operating manual for the cell itself, in the way a recipe tells a chef how to combine all the right ingredients at just the right time and in just the right way to make a fabulous soufflé. When we're young, the recipe works fine. But imagine a recipe whose key instructions slowly become blotted out with dabs of butter, or some misplaced relish. Or imagine the words disappearing to the point where the cook starts guessing at, or eliminating, the recipe's instructions. Then the soufflé might not work so well.

Thus it is with living and dying—or at least, that's what many researchers think. The more smudged and ragged the DNA, the more proteins and ribosomes and enzymes cease to do what they once did so well in their youth—the more death stalks us. The instructions DNA sends—for building muscle and collagen, or white blood cells, heart cells, or sheathing for nerves—begin to unravel; as a result, proteins stop folding the way they should. After a while, individual cells become so compromised that they no longer function properly, at which point still more unraveling occurs.

In some cases, the cell concludes that it's doing more damage than good and commits hara-kiri—something biologists call apoptosis. One theory is that a cell's decision to kill itself is evolution's way of reducing cancer, which happens when cells go sideways and begin dividing uncontrollably. Apoptosis is a fine evolutionary fix that removes damaged cells in the short term, like the weekly trash pickup when you are young. But in the course of life, even the trash system starts to break down and fails to show up, leaving even more dead and damaged cells behind.

Scientists had also learned that not all damaged cells repair themselves or commit suicide. Some simply become "senescent"—useless, but alive enough that they aren't scooped up and removed as dead. They serve no other purpose except to cause trouble, a little like the zombies of *The Walking Dead*. And over time, they accumulate. Unlike cells that kill themselves, senescent cells *can* lead to cancer, which is one theory that explains why cancer increases with age. And if they don't cause cancer, then their misfiring DNA can produce proteins and enzymes the body doesn't need or want: loose cannons that begin ransacking the body's good cells, burdening an already battered body as it ages. In the end, hearing and eyes falter, major organs—including the brain—fail, strength diminishes, the heart stops, and we die.

Clearly, where aging was concerned, there was no shortage of Need. The market and the desire for a long and healthy life were immense. But was there anybody out there with the Will to actually *do* something about our inevitable and universal demise?

As it turned out, there was.

PART TWO

WILL

I sing the body electric.

—WALT WHITMAN,
Leaves of Grass

5 | CALICO

The evening of October 18, 2012, was warm and cloudless the way Silicon Valley evenings often are. Art Levinson had just departed Laurene Jobs's home and was motoring along in his aging Lexus to see Larry Page, and a few others, for dinner at his house in Palo Alto. Laurene was Steve Jobs's widow, and as Apple's chairman Levinson had driven down earlier from San Francisco to review a few matters with her.

On and off, Levinson had been thinking about the get-together with Page. He was skeptical, but that wasn't unusual for him. He was always skeptical. But this particular idea . . . well, it was intriguing. *Very* intriguing.

A few weeks earlier, Bill Maris had contacted him, and that had led to the dinner. Along with Sergey Brin, Page was the co-founder of Google. A little more than a year earlier, he had taken over from Eric Schmidt as the company's CEO, reins he and Brin had voluntarily handed Schmidt in 2001, when the company was still in its infancy. Maris was the head of Google Ventures (also known as GV), a fund that since 2008 had thrown hundreds of millions of dollars at cutting-edge start-ups like Uber, Nest, 23andMe, and a long catalog of others. Together, those businesses had made Maris one of the most successful venture capitalists in Silicon Valley.

Maris reached out to Levinson and told him about his idea. Maris knew it might seem a little out of the ordinary—well, maybe way out of the ordinary—but he hoped to get Levinson's feedback. He wanted to create a start-up designed to cure aging—even death itself.

Levinson had been aware, vaguely, of various efforts to extend life. He had heard of Ray Kurzweil's prescriptions for radical life extension, had come across Aubrey de Grey's work on abolishing aging here and there, and suspected the National Institute on Aging (NIA), Harvard, MIT, and other organizations of that ilk had likewise dabbled in the question. But this was a different beast entirely. Google was involved, and Google had a way of bending the fabric of culture and economics the way black holes bend light and gravity.

Levinson knew this because not long ago, he had been a member of Google's board himself. This was not likely to be some small-time, lab coat, federal grant effort where a few mice were run around the maze and written up in another peer-reviewed science paper. Google had cash, lots of it, and serious intellectual firepower. And that meant any endeavor it brought to the table would also bring serious muscle.

So, Maris asked, was Art willing to talk?

Yes. He was.

THIS THRILLED BILL MARIS to no end. He had been pondering his Big Idea for a while now, and having a heavyweight like Levinson interested vastly improved the chances of the whole endeavor advancing from concept to reality.

Maris had begun to cook up his concept after noticing in the late 2000s that just about every health care company in the world seemed to be either building a computerized diagnostic company of some sort, or a high-tech hardware device designed to improve health. Clearly, biology and computer science were melding. He had also seen this with J. Craig Venter's work during the Human Genome Project in 2000. Venter had accelerated the use of computers to translate DNA's molecular messages into digits. That meant researchers could, at least theoretically, reorganize them in all sorts of absorbing ways to unlock the mysteries of the human genome—as well as the drugs that might improve their shortcomings.

But it was one thing to have an idea, and another to make it a reality. And that was why Levinson was important. Truthfully, Maris hadn't thought he had a chance in hell of getting to Arthur D. Levinson, chair of Apple Inc., and CEO and chair of Genentech, the world's first biotechnology company.

Blake Byers, a Google Ventures colleague and biomedical engineer, had told Maris that if anyone could build a company that could cure aging, Levinson was the guy. Byers knew this because his father, Brook, was one of the original founders of Kleiner, Perkins, Caufield, and Byers (KPCB), arguably Silicon Valley's most powerful venture capital firm. KPCB had been an early investor in Apple, Google, Amazon, and Genentech. Genentech not only went on to revolutionize medicine and the pharmaceutical industry; it also became one of the inspirations for Michael Crichton's best-selling novel *Jurassic Park*. Everyone in Silicon Valley knew what a force Genentech had become in the 1980s, 1990s, and 2000s, and that made Levinson a particularly appealing candidate. Nevertheless, Byers was also pretty sure Levinson would never be interested in getting involved in Maris's idea. At age 62, Levinson was winding down from Genentech—and except for Apple, was downsizing from other boards and various corporate undertakings.

"You'll never get him," Byers told Maris. "Let's go over some other people."

"Wait," said Maris. "Let's not do Art's thinking for him. Why not feel him out? If he's not interested, let *him* say so. What's the worst that can happen?"

ART LEVINSON WAS HARDLY a household name, despite his impressive pedigree. He was that low-key. But inside the fabled worlds of Silicon Valley and the pharmaceutical industry, otherwise known as Big Pharma, everyone knew precisely who he was. Genentech was up there in the pantheon of Silicon Valley companies with Hewlett-Packard and Intel. It was founded after Herb Boyer, Stanley Cohen, and Paul Berg co-invented recombinant DNA, among the truly epic pharmaceutical advances of the 20th century. Boyer then went on to co-create the company in 1976 after an out-of-work venture capitalist named Bob Swanson contacted him. The founding revolutionized medicine. Later, Boyer hired Levinson as a bench scientist, back when he was a bright postdoctoral student at the University of California at San Francisco. That was in 1980. Within 15 years, Levinson was running the company.

And it wasn't just because he was a suit. He was a serious molecular biologist—a doctorate in biochemistry at Princeton, more than 80 scientific papers, 11 patents, and a long list of awards that included the National Medal of Technology and Innovation, the top science honor in the United States. In 2006, *Barron's* listed Levinson as one of "The World's Most Respected CEOs," and Glassdoor rated him the "nicest" CEO of 2008, with a 93 percent approval rating.

There's a picture of Art Levinson when he was a kid. He's around seven years old. His hair is tousled and blond, and he's wearing a pair of flannel pj's, striped with buttons up the front—the kind every boy in American seemed to wear in the late 1950s, bought right out of the children's clothing section of J. C. Penney.

Levinson still had a bit of that boy in him. In some ways he was a throwback to the 1950s, like Timmy in *Lassie* or the Beave in *Leave It to Beaver*. But it wasn't that simple. This was a man who had once simultaneously sat on the boards of Genentech, Apple, and Google. Bob Cohen, who worked with Levinson at Genentech, said he never feared Levinson entering a meeting with another CEO because everyone knew Levinson was the smartest man in the room. (Levinson said that was probably more a comment on the insights of CEOs than his own intelligence.)

The point was, boyish wasn't quite the right word to describe Levinson. He was savvy. Maybe he had that Cub Scout vibe, but he also had a bear trap for a mind and a disarming honesty that might border on bluntness if he weren't so polite. Thus, despite his good-guy reputation, Levinson never did anything he didn't want to do. He could be stubborn that way. He had his own methods for thinking things through, and they often didn't sync with what others might consider perfectly obvious.

When Levinson first sat down with Herb Boyer in 1980, most of his friends and colleagues told him to run away as fast as his legs could carry him. In those days, nobody in the academic and biological worlds actually got into bed with a *business!* The proper approach was to rise up the academic pyramid by doing research that would be accepted for publication in one of the peer-reviewed journals like *Nature* or *Cell* or *Science*. If somewhere down the line, some corporation absorbed your research for practical use—well, that was for bankers and executives and others of their kind who sullied their hands with commerce. But academicians, pure of heart and mind, were to be driven not by greed but by the virgin pursuits of knowledge, and knowledge alone.

Boyer, in particular, had nearly been skinned alive for his incursions into the world of business when he and Swanson created Genentech. Despite Boyer's reputation for groundbreaking research (or maybe because of it), some of his academic colleagues considered him a traitor of the most perfidious sort.

Levinson had heard about the way people treated Boyer, and it bothered him mightily. But what really got under Levinson's skin was when they went after *him*. Once he had decided to take the Genentech job, one of Levinson's professors looked him right in the face and said, "I think it's disgusting what you're doing, and as far as I'm concerned if I never see you again that will be just fine with me."

Well, for Levinson, that only made the move *more* appealing. He had a bit of a libertarian, I'll-crawl-you streak in him, and sometimes it got the better of him. He used to feel sorry for his wife, Rita, when they were first married because sometimes, when the two of them attended a neighborhood get-together, someone would say something arrogant. It really fried him when people looked down their noses at others, and sometimes he would just go off on them. Then Rita would have to calm him down before things got out of hand. What could he say? He liked going against the grain. It must have been in his DNA.

Thus when it came to Genentech, what did Levinson care if investors or a government or foundations funded it? Let the scientists and researchers sneer and roll their eyes and *tsk* their *tsk*'s. If the crowd was following a particular trend, if a lot of "groupthinking" was going on, in Levinson's mind that was a sure sign that it should be questioned. Not that he wanted to be difficult. Far from it. His father, a Seattle doctor, had always counseled him to work hard and be honest. "Do good work," was his motto. "And don't waste your talent." His mother had drilled into him the importance of being civil and respectful, but that didn't mean you couldn't go your own way. What were we, sheep? Never follow the masses, at least not until you had gone back to first principles and thought the thing through.

Much later, when he was moving up the corporate ladder at Genentech, Levinson met Steve Jobs and eventually joined the Apple board. Then, in 2004, he was asked to join Google's board, where he remained for five years until the corporate orbits of Apple and Google began to collide. Nevertheless, even after Steve Jobs's death in 2011, when Apple's board made Levinson chair, he remained on good terms with Page and Brin and Schmidt at Google. That was the way Levinson was: He seemed to get along with everyone.

6 | THE DINNER

Just as Art Levinson wasn't your average dyed-in-the-wool scientist, Bill Maris wasn't your average number-crunching venture capitalist. This was one of the things the Google hierarchy liked about him: He was a true idealist.

Maris grew up in New Jersey in a big family. His grandparents on his dad's side were both deaf and used sign language to speak. As a kid in the 1980s, he recalled his parents had been so broke they actually made tomato soup out of ketchup and hot water. Despite these experiences, Maris's general view of the world was that people weren't put on Earth to get rich; they were there to improve the human condition.

This was one reason why it hit him hard when he watched his grandmother wasting away with dementia and witnessed his father dying of a brain tumor at age 67. He was 26 at the time. One minute his life was great and the whole world was riding high; the next, he was facing the worst day of his life. That taught him that the only thing that really mattered was your health. And it made him wonder, why should his grandmother, or anyone's grandmother, have to suffer the way she did, losing her mind, inch by inch? And why did his father have to have his brain obliterated by cancer? Why did people have to die at all?

If he were to write up on a whiteboard all the symptoms of aging without actually calling them aging, Maris figured it would look like any other degenerative, genetic disease that would eventually kill you. Surely science could find ways to stop such a sickness—even reverse it. But if that was true, where was the company that was getting on it?

When Maris looked around in 2012, he found the answer was no one. Some nonprofit organizations like Oracle co-founder Larry Ellison's Medical Foundation and the Buck Institute for Research on Aging were exploring ways to eradicate aging diseases like cancer and Alzheimer's. But none of these delivered the heft needed to really get at the problem in a truly fundamental way. To make matters worse, Ellison had recently decided to gut funding for any new antiaging projects after throwing almost $350 million at the problem over 15 years with little more to show for it than a lot of his Oracle profits disappearing down a black hole.

As recently as five years ago, the great pashas at NIH, as well as others among the towering spires of academia, looked upon aging research as largely crackpot: nothing any *real* researchers would deign to contemplate. The Food and Drug Administration (FDA) didn't even consider aging to be a disease! If it wasn't a disease, how could there be drug trials? And if there were no FDA trials, why would anyone develop any serious science or even a single useful drug therapy?

In the midst of all these contemplations, Maris met Ray Kurzweil. He had already heard about the celebrated futurist's inventions, documentaries, and lectures, and had read his books, including *The Singularity Is Near; Fantastic Voyage: Live*

Long Enough to Live Forever; and *Transcend: Nine Steps to Living Well Forever.* By now, Kurzweil was considered a kind of guru among the ranks of the geekerati. Four years earlier, in 2008, he and Peter Diamandis, the man who invented the XPRIZE, had conceived the idea for Singularity University.

"Singularity" was Kurzweil's term for explaining that by 2045, the rapid rise of artificial superintelligence would trigger runaway technological growth, resulting in changes in human civilization so radical they would be impossible to describe. Diamandis, therefore, suggested creating a university that would prepare people from all walks of business and science and culture for a future when the Singularity would come. He asked Kurzweil to join him. Larry Page embraced the idea, and Google became one of Singularity University's biggest supporters. So did Genentech.

Kurzweil believed that the same artificial intelligence that would lead to the Singularity could also cure death. That thinking had spurred Maris's belief that it was about time to create a company that could truly attack aging. And it was around that time that he began percolating a series of longevity ideas. His first thought was to create a grant-making institution, using Google Ventures (GV) money, load it with 50 really smart scientists funded to the tune of two million or three million dollars each, and then let them have at it. But he quickly realized that, like the Buck and Ellison foundations, those efforts just wouldn't deliver the muscle and focus needed to truly get the job done.

Next, Maris thought he might create Google's version of NIH, except for profit. Hire a platoon of scientists and have them start whittling down the aging problem. He might even run the operation himself. But the more he thought about that, the more he realized a for-profit venture that big and complex would require truly serious capital, as in a good $500 million. Maris could carry some pretty heavy water inside GV—in the tens of millions—but nothing that monstrous. For that he would need outside venture capitalists of the Kleiner Perkins, Accel Partners, or Intel Capital variety. And that meant taking discussions to quite another level.

One of the people Maris admired most at Google was John Doerr, Kleiner Perkins's chairman and a longtime Google board member. Compared with Doerr, Maris considered himself a neophyte. He was in his mid-30s. Doerr was somewhere in his early 60s, a legendary investor who, under Barack Obama, had been asked to join the President's Economic Recovery Advisory Board to repair the shambles of the Great Recession. Doerr had seen more Silicon Valley venture proposals than pileups on the 101 Freeway.

Before he met with Doerr, Maris thought it might make sense to create a deck that outlined the heart of his Big Idea. He wanted to shape something powerful, not goofy. And if it was goofy, he figured Doerr would be the man to tell him so straight out.

Maris met with Doerr at Kleiner Perkins's offices in Menlo Park and put the idea to him this way: John, imagine you're walking along a beach and you find a lamp, and in this lamp you also find a genie. Naturally, it has three wishes. So what do you wish for first? What is the one thing none of us can control? Time, right? At your age, if all goes well, maybe you'll live another 30 years? That's 365 x 30, so let's say 10,000 days." (That got Doerr's attention. The idea of days somehow didn't seem to feel as far away as years.) But wait, it could be worse: What about zero days?

Maris told the story of his father's brain cancer diagnosis. His father asked the doctor how much time he had. The doctor said he never made those predictions anymore, because one time he told a cancer patient that he only had six months to live: 180 days. Well, the man thought, at least I have time to get my affairs in order. So he walked out of the doctor's office feeling all would be well enough, and was flattened by a bus. Literally. The poor man was killed by the proverbial bus. He didn't even get six hours, let alone six months!

The point Maris wanted to make was that none of us can take anything for granted. Here we are, this remarkable assemblage of atoms and cells that somehow add up to us. And every day we are alive is a blessing, a miraculous gift. But every day those gifts grow smaller; the sands of time dribble away. And that's where the genie comes in. Because then you could ask your genie to add all the fresh days you wanted onto the back end of your life as quickly as they were being lost at the front end. In other words, the genie could just stop the clock and keep you young and healthy . . . forever.

And, Maris reminded him, it's not insane that this could happen. His conversations with Ray Kurzweil had reminded him that computing was revolutionizing the life sciences. The fact that Craig Venter and his team at Celera had completed sequencing the human genome in 2000 made it abundantly clear that it was only a matter of time before science understood what our genes were telling us and how we could repair them. Given the right resources, *that* was what the genie could do: *Buy time!* Maris dragged his hand across his hair and gazed expectantly at Doerr. "That is the kind of company I am describing," he said. "What do you think?"

Long pause. But not because Doerr didn't like the idea. Because the man was floored. *No death? Or at least a very long life? And a good one at that?* Stunning! He told Maris the idea may have been the most compelling pitch he had ever heard. So, asked Maris, would Doerr support the idea? Absolutely. He would put money in it himself! Maris had already run the concept informally by Sergey Brin, Google's co-founder, and he liked it too. Should we share it with Larry Page, he asked? Yes, said Doerr. Of course, talk to Larry.

Page loved the idea too. This was precisely the delicious sort of thinking he embraced: long-range, outrageous businesses to invest in that had the potential to create truly radical change. This was why the folks over at the Googleplex offices in Mountain View had come to call the big ideas they were brewing "moonshots." That was, of course, a reference to John Kennedy's famous 1962 speech declaring that the United States would, inside of 10 years, put a man on the moon. *We do these things not because they are easy, but because they are hard*—that was the way Kennedy had put it. And that sentiment was right in Page's wheelhouse. Page liked Maris's idea so much that he suggested Google fund the whole company. Keep it simple.

But this brought everyone back to the key question: Who was the right person to undertake such a monumental effort? And more importantly, who was the person most likely to actually wrestle the damned beast to the ground?

Thus did Art Levinson find himself motoring along the ribbons of Silicon Valley highway on October 18, 2012, headed to Larry Page's house where he would soon be discussing the extermination of death.

BEFORE ART LEVINSON'S ARRIVAL, Page reviewed the thinking he hoped would win the man's heart and mind. Even though he was shy, Larry Page was driven and competitive, and he wanted the meeting to go well. Page already trusted Levinson from his days as a Google board member. That was important. And he knew Levinson was a grand master of the pharmaceutical arts. He understood molecular biology at a granular level, and had helped Genentech through some of its toughest times when he took over as CEO in 1995. And like Page, he was unusually focused and didn't care much for failure.

Art was the right man for the job, all right, but would he accept it? Page and Maris weren't sure because Levinson often said no to ideas that anyone else would have leaped to take on. That made him one of the more refreshing characters in Silicon Valley, but it also made him unpredictable. Money and power were usually the big drivers in the Valley, but Levinson didn't really care much about either. For him it was about the hunt, and the reward of solving complicated problems. Well, Page had a whopper for him now.

The dinner was easygoing enough. At the Pages', there were generally no fancy preparations or elaborate meals. Those convened included Page and Maris, Levinson and Brin, the kids and Lucy, Page's wife, plus a longtime Google associate, Salar Kamangar, who was running YouTube at the time. After dinner, everyone got down to kicking around the Big Idea. At this point Levinson still didn't know that anyone was interested in him actually heading up the new venture. As far as he was concerned, they were all there having a nice chat and running a few hypotheses up the flagpole. Page quickly laid out all the thinking he and Maris had discussed. What did Levinson think? Was this a business that had any chance of working?

Levinson proceeded to explain that there were a million reasons why eliminating aging was just about impossible. And why it would therefore make little sense to build a business around it. He wasn't trying to be argumentative or difficult, you understand, but, at least from his scientific viewpoint, why sugarcoat the truth? Aging was an unbelievably complex biological problem. And figuring out why we age—let alone how we age, let alone how to *stop* aging—well, you didn't have to be a molecular biologist to see that on a scale of difficulty from one to 10, this was a 20. And because Levinson *was* a molecular biologist, he put it pretty unequivocally that a business like this probably wouldn't stand a chance.

First, there was the issue of the FDA not considering aging a disease. Second, launching a company would demand starting from scratch, because that was basically where the science truly stood. You could work 10, 25—who knew, maybe 100 years—and then you might still conclude the whole business was for naught. Finally, it would be outrageously expensive. The unvarnished truth was you could spend a helluva lot of time, effort, money, and human capital on the problem and every bit of it could go up in a great plume of black smoke.

Page patiently listened to everything Levinson laid out, and then he looked at him and said, as matter-of-fact as pie, "I don't find any of those arguments compelling." What if, Page said, we had all the time and money and resources we needed? What if we could really dig in and solve the problem, do whatever it takes? *Then,* tell me why this is a bad idea.

"Well," said Levinson, "when you put it that way, I really can't."

And here Page delivered the coup de grâce, the surprise Levinson hadn't seen coming. "Then, will *you* do it?"

It was a rare thing for Art Levinson to make a snap judgment, but how could he say no to this? The whole question was at the very heart of human happiness. It ranked up there with the top two or three most important challenges he could imagine. If you solved aging, it would change every aspect of human endeavor. *And* he was looking at one of the most exquisitely complex biological problems ever. He once said that he had always been attached to mystery. Well, here was just about the juiciest mystery of them all, and he was being given carte blanche to hunt it down.

7 | LEVINSON

To be perfectly clear, there had been two meetings, not one, when Art Levinson made his October pilgrimages to Larry Page's house in 2012. There was the first one on October 18, in which Page laid out the Big Idea, and the second, which focused more on getting down to the business of making the new company a reality. That came on October 30, the night before the dead come out to show themselves. If there was any irony in that, no one mentioned it.

The group at the meeting worked well together. Levinson and Page in particular liked one another; anyone could see the similarities between them. Both were quiet, almost shy, and very focused. Levinson was famous for asking penetrating questions—something Page excelled at too. He also liked to go back to first principles and sweep away any prior, preconceived thinking in the face of a new challenge.

Following their second meeting, Levinson headed back home to the Bay Area. It was windy, cool, and dark—a time for reflection. What really was at stake here? Well, first was the bald, titanic question of the Ultimate Problem. Death. No pressure there. How strange the twists and turns of life could be, and how ironic to suddenly find himself face-to-face with problems that had haunted and fascinated him since childhood.

If there were any central themes in Art Levinson's life, they probably boiled down to two things: curiosity and death. Curiosity was celebrated. Death, on the other hand, was not looked upon so kindly. Levinson's parents lived in a tiny section of northeast Seattle called Hawthorne Hills. His father, Sol, was a prosperous doctor. When Levinson was maybe five or six, the family would often return home on weekend afternoons following a trip into the city to run errands, pick up groceries, and whatnot. Each time, he noticed a big hill that rose between Seattle and home, and right there among all the houses on this hill laid a wide swath of green.

That was strange. Why this big green field in the middle of all the houses? So from the back seat of the car, he would point out the green patch, and ask his parents what it was. Silence . . . long and deafening. And then they would drive on home. One time his mother, Malvina, started to answer, but Levinson's father, who was normally pretty warm and approachable, barked, "We are not going to talk about that!"

Still, on subsequent trips, Levinson, mesmerized by the mystery, persisted and finally one day his mother told him the answer. It was a cemetery. Levinson's father was not happy with that revelation. Death was something to be avoided at all times, especially if one was a doctor whose job was to keep people *from* dying. In fact, Dr. Sol Levinson so despised The End that he never signed a single death certificate. Not one! An astounding feat for an M.D.

Levinson never thought much about it as a kid, but later he wondered if little episodes like those with his parents reinforced a subconscious message that the specter of death was always there, even if any admission of it was to be avoided at all costs.

But truthfully, it probably wasn't comments like these that made young Art feel the insistent passage of time and life. It was death itself. His mother had lost an older brother, Norman, as a young man. And then, about nine years after telling Art about the cemetery, his mother died of the same disease, a rare inflammatory autoimmune disease that slowly destroys the kidneys. She was 35. Levinson was 14.

Eleven years after that, Levinson's father died of a heart attack, as men in those days often did. Sol didn't feel well one day in May 1975, and told Art's younger sister he needed to take a day off. It was the first time he ever took a sick day. Then he took another one, and died.

When Levinson was around seven, something else struck him about death and dying. It came to him by way of his uncle Howard, his father's younger brother and one of the more lovable characters in his life. A few years earlier, Uncle Howard had begun sending him books every week or two. Usually Art passed on the novels and history, but he devoured the geography and science and anything about the future. One day, a particularly special box arrived. It contained *The World Almanac,* page after page of tables and trivia and statistics. The population of New York City, how much wheat was grown and shipped in Russia in 1958, rainfall in Arizona, geography, populations, rivers, stars, the planets. Sweet bliss!

While Levinson was poring through the columns of data, he noticed a startling piece of information. If you lived to age 80, it said, then age eight was the best time in all of your life to be alive, statistically speaking—because after that, the chances of dying did nothing but rapidly increase. He saw it right there in the tables. Once a human being got past the danger of being wiped out in childbirth or by some horrible disease early in life, you hit this sweet spot when you and death were least likely to cross paths.

This was not good news to young Art. It made enjoying the idea of celebrating his seventh birthday awfully difficult, because that would naturally lead to an eighth, at which point the inevitable decline toward death would begin! He knew right then how much he didn't care for death. When he lost his mother, and then his father, he knew it even more.

IN 1968, LEVINSON MATRICULATED to the University of Washington, just down the road from Hawthorne Hills in Seattle. He became a biology major, figuring he would become a doctor like his father. But truthfully, he wasn't enjoying it much. One day, he came across a book cowritten by two astronomers: a young Carl Sagan and a Russian scientist named I. S. Shklovskii. The book was called *Intelligent Life in the Universe*. When Levinson read it, he immediately saw biology in an entirely new light. It didn't have to be about dissecting rats or mitosis or chlorophyll. It could be about chemistry and DNA, the structure of genes and the complex ways those interactions created, or unraveled, a human being.

In no time he finished the book, and then the first day of his junior year he switched his major to molecular biology. Or more accurately, because the university didn't have a molecular biology program in those days, he fashioned one of his own, adding classes in physics and molecular biology and advanced genetics to his docket. He wanted to be one of *those* scientists—

the kind that got way, way down into the tiniest particulars of biological systems to figure out how they work.

Two years later, Levinson graduated from the University of Washington. By 1977, he had earned his Ph.D. at Princeton in biochemistry, and in time headed back west to do postdoctoral work at the University of California at San Francisco (UCSF).

By now, Harold Varmus and Mike Bishop had arrived at UCSF from the National Institutes of Health. In 1989, both would be awarded the Nobel Prize in physiology for essentially figuring out how normal cells transform themselves into cancer cells. Levinson was fascinated by the work Bishop and Varmus were doing. They loved exploring the noisy molecular stuff, from retroviruses and reverse transcriptase to viral DNA and gene regulation, and he did too. Soon he joined them as a postdoctoral student, where he studied the mysteries and origins of different cancers.

Unfortunately, in the academic world, grants for postdocs last only so long, and as 1980 rolled around, Levinson found himself facing a dilemma. His plan had been to land at MIT or some nice Ivy League school like Harvard, conduct some interesting research, and write the sort of peer-reviewed papers that would ascend him up the scientific food chain. Who could say, maybe he would pull a few biological rabbits out of his hat and change the face of cancer?

But he had a problem. Rita, his new wife, needed to complete her last year in computer science at Berkeley. That was when he ran into Herb Boyer and landed the job at Genentech.

The big breakthrough that led to Genentech had come in 1972, at a meeting in Hawaii over sandwiches, when Boyer (who was then working at UCSF) and Stanford geneticist Stanley Cohen discovered a way to snip sections of DNA from one organism and recombine them with another, something that up until then could only happen in the natural world. This meant that a simple bacterium—*Escherichia coli,* for example—could be hijacked to grow specific proteins, like insulin or human growth hormone, in large quantities as the organism itself multiplied.

That discovery revolutionized the biological and pharmaceutical worlds, creating not only a new field—biotechnology— but also an entirely new form of evolution: one driven by human technology, not the ancient and random interactions of natural selection. Until that time, hormones like insulin had to be painstakingly drawn from other animals like pigs, not a simple or cheap process. Now they could be created artificially, and in huge amounts. It was a remarkable innovation. If not for the advance of recombinant DNA, thousands of drugs that billions of people today take to help control their diabetes, cancer, Parkinson's, or arthritis would be nothing more than a wispy dream.

When Boyer hired Levinson to join the small but growing ranks of Genentech's other bench scientists, his job was to see what secrets he could pry out of life's genetic riddles. In particular Boyer suggested Levinson spend half of his time on the gene incompatibility expression problem.

"And what about the other half?"

"Just make yourself useful," Boyer said.

The gene incompatibility expression problem was indeed thorny, and had been frustrating Genentech researchers for some time. It was related to hepatitis B, a disease that afflicted billions of people. Over time it destroyed their livers, and eventually, the rest of their bodies. An effective vaccine, if it could be created, would save millions of lives. Genentech was struggling to use recombinant DNA to create large batches of hep B vaccine, something that would deliver a major breakthrough in the treatment.

The standard approach for growing a protein in 1980 was to use Boyer and Cohen's approach: Insert it into the *E. coli* bacteria, and then place it in large fermenters where the bacteria would create millions more copies of the desired protein. This had worked with insulin, but it wasn't working with hep B, and no one could understand why. The research team would insert the hep B virus into the *E. coli,* but the bacteria, for reasons no one could fathom, would promptly turn itself and the virus into glue, which naturally destroyed any chance of a successful vaccine.

Levinson, having spent most of his time in cancer biology, where mammals were used in research, thought: Why not replace the *E. coli* with cells from mammals—hamsters, for example? And when he did, it worked! The reason was simple. The hepatitis virus and mammalian cells had, unlike the *E. coli,* been evolving together for millions of years; in fact, they were on the most intimate of terms. So now, when the vaccine proteins entered the mammal cells, they were accepted and duplicated like a house on fire.

When Levinson told the manufacturing department about his new method, they dismissed it out of hand. After all, everyone knew that *E. coli* was the one and only cost-effective way to mass-produce proteins. Nevertheless, Levinson persisted. "Try it," he said.

"We'll run some numbers and get back to you." A week later, they returned with their verdict: It's too expensive.

Levinson persisted some more. "Can you show me the math?"

"Trust us. We've been very thorough, and it can't be done."

Levinson: "Show me the math . . . please."

The bean counters shared the math, reluctantly. Levinson went away and pored through it all, including the underlying assumptions, and confirmed his suspicions: They were wrong. Way wrong. Orders of magnitude wrong.

Diplomatically, he told them so. Of course, they had to go back and forth a few times before the manufacturing department saw the light, which was suddenly very bright and promising because the new vaccine wasn't just pretty good, it was marvelous! Even today, flu vaccines are 70 percent effective in a good year, and sometimes as low as 30 or 40 percent. But this vaccine was at least 95 percent effective. It stopped the disease in its biological tracks! Not only that, the new method improved Genentech's yield tenfold *and* cut costs. The approach revolutionized biotech manufacturing and became the standard for cloning proteins in the pharmaceutical industry. Herb Boyer later told me that not many people understood how pivotal Levinson's discovery was. He called it one of the most important breakthroughs in biotechnology, ever.

At the time, Levinson was 31 years old.

AFTER THAT, LEVINSON never really looked back—although it wasn't his intention to someday run an entire company, even Genentech. He preferred science but found himself pulled more and more into the management side of the company, and was quickly run up the corporate ladder. In 1989, he became Genentech's vice president of research technology; a year later, he was named vice president of research, then senior vice president of research and development in 1993. In 1995, with Boyer's support on the board, Levinson became Genentech's president and chief executive officer, and in 1999 he took on the chairmanship.

Under his watch, the company developed multiple genetically engineered pharmaceuticals: real breakthroughs like Herceptin for breast cancer; Tarceva, to treat lung and pancreatic cancer; Esbriet, an anti–pulmonary fibrosis drug; and Cotellic for melanoma. Meanwhile, Genentech's stock just kept going up.

By 2009, though, Genentech had been folded into Roche, a huge pharmaceutical conglomerate, after Levinson arranged a $46.8 billion merger. He was ready to move on. So he began planning a nice early retirement to spend more time with Rita, maybe play a little tennis now and again, and dial back his board memberships, except for his duties as Apple chairman. It was all good.

And then he gets the call from Google Ventures. Out of nowhere he finds himself facing one of the greatest scientific mysteries ever. It was as if someone had tapped him on the shoulder and said, "Ahem. Would you care to save a few million lives, and utterly transform the course of human history?"

8 | KURZWEIL

I t was still winter in 2012 when Ray Kurzweil decided to send an early manuscript of his latest book, *How to Create a Mind*, to Larry Page. The book described Kurzweil's methods for developing human-level artificial intelligence, one of his great obsessions. Now that the book was complete, he was seeking funds to launch a company that could build on it. That was often the way it worked with Kurzweil. He hatched ideas, honed them in speeches and interviews, and wrote books about them. Sometimes, the books became businesses.

Page enjoyed the manuscript, and that summer it eventually led Kurzweil to Bill Maris and Google Ventures at just about the same time Maris was kicking around his ideas about some sort of longevity company—the one that would eventually bring Art Levinson into the fold. Maris found Kurzweil's thinking about almost everything flat-out inspiring, but he particularly liked his thoughts on longevity. Kurzweil was arguably the first mainstream thinker to make logical, scientific arguments for living radically long—so when the two met and talked, they reinforced one another's common interests.

"You really ought to try to solve this death thing," Kurzweil remembers saying to Maris.

Kurzweil had that effect on people. He was remarkably effective at describing truly outlandish concepts, and then making them sound sensible. Ideas like living forever, or machines melding with the human race to create a species of superhumans; all of it couched in a world where technology was accelerating at a blistering pace. Initially, this talk could come across like the wildest sort of science fiction. But Kurzweil's personality and writing had this restrained, laid-back vibe that was so quietly methodical and logical, and so laden with science, that after a while people would find themselves thinking *You know, I believe he might actually be onto something!*

And truthfully, you couldn't dismiss the man. His many inventions included the K250 music synthesizer, also known as the Kurzweil piano, a machine that could flawlessly imitate the sound of a grand piano (and just about any other instrument); hardware and software that created the first flatbed scanners; the first machines to read and synthesize written words for the blind; some of the earliest speech-recognition software; and a variety of other futuristic and humanitarian technologies.

People take these advancements for granted now, but they didn't before Kurzweil created them. For his achievements, President Clinton awarded him the 1999 National Medal of Technology and Innovation, 14 years before Levinson received his medal and eight years before Venter got his. Levinson himself told me that Kurzweil's books and ideas on the Singularity, as well as his thinking on rapid exponential growth, influenced his thinking at Calico.

Among Kurzweil's edgier ideas was his belief that by 2045, the human race would meld with advanced artificial intelligence. That sort of thinking had made him a darling of the transhumanist movement—or, as it was known in some circles, the H+ Community (H standing for human). "Transhumanism" had been around in one form or another since Julian Huxley (the brother of Aldous, who wrote *Brave New World*) coined the term in a 1957 article. Transhumanism was, he said, "man remaining man, but transcending himself, by realizing new possibilities of and for his human nature."

That was the idea: the improvement of humankind by any means possible. Take the human race to new, some might say, angelic, levels. Max More, an Oxford University graduate and the CEO of Alcor, had long been one of the leading lights in the H+ Community; he and Kurzweil had known one another since the early 2000s, when Kurzweil first signed up to become a cryonaut. Bill Maris had developed an interest in transhumanism too and was planning on becoming an Alcor member like Kurzweil, once he completed all the paperwork.

There was, in fact, nothing about Ray Kurzweil that any right-minded person could possibly describe as normal. Eccentric maybe; quirky, brilliant, nerdy, even rebellious in a quiet, mannerly sort of way. But normal? No. He took hundreds of supplements a day to maximally extend his life, and exercised on a crazy-looking $14,000 contraption called a QuickGym/ ROM machine that looked like a Dr. Seuss bamboozler. He was at once a thoroughly sincere idealist and a shameless self-promoter. Way ahead of his time, in 2001, he even created a virtual female rock star version of himself, named Ramona, who performed at a TED event with Kurzweil wearing sensors that projected the avatar of the digital singer onto a giant screen. All of this was just fine with Kurzweil. The way he saw it, why would anyone want to dwell inside the numbing mediocrity of the bell curve when playing outside of it was so much more fun?

Kurzweil had always been built this way. In 1952, when he was just five, he would roam the streets of Jackson Heights in Queens, his childhood home, in search of the stuff he required to make his inventions. He hauled broken bicycles and radios, gears and gadgets, and all manner of parts back to the house. In those days, five-year-old kids—even small and curious ones with inky hair and dark, inquisitive eyes—could get away with that sort of thing and not get hurt. It was a simpler time: the age of Nancy Drew mysteries and the Hardy Boys and, for Kurzweil, Tom Swift, boy scientist—*Swift by name and swift by nature!*—whose adventures he devoured, wide-eyed. What could be better than to be a kid-scientist just like Tom, traveling the globe with inventions that kept bad guys at bay and made the world a better place?

After a while, people in Jackson Heights began to wonder what was up with the little kid who hauled around all this junk. So one day a couple of 10-year-old girls just came right out and asked him.

"Well," he said pretty matter-of-factly. "I am going to build machines that can do . . . anything."

They just looked at him.

"You know, machines that can fly anywhere, or see through walls. When I figure out how to put these things together the right way, I'll be able to solve any problem in the world!" *Just like Tom Swift.*

They rolled their eyes and laughed, amused but not mocking.

"Well, that's quite an imagination you have there."

If they only knew.

Later, Kurzweil traded his solitary Jackson Heights excursions for adolescent trips to Canal Street in Manhattan, where he trolled the parts stores in endless fascination. Canal Street, even in the 1960s, was nerd heaven. You could find just about anything on Earth there—relay switches, capacitors, vacuum tubes, wire by the yards—the sorts of things that were capable of moving information from one place to another in a blink. By the time Kurzweil was in high school, the pilgrimages primarily involved searches for the devices he needed to build his very own thinking machine.

Kurzweil had developed a certain familiarity with thinking machines because he was actually working with one: an IBM 1620. It resided on 105th Street in Spanish Harlem at the Flower-Fifth Avenue Hospital. At the time, you could count the number of computers in New York on one hand. The 1620 was a monstrosity, but it was a brilliant numbers cruncher. Kurzweil's job was to program the hospital's accounts, which he did, mostly working the midnight to 8 a.m. shift in high school. While he was at it, he completely revamped and automated the hospital's accounting system.

Around this time Kurzweil decided to compete in the national Westinghouse Science Talent Search. The talent search was the biggest of deals if you were one of *those* high school students in the 1960s; only the nerdiest cream of the crop made it to the top rungs of the competition. Eight of the finalists would one day win the Nobel Prize, and five would win either the National Medal of Technology and Innovation or the National Medal of Science. Including Kurzweil.

Not surprisingly, Kurzweil's entry in the talent search was out of the ordinary. He loved music. His father was a Viennese concert pianist, composer, and music educator who had conducted symphony orchestras and opera companies at Queens College in New York, Chatham College in Pittsburgh, and the St. Louis Grand Opera. He had even performed as a concert pianist at Carnegie Hall. Music, art, science, and technology were all subjects that regularly came up for discussion at the family dinner table. So Ray found himself wondering: *Could a machine learn to make music?*

Well, clearly that was silly. Anyone who knew anything about computers in those days knew they were for crunching census numbers or calculating ballistic trajectories and payrolls. But music?

Yet, in Kurzweil's mind, why not? *Tom Swift!* Any problem could be solved, right? And so he put together his presentation, and began to build the machine.

In 1965, after hundreds of hours of labor, and round after round of competitions, Kurzweil was named a finalist. There's a picture of young Ray and some of the other finalists meeting the 36th president of the United States, Lyndon Baines Johnson. Kurzweil is standing right there with him, shaking the great man's hand.

Soon after his White House trip, Kurzweil received a letter in the mail. Would he be interested in being a featured guest on *I've Got a Secret,* one of the nation's most popular television shows? The producers had come across his music project and thought it might make a good segment.

It was slick the way they set up the whole show. Kurzweil would be introduced by the host, Steve Allen, as the man with the "secret." Steve Allen was a legend. In the 1960s, he was one of the best known personalities in America. He had been the original host of *The Tonight Show,* had written several hit songs, was a playwright, author, and musician—a real main-street Renaissance man.

Once he was introduced, Kurzweil's job was to play a short piece of music on the piano. After that was done, the interrogation would begin. A panel of star personalities were assembled to grill him in the style of the game "20 Questions" until they either figured out the secret or gave up, stumped.

Kurzweil was nervous about only one thing. He had no problem speaking live in front of millions of people or meeting the famous Steve Allen. No, the thing that petrified him was playing the little piece of music on the piano. Earlier in his life he had performed at a piano recital, and right in the middle of playing, the next bar of music disappeared out of his head: a massive white, paralyzing blank! He recovered, but only by starting over from the beginning, and never got over the unspeakable embarrassment.

So for the show he practiced and practiced. But how could he be sure he wouldn't make the same mistake? The mind was a strange and mysterious thing. Even if the music was embedded deep in the gray matter behind his forehead, even after repeated practices, it could all still fail him. The human brain was flawed that way.

At last, the evening came. Raymond Kurzweil, the nice, diminutive Jewish boy from Queens, walks on stage. Steve Allen towers over him. Ray looks remarkably calm for a shy teenager facing the hordes of viewers as he peers at the other end of those huge, cyclopean studio cameras. His hair is black and thick. His face is dimpled and handsome. And he is ready. "My name is Raymond Kurzweil. And I'm from Queens," he says.

There, to his left, is the piano—just a simple upright, its sheet of music beckoning him. He sits down and begins to play this short, very lyric, classical melody. And it all goes down without a hitch, even if the piano is pretty badly out of tune. Immense relief! His brain didn't fail him.

Next, he sits down with Steve Allen and the panel starts in. One of the first questions comes from Bess Myerson, a former Miss America. She asks him if he composed the music.

"It's very unlikely sounding," she says. "Did you write it?"

A slight shake of the head, and a close-lipped smile, "No, I didn't."

There are a few more panel questions, but no one is making any progress, and then it's Henry Morgan's turn. Morgan (his real name was Henry Lerner Von Ost, Jr.) was a famous radio personality—sort of the Howard Stern of his time—and a master of the ad-lib. But here, there is no ad-libbing. Morgan just looks at Kurzweil and comes right out with it. "Was that thing written by a computer?"

If Kurzweil is disappointed, he doesn't show it. He just flashes this big-kid grin and nods, seemingly thrilled. But it turns out this is really only part of the secret. Because if this "thing" was in fact written by a computer, how did *that* happen?

Well, Ray explains to the audience, he built it. "By feeding it certain relationships in music, I was able to program it so that it would write music in the style of Mozart," says Ray. *A computer that writes its own music!* And this mere boy, this kid, actually builds the thing with his own hands from collected parts that he has gathered and fitted together like some terrifically complicated typewriter? And then he *instructs* the computer to create the music in this alien language called Fortran? *A language for talking to computers! Imagine that.*

But there's more: Steve Allen now reveals the computer itself. A curtain parts and there the thing is—a machine that writes music! But wasn't music the exclusive domain of the *human* mind, not machines? And weren't computers usually the size of rooms? Not that Kurzweil's machine was small. It was still about the size of a grand piano and then some. But wow, this kid had built it!

Steve Allen turns to Kurzweil and asks, "Ray, how old are you?"

"Seventeen years old," Ray answers.

There's a pause as Allen regards the young man. "Do your parents know what you're up to?"

Thunderous laughter. That was classic Steve Allen. His famous wit. But then, the teenager calmly replies, absolutely deadpan: "My father is a musician, and he doesn't care for the competition." More thunderous laughter. *Did he just upstage Steve Allen?!*

"Raymond," Allen says, "I'm amazed that anyone can do anything at all of this sort. And I predict a great future for you."

And with that, Ray walks off the stage: the junk kid from Queens who makes music with artificially intelligent machines.

IT WASN'T LONG AFTER his debut on national television that Ray Kurzweil found his way to the Massachusetts Institute of Technology. While in high school he had sought out and written to Marvin Minsky, then considered one of the two great artificial intelligence experts in the world, to see if he might be able to apply to his school. The other expert was Cornell's Frank Rosenblatt. Both men agreed to meet with Kurzweil, but it was Minsky who soon arranged for his acceptance to MIT.[6]

From the beginning of his arrival on campus in the fall of 1967, the act of attending class became almost a hobby for Kurzweil. At least that's the way it seemed to Aaron Kleiner, Kurzweil's freshman roommate.[7] Kurzweil and Kleiner both were cut from the same cloth—hardworking, mathematically gifted kids from the East Coast. They both joined the same fraternity, Tau Epsilon Phi, your run-of-the-mill 1960s frat house. Ray immediately became the social chairman, and under his stewardship the rock bands and songs he lined up for dances were totally rad and the parties right on! Around the fraternity, they called Kurzweil the "Phantom," because one minute he was there, talking, meeting, spouting ideas, and the next he was gone, sometimes for days. No one knew where the hell he went, and when he returned, he never offered any explanations.

One night, Kleiner was at the frat house, sweating over a physics final, when the Phantom sauntered by and saw him studying.

"Oh, yeah," Kurzweil said, slightly distracted, "We have that physics exam tomorrow, don't we?"

Kleiner thought, *You're just remembering this now? The night before the exam?*

"Can you lend me your book?" Kurzweil asked. Kleiner was reluctant. He was a good egg and all, and wanted to help out the Phantom. Hell, the man didn't even have a copy of the book. But Physics 802 at MIT was not easy, and he needed every minute himself to cram.

"Just for a little bit," Kurzweil nudged.

So Kleiner took a short break while Kurzweil looked over the book. Not long afterward, Kleiner returned, and Kurzweil started asking him questions. They were awful! *He's going to bomb this test like the* Enola Gay.

"Let me borrow the book a little longer," Kurzweil said. Once again, Kleiner was less than happy, but what could he do? The guy needed help! A half hour later, Kurzweil returned a second time. Again he began with the questions, but this time he knew it cold! *How could this be?*

The next day Kleiner and Kurzweil filed into some nameless MIT classroom and sat down to take the test. Kurzweil aced it. Kleiner managed a C. A "C"! *After days bleeding from the forehead! After months attending every class—not one of which Kurzweil has even drifted by the whole semester—he pages through the book for an hour and aces it?*

The man was an alien.

Given his aptitude for mathematics, anyone who didn't know Kurzweil might have assumed he would go on to acquire his master's and Ph.D., and then settle in among the ivy-covered palisades of academia. Kurzweil could have worked with Minsky and been the pick of the scholarly litter. But that's not the way it went.

Instead, he simply began creating whatever new and absorbing ideas engaged the Kurzweilian cranium. He called these intrigues his "projects," and they spilled out in endless streams. Before he graduated, he sold his first company—the Select College Consulting program—to Harcourt, Brace & World for a cool $100,000 plus royalties. (Turns out, *that* was where the Phantom was spending most of his college time.)

The thing that caught Harcourt, Brace's attention was the computer program Kurzweil wrote. It optimized methods for helping high school students find the college of their choice by loading more than two million facts about 3,000 colleges into one of New England's most advanced computers, at a cost of $1,000 an hour—a kind of computer dating service for college.

After that, Kurzweil became a hopeless serial entrepreneur. He had little interest in academics except as a starting point. He wanted to *do* things, not just think about them. Make an impact. In time he created nine companies, each one based on his various inventions, like the Kurzweil piano.

The seminal concept behind each of these inventions was "pattern recognition," a concept at the heart of his view of artificial intelligence. Everything to Kurzweil was a pattern, from human consciousness to the sound of a plucked violin string to the letter "B" (what defines the "B"-ness of a "B"?). His inventioneering made him very acceptable sums of money, and also led to an assortment of prestigious prizes: the Lemelson-MIT Prize, Carnegie Mellon's Dickson Prize, and the Grace Murray Hopper Award. Kurzweil soon found himself operating more in the mold of Edison or Buckminster Fuller than your average, workaday academic: a gifted inventor who sprayed ideas, software, and gadgets around like confetti.

But all of that would come later. For now, Kurzweil was simply enjoying the benisons of life at MIT. He liked the room-size computers, the constant projects, and the ethereal confines of one of Cambridge's finest schools. He was young and smart and a baby boomer. What could be better than that?

And then Ray got the phone call from his father.

It was the late summer of 1970, just before his senior year. Kurzweil could hear the melancholy tone of his father's voice. He was lonely, his father said, and he missed Ray. That was strange. Kurzweil could hardly recall a time when his father spoke with that sort of emotion. Something had to be up.

While Kurzweil was still a teen building his machines, he had begun to notice his dad slowing down. Fredric hadn't been dealt a very good genetic hand and suffered from what, in those days, they called "a weak heart." The first heart attack came when Ray was 15. In those days, nothing could be done about heart disease. Nevertheless, Fredric soldiered on. He even founded the music department at Queensborough Community College.

But now, on the phone, the weariness and sadness in his father's voice was palpable. It wasn't a long conversation. They chatted about nothing in particular, and soon Ray hung up. Those were the last words he heard his father speak. A few weeks later, Fredric had his second heart attack. Massive heart failure. He was 58.

Fredric must have known something was up when he made that phone call. That's the way Ray came to see it. It was his way of saying goodbye. Kurzweil never did get over it. The call planted in him an abiding resentment of dying and death that would fuse his lifelong fascination with artificial intelligence to his belief that even death could be outsmarted.

Even before his father's illness, as a kid, Kurzweil couldn't tolerate the loneliness he associated with dying. That was when he first started having the recurring nightmares. In them he would be exploring this endless succession of bare and empty rooms, wandering from one dark and cavernous space to the next, looking to make contact with someone, but finding no one, never getting anywhere. There was this profound, inexplicable anxiety about being... hopelessly abandoned. As a kid he would sometimes wake up sobbing, and the only thing that would help was being held.

In time, Kurzweil came to see the recurring nightmares as perfect descriptions of death. Separation, total and complete. It was unbearable.

This was before all the accolades and prognostications. Before the inventions and patents and medals. And long before he wrote any of his books that laid out the argument that everyone could live forever. That idea hadn't yet fully formed in his mind.

Not yet. But it would.

9 | VENTER

Around the time Ray Kurzweil was hand-building a computer that would show the world what a genius he was, John Craig Venter was honing his surfing skills at "the Wedge" in Newport Beach, California. That was after he had moved from Millbrae, near San Francisco, where he had spent much of the previous year passing his evenings climbing into his girlfriend's window late at night for the occasional tête-à-tête. He would scramble along a rope ladder rigged from his second-story bedroom window, silently roll the family car down the street, and disappear into the cool California night. Until, that is, his dad figured out what he was up to, and passed the news on to the girl's father, who promptly stuck a gun in Venter's face and told him he'd shoot if he ever caught him again.

If anyone was looking to pinpoint someone who would one day upend the scientific worlds of biology and genomics and become one of the planet's best known scientists, they might have been forgiven if they overlooked Craig Venter. Among the four children in his family, he was an unrelenting disappointment. His grades were lousy, his teachers didn't care for his insolent attitude—and even in his senior year at Mills High, he hadn't given an ounce of thought to college or career. Why worry about it? He was blond and handsome and slim, with a manly command of the surfer lifestyle. A Beach Boy incarnate. And he was a champion swimmer, despite ignoring his coach's advice for improving his unconventional stroke. The point was: Who needed to bother themselves with the future when there was such a vast and unlimited supply of it?!

Yet three years later, he found himself standing on China Beach in Vietnam, naked as a mole rat, contemplating suicide.

DEATH BY SWIMMING was the plan. Venter had just departed the corrugated, festering Quonset hut where he had been coexisting with his fellow recruits and corpsmen at the Da Nang naval hospital, and walked down to the beach. There he stripped naked and gazed at the South China Sea. Swimming seemed an easy, sensible way to go. The water was right there, and if he was good at one thing, it was swimming. Why not go out doing something he enjoyed, and then, when the exhaustion set in, slip into the black water's deep embrace?

Venter had been contemplating suicide for a while. Again and again he described the horror of the past several months in long and vivid detail to his girlfriend Kathy back home. He couldn't take it anymore: the death, the dying, the endless stream of bodies coming in on the choppers from the jungles and bomb-scarred rice paddies, the thatch-and-mud-wattle hamlets scattered in the congealed, jungle heat. He had already watched hundreds of soldiers die, some of them while he held their hearts in his own hands, literally, slithering and shuddering as he struggled to massage them to life.

How appallingly fragile the human body was. And how little could be done as the corpsman gazed upon the young soldiers' faces when the horrible and inescapable truth hit them: *I am dying!* These young men, with their legs blown off or their guts hanging half out of their bellies shredded with gunfire, lying sewn up in their beds, waiting for death (or, if they were lucky, a medevac to Japan)—either way, their minds thoroughly ransacked with trauma. The University of Death was how Venter later described it.

Kathy's response had been a "Dear John" letter. They had to break up. She couldn't handle the grisly descriptions anymore. So now she was gone too, but there was still the sea. Very good for drowning.

He walked into the surf and began to swim. The riptide was strong—it almost always was—and it carried him quickly beyond the breaking waves into the expanding basin of the sea. He struck out in the general direction of Manila, the Marble Mountains on one side and Monkey Mountain on the other. For a while it would be just him, the barracudas, and the sea snakes: ugly creatures, and deadly, if they got their fangs into you. That would be an unpleasant way to go. Sometimes they swam in schools miles long and up to half a mile wide. He'd rather avoid that. Farther out were the sharks. No venom there. Just jaws and lots and lots of teeth.

Venter had arrived in Vietnam five months earlier on August 25, 1967, diving through the air in a chartered plane like an oversize dart toward the airstrip at Da Nang Harbor. Bright bursts of incoming flack illuminated the dark cabin that held him and the others as the plane bounced to earth. It was a long, long way from surfing the Wedge, winning championship swimming medals in high school, and exploring the ripe joys of teenage sex. A very long way.

Venter had thoroughly screwed the pooch; there was no other way to put it. C's and D's throughout high school, except in shop, PE, and swimming. He would purposely bomb tests and quizzes, refuse to answer questions, or sometimes take no tests at all. He didn't apply to college until after he graduated, and by then it was too late. Somehow, while growing tan and riding the Pacific surf, he had missed the turn of certain political events in the mid-1960s that made it suddenly apparent that an exciting, but possibly very brief, career as an Army infantryman in Vietnam lay in his future.

Soon Venter was drafted, and avoided the Army only by following a piece of advice from his father, an ex-Marine: Enlist in the Navy. It was the best advice his father ever gave him. And it wasn't a bad deal—at least, it didn't look that way at the outset. Thanks to his swimming record, the recruiter said he could rotate out of service after three years rather than four, and, in the meantime, serve his country as a member of the Navy swim team. He might even get a chance to compete in the Pan American Games. It never dawned on him that he might end up in Vietnam.

But then, two-thirds of the way through boot camp in San Diego, President Johnson (the very same president who had so graciously stuck his hand out to greet Ray Kurzweil) escalated the war in Vietnam, and said that all armed services sports teams were canceled. Still, surely he wouldn't be among the unlucky destined to ship out to some place called Da Nang, 7,936 miles from home?

Well, guess what.

Not that Venter was stupid. Maybe he hadn't been the golden boy his older brother Gary was—he of the soaring grades, academic awards, and sparkling athletics, the brother who was now studying at Berkeley and whom his parents adored beyond measure. *Why couldn't he be more like Gary?* That seemed to be the big mystery his whole life: the nagging, never ending question he kept hearing from his mother and father. If that was the situation, why even try to compete? Who could beat perfection? So he had gone the other way, the bombing-tests-sneaking-out-wearing-insolence-like-a-badge-of-honor way.

AFTER SWIMMING AWHILE, Venter turned and looked back. He was now more than a mile from shore. To one side of him, he saw a school of sea snakes come up for air, their taut necks rising out of the water like so many reptilian prairie dogs. That was disconcerting. He treaded water and looked around. His 22-year-old mind began to wonder. *Is this really a good idea?* But then, after a moment, the thought passed and he swam on. By now the shore was out of sight, and he was truly alone. That was when he felt it: a shivering, primordial prod from a creature in the sea. A shark! In "bump and bite" mode, testing him.

His first thought was *How dare this creature disrupt my plans!* He turned and kept swimming, except now his determination was flagging. Here was this sleek, invisible killing machine that could rattle him like a doll once it sank those razor teeth into him before shredding him into disjointed chum. A strike, searing pain, and then, at last, the killing blow. He trod water again. His head swiveled. Where *was* the damned shore?

Then without warning he was gripped by a new fear so complete and primal that it consumed him whole. *What am I thinking?? I don't want to die!* It hit him like a thunderbolt. He had seen so many men die, had seen what a waste that was.

How could sending his own life down the toilet help? If he went down, one more dead 20-something American wouldn't mean a thing to the rest of the world. He had been given this gift: his life. And now it was up to him to do something meaningful with it.

He looked again for the shore, and dug in on pure adrenaline. Now a new fear struck home: the possibility that he might not make it back. How far out had he gone? Was he moving in the right direction? He swam and swam until his arms had turned to taffy. And then, at last, he saw land, and then the edge of the breakers.

But now there was the riptide. It kept pulling him back like a long and beckoning hand. He dug on. Finally, he caught a wave, then a second and a third. He rode each like a lump of flotsam coughed up by the sea, just this sorry bag of soaked cells in the surf, until at last, his feet found the sandy bottom. And there he collapsed on China Beach—utterly drained, but relieved beyond all imagining. In spite of his own impudence, he was alive! In his exhaustion, a kind of purity filled him. An energy, entirely new: a determination to accomplish something worthy.

10 | A LIFE WORTH LIVING

Craig Venter made good on his promise that day on China Beach. In fact, he had made just about as big a stir as any scientist in the world could. But all of that was still more than 25 years down the road. Now, in 1968, after the Navy discharged him, his goals were modest. First, he wanted to get a college education, and then, if he was lucky, a decent-paying job. So he returned to Millbrae and applied to a community college in San Mateo. Because of his lousy high school grades, he didn't think he could get in anywhere else, and he severely doubted he had the academic chops to succeed in a better school. But a couple of semesters later, he succeeded in transferring to the University of California, San Diego and put his academic career into high gear.

Venter's original plan had been to become a doctor, the same as Art Levinson. He had already performed more surgeries in his ugly Da Nang Quonset hut as a combat Navy corpsman than some doctors performed after years working in the States. But while studying under Nathan O. Kaplan, a biochemist who had done historic work on cancer, he decided to go into research and up the ante of what constituted a life worth living. A doctor, he figured, assuming he was good, might save a few hundred lives in a lifetime. But a researcher could save the whole world, *if* he made the right breakthroughs.

And so in 1972, Venter landed a degree in biochemistry, and by 1975 had blown through his Ph.D. in physiology and pharmacology. The question now was what to do next. He had the will—but how exactly was he supposed to go about saving the world?

He decided to skip the next step most students undertake in their academic careers: the postdoc. Instead he accepted an offer from the State University of New York at Buffalo. It was a junior faculty position, and a long way from the sunny shores of San Diego, but one takes what opportunities the universe supplies.

At Buffalo, Venter immediately made an impression on his colleagues—but not in a good way. He strode the academic corridors with a ragged beard and a ponytail of long, thinning hair, wearing bell-bottoms embossed with roses and outfits whose colors clashed so luridly they could induce a migraine.

To these quaint behaviors, Venter added his personal brand of unreserved bluntness. He had a habit of telling people precisely what he thought, no punches pulled, but seemed to be utterly clueless as to why anyone had a problem when the punches hit home. On his first day at the university, he was invited to sit in on a student's defense of her thesis. The student was a favorite of the professor who invited him and he was clearly delighted with his star pupil. But that was lost on Venter, who upon being asked his opinion of the defense commented, "That was the most mediocre load of shit I've ever heard."

Still, Venter was an avid and creative researcher. He continued the work he had begun under Nathan Kaplan in San

Diego on how adrenaline affected the cells of the brain and body. If he could just find the gene related to the adrenaline receptor, maybe it would reveal how messages of all kinds were communicated in the brain. And if he could do that, perhaps he would someday fathom why humans behaved the way they did. Even humans like him.

But after several years at Buffalo, Venter grew frustrated. How could he ever truly make a difference? Where was the world-changing science? Then, in 1986, he and his second wife, Claire Fraser, also a scientist, landed appointments at the National Institute of Neurological Disorders and Stroke, a division of the National Institutes of Health. Neither of them wasted a minute moving to Maryland. Maybe at NIH he could at last find a way to make an impact.

As it turned out, he did.

Word was that a new and breathtaking concept was kicking around the scientific community, one that involved sequencing the entire human genome. Many considered the idea insane, far too ambitious. But there was scuttlebutt that the great James Watson was interested. Watson, together with Francis Crick, Maurice Wilkins, and Rosalind Franklin, had revealed the structure of DNA in 1953. In 1962, Watson, Crick, and Wilkins were awarded the Nobel Prize; Franklin had died four years earlier and therefore was not included, even though her discovery of the DNA molecule in an x-ray she had taken was crucial to the work.[8] Either way, their discovery marked one of the great scientific advancements of all time.

Since then, Watson had grown to become one of those statesman-scientists that often emerge after winning Nobels. He taught at Harvard and ran the legendary Cold Spring Harbor Laboratory. In 1965, he literally wrote the book on genetics, *Molecular Biology of the Gene,* which he followed three years later with one of the best-selling science books ever, *The Double Helix.*

It had taken 10 years of excruciating labor before Venter had finally nailed down an understanding of one stubborn protein—the adrenaline gene—and he knew as well as anyone that discovering the other hundreds of thousands out there was going to take a very long time. But he didn't have time for progress that glacial. So if there was a new and quicker way to unlock the meaning behind every human gene, he wanted in.

Venter didn't know it yet, but that undertaking was about to utterly change his life—and with it, the fundamental science needed to solve aging.

PART THREE

RESOURCES

———

Yea, though I walk through the valley

of the shadow of death, I will fear no evil:

for thou art with me; thy rod and

thy staff they comfort me.

—PSALMS 23:4

11 | THE HUMAN GENOME

ven before Craig Venter had settled into his job at NIH, the panjandrums of the biological sciences had met at Cold Spring to explore the idea of decoding human DNA. This even though the very concept of a "genome" was alien. At one point, a bioethicist had asked some state legislators in Pennsylvania where their genome was located. A third of them answered that it was in their brain; another third thought maybe it was in their gonads. The remaining legislators didn't have a clue. In the 1990s, Microsoft Word's spell-check would routinely autocorrect "genome" to "gnome," as if the fabric of human life were some ugly, knob-faced troll. Even Herb Boyer, at Genentech, thought there was no way the genome would *ever* be sequenced. It was too complicated and would take forever.

And truthfully, in 1986, it was blindingly difficult to read DNA proteins—invisible, biological molecules of exquisite complexity and design. Scientists had known for decades that DNA spelled out all of the information needed for the growth and operation of a human being. It was, in effect, a molecular software program that used four chemicals in different combinations to describe how to grow bodies and brains from a single fertilized egg, and then turn them into fully functioning humans. All over the world people rose and went off to their jobs, bounced their babies, watched life go on in all of its variety and complexity, and rarely gave a single thought to the strange and ancient substance that made it all possible. Nor did they know that the vast majority of human DNA had hardly changed for a good two billion years, although there had obviously been a few crucial amendments.

The four chemicals in any genome—adenine (A), guanine (G), cytosine (C), and thymine (T)—were attached to one another in the shape of a ladder, which twisted into a spiral so tight that it fit within each of the body's 100 trillion cells. The whole spiral is a mere 79 billionths of an inch wide, invisible to the naked eye. The sequence of the paired rungs forms chunks of information called genes; the order of those genes describes how they create all the cells a body needs to operate, as well as all the ongoing work each requires to stay alive from one day to the next.

Some DNA proteins might deliver the building blocks of an enzyme that helps digest popcorn, or a hormone that fires sexual desire, or a series of molecular interactions that spark a neuron. Or they could form a gene that goes haywire and creates a disease. It was known, even in the 1980s, that genes often serve multiple purposes in combination with other genes—but what those combinations were was almost entirely unknown. Those that *were* known had been painstakingly hunted down by researchers who squinted at x-rayed images of fuzzy columns on a gel that then revealed the strings of each tagged base pair of DNA by their color: an A (green) or a C (magenta) or a G (blue) or a T (red). It was brutal work.

Scientists who supported what came to be called the Human Genome Project, or HGP, wanted to get to the bottom of what all those genes communicated. In them, they believed, lay the precise blueprint of *all* humans at the same time it delivered the personal recipe for *each* human.

Biologists were just beginning to use the growing power of computers to unravel the whole mess, but the process was still slow. In the mid-1980s, scientists at Stanford ran a computer simulation of a single cell dividing. It required half a gigabyte of data and took 10 hours to generate. And that was the gold standard! The experts were quite certain the whole undertaking would require an unprecedented leap in computing power—because ultimately, that was where the information about the genome would have to reside. It was the only way.

Despite these colossal difficulties, Walter Gilbert, a Nobel laureate from Harvard, had stood up at the Cold Spring meeting and argued that the human genome was nothing less than "the holy grail" of biology. True, it would be expensive and massively difficult—but doable *if* science and government threw "thirty thousand person years" and three billion dollars at the job. That came down to a dollar per DNA base pair. Even for the federal government, that was a lot of cash.

Stanford geneticist David Botstein, a basso-voiced firebrand, stormed the podium, saying that the whole idea was a senseless waste of resources. Only so many science dollars were out there, and that sucking sound you would hear from sequencing the human genome signified far worthier projects disappearing down a black hole—indenturing scientists, especially young ones, to some monster project that would rob them of their own creative efforts. Loud applause.

Thus, the project looked doomed. Except it wasn't—not entirely. For the next two years, the idea managed to crawl along with just enough support to keep it from entirely vanishing. And then one day James Watson agreed to run the project. Instantly, everyone snapped to attention.

"A mover of people" was how Watson saw himself. And that was a fair description, because when it came to the nexus of genetic research and academic politics, he was, indisputably, the 800-pound gorilla. Thus, on October 1, 1990, the announcement was made in cooperation with researchers from Great Britain, Japan, Germany, China, and France. With a billion dollars in federal funding and Watson at the helm, the HGP was officially launched. A 15-year deadline was set to complete the project, now titled the National Human Genome Research Institute (NHGRI). At least that was the plan. Plans, however, sometimes have a way of going sideways.

AT FIRST THE WORK BEING DONE at NHGRI was fine and good from Craig Venter's point of view. But as time passed, the sluggish pace at which the project was moving increasingly got under his skin. And after a while, he began to make his opinions known.

In the mid-1980s, Craig Venter was just another among the battalions of researchers at NIH. He was considered a good enough biochemist, but hardly a man who could strap it on with the likes of James Watson. But now, 10 years later, while Art Levinson was busily moving up Genentech's corporate ranks, and Ray Kurzweil was making a national name for himself as one of the country's most promising inventors, Venter's career had advanced too.

The big leap came when he ran across his first automated DNA sequencer: a machine that could identify genes by shining lasers on all four DNA bases, instantly revealing whether they were an A, C, T, or G, and then record the information sequentially in a computer. Right away, Venter saw that the sequence of each gene could be recorded far more rapidly with this machine than any other technology. Immediately, he boarded a jet and headed to Foster City, California, to meet with one of the instrument's creators, a scientist named Mike Hunkapiller. Such a machine was a beautiful thing to behold. Venter didn't buy one. He immediately bought two.

Sequencing the human genome the way Hunkapiller's machine did, inside a computer, meant scientists could now theoretically track all the genome's linked letters in the order they existed—something like an extraordinarily long list of telephone numbers—and they could do it at blinding speed. And yet, even after Venter shared this new discovery, the approach wasn't adopted at NHGRI.

The reasons were complicated.

By 1993, a new scientist had taken over for James Watson at NHGRI. His name was Francis Collins. Collins was considered an all-star gene hunter, and a man of serious scientific distinction. Even though he was only 43 years old, he ran a richly funded genetics laboratory at the University of Michigan. In collaboration with other scientists, he had used a method called "chromosome jumping" to uncover the genetics behind cystic fibrosis, Huntington's disease, and Hutchinson-Gilford, an affliction that rapidly aged its victims.

Right out of the gate, Collins had his hands full at NHGRI. He could already see that the HGP was never going to hit its self-imposed 15-year deadline. And despite Venter and

Hunkapiller's new, faster approach, the institute still wasn't certain that was the best way to accurately sequence the genome. Collins felt Hunkapiller's machines were too sloppy, and he believed, adamantly, that the project's accuracy should never be sacrificed for the sake of speed. A standard was set that had to "stand the test of time," he said: No more than one base pair could be misspelled out of every 10,000. And that was that!

This drove Venter crazy. The central vector in his universe—the one that struck at the very heart of his view of science, and really his view of life—had been drilled into him by his mentor Nate Kaplan at University of California, San Diego.

Every scientist, Kaplan told him, had to "do the experiment." They had to be willing to try new solutions to old problems. Yet so many were afraid to try anything new. Why? Because in their heart of hearts they feared what they might find: the horrifying truth that their theories, their ideas, the comfortable concepts that they had wrapped their minds around for so long, might be wrong! What if they tried something new and it shattered their hypotheses? So rather than move forward, rather than push the envelope, too many scientists found it convenient to avoid the experiment and cling to the status quo.

Venter never forgot Kaplan's words. He made The Experiment a fire-breathing metaphor for his life. Take chances. Knowledge was power, even if it obliterated what you held dear. It was the only way science, humanity, or anyone at all could hope to advance. And it was the best way to meet the holy promise he had made that day on China Beach: *Make something worthy of your life!*

Nevertheless, Collins held to his "must stand the test of time" standard. It was slower, but at least it was reliable.

It wasn't that either scientist cared about the undertaking more than the other. Both viewed it as one of the great—perhaps *the* greatest—scientific endeavors ever. Collins himself considered it bigger than splitting the atom, and he had dubbed the human genome the "book of life" in his lectures. Yes, they could both agree the project represented noble, high-minded, historic work. But that was where the common ground ended.

Whole books and uncounted articles have been written about the political and scientific knife fights that ensued during this period. But in the end, it came down to this: With backing from PerkinElmer, a big, Connecticut-based analytics and computer science company that had brought in Hunkapiller's gene sequencing company, Venter created Celera Corporation, a for-profit company that could, all on its own, sequence the human genome. The company had all the backing it needed to complete the entire job: $300 million. In short, Venter was ready to move ahead, and he didn't need NHGRI or Francis Collins or anyone else to make it happen.

In a dramatic meeting at the Red Carpet Club at Dulles Airport on the afternoon of May 8, 1998, the two scientists faced off: Venter, the California kid and ex-Navy corpsman with the blue-volt eyes, now bald and shorn of his golden California locks but still carrying the outlines of his swimmer's body, and Collins, lanky and bookish, with a great mop of dark brown hair sweeping across his large forehead.

Venter was respectful, but direct. "We don't think people want to wait another seven years for you to finish the genome," he said. "Perkin Elmer and I have teamed up to form a new company. Our goal is to do it ourselves, using a couple hundred of Mike's new sequencing machines. We are going to make the genome free and available to everyone, same as you. The main difference is, we estimate we'll be done in 2001, four years ahead of your schedule."

Venter's scheme was a huge gamble. Nothing like this had ever been attempted before—certainly not in the annals of biology. Every technical component had to work seamlessly, or the whole undertaking would go down in a howling ball of public flame, with Venter hung out to dry like a sack of wet laundry. But that was okay with him. Maybe the entire endeavor would fall flat on its ass, he told Collins. Maybe not. The point was: It had to be tried! *Do the experiment!* And that was precisely what he was going to do.

CELERA DIDN'T COMPLETE sequencing the human genome in three years, by 2001; it did it in two—by July 1, 2000, to be exact. During that time, all parties—NHGRI and Celera—eventually negotiated an agreement, and announced that the genome had been sequenced as a joint effort. Everyone bought in: Venter, Collins, President Clinton, and all the other organizations involved from around the world. The big day, at last, had come.

Six hundred members of the world press arrived on cue to get the word: TV crews with their glaring lights and lenses; journalists from the most influential magazines and newspapers, notebooks and recorders poised, eyes wide; photographers and assistants, all scrambling like some immense, many-legged beast to learn how science had accomplished what the president of the United States himself described as "the most important, most wondrous map ever produced by humankind": the map of the human genome.

Venter had waited a very long time for this day—fought for years, viciously, some said, although that was a matter of opinion. One man's vicious was another man's tenacious. He had been vilified, marginalized, and labeled crazy—but in the end, he had found a way. More than one among the gleaming towers of academe had called him a cantankerous megalomaniac hellbent on destroying the high-minded aspirations of the original government team while seeking to place himself in the limelight. One scientist, in a *New Yorker* article, had flat out called him an asshole! But it was either create Celera or sit on the sidelines like some spear-carrier as the NHGRI dawdled and threw valuable time and money away.

Still, Venter would have preferred to be well liked and appreciated. He had said again and again that he didn't want the approval of NHGRI's top brass, but that wasn't entirely true. One of the great ironies of Venter's life was that he craved the approval of the very people whose noses he so often thumbed: his older brother, his father, the academic insiders, and the anointed.

But today, at least for a little bit, he had it all. He had stood at the right hand of the president himself. He had done the experiment, and on the big day said his piece, right there in the East Room where Meriwether Lewis had once sat with Thomas Jefferson to map another vast and mysterious place: the Louisiana Territory. Now, he was certain that by sequencing the genetic code—this remarkable string of molecules that made the human race possible—science could at last get down to the business of taking on the diseases that unraveled us all: cancer, diabetes, Parkinson's, Alzheimer's, the whole messy lot. Countless lives would be saved, and that, he was certain, would absolutely transform the medical world. It was just a matter of time.

12 | THE ACCELERATION OF ACCELERATION

arch was one of the nicer times of year to be in Washington, D.C.—as long as you discounted the politics. It was generally free of the oppressive swamp heat and shirt-soaking humidity of summer, when the throngs clogged the National Mall and the endless procession of tour buses belched and threaded their way through the capital. In early spring the weather grew mild with the cherry blossoms on the cusp. But that wasn't the case on March 14, 2000, as Ray Kurzweil blithely made his way to the East Room of the White House wearing a dark suit and a muted red tie. Today it was cool, with a stiff breeze out of the south blowing bright cumulus clouds above the city's grand monuments.

Life was good for Raymond Kurzweil as he dipped his toes into the shallow waters of the 21st century. He was on his way to spend some time with the president of the United States, William Jefferson Clinton, who would that day hang the National Medal of Technology around his neck. Not only was he being feted at the White House, but he also had finally begun fusing his prescriptions for immortality and artificial intelligence with the publication of his latest book the previous October, *The Age of Spiritual Machines*. That was 29 years after his father's death and 32 years after he created his first computer. Apparently, even for Ray Kurzweil, big ideas took time to percolate.

Kurzweil wouldn't be alone that day when he received his medal, of course. He would be joining 16 other scientists who were also receiving theirs. (One award was posthumous: Bob Swanson, co-founder of Genentech, who had died of brain cancer only a few months earlier.) Craig Venter would not be among the awardees either. He wouldn't win his National Medal for another eight years. Nevertheless, all of the explorers assembled in the room that day could feel Venter's presence. Three and a half months from now he would, at the very same podium, in the very same room at the White House with Clinton, make his human genome speech—the one the whole world would watch. Anyone listening closely enough, in fact, might have thought the National Medal ceremony was more about the Human Genome Project than the collective accomplishments of the scientists assembled. On that day, Clinton— before distributing the heavily ribboned medals—announced that the United States and Britain had agreed that very morning that all genetic information, once the Human Genome Project finally shared it, must be, "Free to scientists everywhere for people everywhere." Clinton felt this was crucial because the advances would not simply change science; they would change everything.

The project's findings were already revealing the genetic links between scourges like leukemia, schizophrenia, and kidney disease, and Clinton felt that soon they would do the same for cancer and heart disease and all the rest. The mysteries of human weakness and mortality, he said, would be laid bare, and then the solutions would follow.

If it had crossed their minds, any number of the bemedaled attendees in the East Room could have switched out the names of all the maladies Clinton had just mentioned and substituted only one: aging. Had they done that, they would have glimpsed an insight that had already begun simmering in Ray Kurzweil's mind five years earlier, in 1995.

The insight was simply this: Unless a meteor struck Earth, the human genome *was,* one way or another, going to be sequenced. What's more, it was obvious that the genetic information pouring out of the HGP was doubling every year, while at the same time the cost of its creation was dropping by half. This meant advances in computer science and biology were merging; in their way, humans and machines had begun to meld. He knew all of this because he had written about it in his books.

So now, as he sat perfectly erect with the other honorees in front of the podium, smiling up at the commander in chief that March morning, Kurzweil thought to himself, *They are finally getting it.* And of course they had to because the Law of Accelerating Returns made it so.

THE LAW OF ACCELERATING RETURNS, or what Ray Kurzweil came to call LOAR, had begun to dawn on him as early as the 1980s, but wasn't really codified until the publication of *The Age of Spiritual Machines.* It started out mostly as a practical matter; he needed a system for timing the rollout of all of those technologies he was continually creating. In Kurzweil's universe there was never a shortage of concepts—

but what good did it do to conjure a good idea, or even a well-executed invention, if there wasn't a market for it? Timing was paramount.

By the 1980s, Kurzweil had gotten pretty good at foreseeing the future. He predicted a computer would beat the world's best human chess players by the year 2000—and lo and behold, in May 1997 it happened. IBM's Deep Blue computer defeated Garry Kasparov, the chess world champion, in one of the highest profile competitions ever. The world gasped.

Kurzweil also foresaw the explosive growth of the internet in the early 1990s, when the world's total population of users was a mere 2.6 million. In 2017, that number would clock in at 3.7 billion, more than a thousandfold increase. Smartphones, cloud computing, and self-driving cars were also among his predictions. Not that he was always right, but he clearly foresaw something in this idea of digitizing the human genome, and all the exponential business that went with it.

In his efforts to predict the future, Kurzweil had turned to Moore's law. Gordon Moore was one of the founders of NM Electronics, which later became the Silicon Valley juggernaut Intel Corporation. By 2000, it easily stood as the world's most dominant manufacturer of advanced silicon chips. In a 1965 article for *Electronics* magazine, Moore noted, almost in passing, that the number of components in the integrated circuits of the day—things like transistors, diodes, and capacitors—appeared to be doubling every year, and probably would continue to do so for at least the next decade. (In 1975, he amended his insight, and changed the rate to every two years.) The point was: Change—at least when it came to integrated chips—was advancing, exponentially. This discovery became the very foundation of Silicon Valley and the explosion of ideas, money, and transformation it generated over the next 40 years.

While Kurzweil pondered Moore's law, he began to suspect it was part of a much larger trend that began not with the invention of the silicon chip, but with the big bang itself. The universe, he argued, had been accelerating its own organization from its first milliseconds right up to the present. First there was the formation of galaxies and stars, and then planets. Next, with the emergence of life on Earth, self-organization took another leap in the form of biological evolution and the natural selection that drove the diversification of the world's life-forms from the first single cells to elephants. Another surge came with the advance of intelligence, human consciousness, and the technologies that a symbol-creating, self-aware creature could conjure: words, language, writing, art, mathematics, and eventually software code, computers, robots, even genetic engineering—each gathering speed as they built on the foundations and developments before them. The more organized it all became, the more quickly it continued to organize. This made Moore's law a subset of a much larger evolutionary vision: the Law of Accelerating Returns—LOAR.

Kurzweil enthusiastically shared all of this thinking with the world. On stages or in conference rooms, he would reveal on great graphs how LOAR played out across the cosmos. It was an adult version of the same thinking he shared as the junk-collecting kid from Jackson Heights: *I'm going to change the world!* He would reveal the benchmark moments of history, and illustrate the way they took the shape of a hockey stick, where advances rose in a perfect exponential curve from the flat surface of the stick's blade to a sudden rocketing up the nearly vertical slope of its shaft.

That's what exponential growth did: It started out slowly and looked almost flat until it reached what he called "the knee of the curve," an inflection point that suddenly shot upward. The human race was now approaching that inflection point, Kurzweil would say, and events that had so long looked level and slow over the incomprehensible epochs were now poised to stagger upward almost vertically. What had been accomplished in 20 years during the 20th century would soon be accomplished in the first 14 years of the 21st, and within 7 years more after that, and 3 and a half after that and so on. By the end of the 21st century, human technology would advance the current equivalent of 20,000 years! It was all writ large in everything from the chemical and molecular interactions that shaped the early universe right up through the advent of DNA, genes, language, and mathematics. And it was gathering speed with the absolute reliability of a Swiss watch.

As proof, Kurzweil still likes to show pictures of Martin Cooper walking around holding the world's first cell phone back in 1973. The thing was huge—like a giant loaf of bread with an antenna on it—and hardly worked at all. But the next thing you know, flip phones are everywhere looking just like the *Star Trek* communicator. Then Apple invents the smartphone, which quickly becomes much more than a phone. Suddenly everyone is carrying around a handheld computer linked to the Cloud with all of its untold knowledge and information right there at their fingertips. Early on, the idea of lugging around some big clunking phone would have seemed like the world's stupidest idea. Kurzweil would often smile wryly at this. Because soon, people found they couldn't imagine life without these things. And then they would say, "Ahh, that's not really a big deal; it's been around for years." They feel that way because of something called recency bias, the sense that a new thing is quickly perceived as old hat because it's become so indispensable. Think of fax machines, microwaves, streaming television, and car doors that open with a gesture.

The race for immortality will behave very much the same way, Kurzweil says. Costs will start high, and the idea of living radically long will look as cockamamy as mobile phones, or self-driving cars. But then costs will plummet. And when they do, that is when they will actually work—because history shows that the only people who pay through the nose for technology that *doesn't* work are the wealthy. They are the early adopters because they can afford to be. But they are also the only ones who lower the costs of new technology enough that the rest of us can afford them.

Thus, in March 2000, there in the East Room, Kurzweil could see that the world was glimpsing an indestructible fact: Human biology was going binary, and that would create a new world. And that, in turn, would lead, one step at a time, to life everlasting.

PART OF RAY KURZWEIL'S BELIEF in his vision of a supremely long life began one year before his visit to the White House. He was in the lunch line at a nanotechnology conference at K. Eric Drexler's Foresight Institute and struck up a conversation with Terry Grossman, a slim, hardy-looking doctor who ran the Grossman Wellness Center in Golden, Colorado. Grossman had recently written a book of his own, *The Baby Boomers' Guide to Living Forever,* and the two men immediately connected. Grossman's Wellness Center was all about youth and health, and he had developed a variety of prescriptions for a longer life, including supernutrients, wellness diets, exercise, and chelation therapy to remove toxic metals from the body.

Kurzweil was fascinated with Grossman's work for the simple reason he agreed with it. In the early 1980s, he had been diagnosed with type 2 diabetes, mainly because of his poor diet. During one of his early entrepreneurial meetings right out of college, he needed to put on a suit. But when he pulled one out of the closet and tried it on, he was forced to leave it buckled but unbuttoned; he had gained that much weight. When drug treatments for the diabetes only seemed to make matters worse, Kurzweil researched and then attacked the problem on his own. He radically changed his eating habits, reduced all sugar, lost weight, consumed large quantities of selected supplements, and published his second book in 1993, *The 10% Solution for a Healthy Life: How to Reduce Fat in Your Diet and Eliminate Virtually All Risk of Heart Disease.*

After their initial meeting, Grossman and Kurzweil exchanged no fewer than 10,000 emails in the ensuing months. That led to a new book, *Fantastic Voyage: Live Long Enough to Live Forever,* which hit bookstores in November 2004. The book's goal was unabashedly optimistic: Do away with death. Others might be satisfied to grow old and die, but Kurzweil was not among them, and neither was Grossman. If anyone wanted to think their prescriptions were kooky or unrealistic, let them take the *Fantastic Voyage* and refute their arguments.

At this point, Kurzweil was approaching age 60; the very idea that death was somehow good, that it gave life meaning, rankled the hell out of him. Aging robbed you of your mental agility, whittled your sensory acuity, and burgled your sexual desire. In time, everything was taken from you until there was not a scintilla of life left to give.

Fantastic Voyage revealed to readers how death would be avoided—and one of the truly big breakthroughs was the Human Genome Project. The HGP would unlock the ins and outs of genetics, reveal why we died and how, and lead to new treatments tailored to each of us. Science would even find ways to grow fresh organs or supercharge old ones or reprogram human genes to reverse the ravages that aging had already wrought. Even foods using recombinant DNA might soon be created that could treat diseases like Parkinson's, Alzheimer's, and AIDS. The possibilities were unlimited!

Kurzweil and Grossman laid out how everyone could live forever using what they called their "three bridges" strategy. Each bridge would be a little like skipping across a creek from one rock to the next. In Bridge One, readers were asked to live a smart, healthy lifestyle to take advantage of Bridge Two, which constituted breakthroughs in biotechnologies largely based on insights from the human genome. This, in turn, led to Bridge Three, Kurzweil's favorite: nanotechnology and artificial intelligence (AI) that would replace our "suboptimal" biology and make radically long life a reality.

Each bridge in the book was plotted out with the detail of a scientific coda—which, in a sense, it was, from the supplements, exercise, and medical tests readers should take to cross the first bridge to the "programmable blood" that nanotechnology would make possible during the third. The book included chapters on diet ("Food and Water," "Fat and Protein"), the scourges that kill us (sugar and inflammation), and ways to overcome it all (hormone therapy, genomics, detoxification, and exercise). It was especially important for baby boomers to stay healthy because Bridge Two, the biotech revolution, had not yet arrived in 2004—and if boomers didn't take good care, they might not survive long enough to take advantage of the biotechnological advances on the horizon.

Did the human race have the tools and technologies in hand to live forever in 2004? No, the authors had to admit. But remember: A defining trait of the human species was that it insisted upon going beyond its limitations. That was one of Kurzweil's clarion calls. Science was not in the habit of slowing down. LOAR was advancing exponentially, and by that calculation, within 10 years, the average American would be adding a year of life expectancy for every year lived. All one had to do was survive in good health until 2015 (and avoid being hit by the proverbial bus), and immortality would be in the cards; kind of like a living version of an Alcor cryonaut. Except without the wait.[9]

THE REACTIONS IN THE SCIENTIFIC WORLD to *Fantastic Voyage* were polite enough, but less than riveting. At least among his artificial intelligence colleagues, the responses were often more along the lines of *Ray is really smart, but these ideas about melding with nanomachines and living forever—well, maybe he's gone a bit off the rails.*

Yet a good deal of evidence supported the general trends *Fantastic Voyage* foresaw, even if the timing of it all might be in dispute. For years Genentech, with Art Levinson as CEO and chair, had been "pharming" artificial insulin, human growth hormone, and proteins that attacked cancer and kidney disease—even asthma and psoriasis—with increasing speed. And Craig Venter was furiously crunching genes to illuminate genomic mysteries of all kinds. These advances were already emerging.

By the time *Fantastic Voyage* and its follow-up, *Transcend—Nine Steps to Living Well Forever,* arrived in 2008, Kurzweil's ubiquitous prognostications continued to gather interest and credibility, and the titans and cognoscenti of Silicon Valley were taking notice. Why not? After all, Kurzweil's personal and persistent visions of the future fit into the Silicon Valley vibe as smoothly as a $1,000 pair of Ferragamo loafers. Legendary venture capitalist and Sun Microsystems co-founder Vinod Khosla invested in his companies. Bill Gates called him a visionary thinker, and would invite him over to the manse now and again to have a bit of dinner. Kurzweil had come a long way since his days as the kid determined to build magical machines that saved the world. He had become an oracle in all things technological—which was to say, all things. Kurzweilian concepts that had once seemed so *out there* began seeping slowly into the public consciousness, becoming sources of insight into the murky future that Silicon Valley wanted so desperately to clarify. Because, as he saw it—and as the Valley was clearly demonstrating—every change in the 21st century was becoming a blazing, exponential bitstream! And hadn't he predicted precisely that? Even if there was still an immense amount of work to be done, hadn't he actually said the words? *Life without death was not only possible. It was inevitable.*

But, in the early 2000s, Kurzweil was not the only eccentric who was gathering the attention of those riding the bleeding edges of science and radical life extension. A lanky, biblically bearded computer scientist with a prodigious thirst for ale had also emerged, seemingly out of nowhere, from among the musty labs and libraries of the University of Cambridge across the Atlantic. He had even influenced the thinking of Kurzweil himself. This man, too, had a way with words and a penchant for combining science and logic with outrageous pronouncements. And he, too, was hell-bent on redefining the sainted meanings of aging and death. His name was Aubrey David Nicholas Jasper de Grey, and the world would soon hear of him.

13 | LIFE EVERLASTING

I t was 4 a.m. in Manhattan Beach, California, and Aubrey de Grey was knackered. Still, he couldn't sleep, partly because his brain was stuck in the British time zone he had departed just yesterday, and partly because he was having a eureka moment. He had flown over from Cambridge and spent June 24, 2000, submerged in roundtable discussions and debates with gerontologists from all over the world. The subject of their discussion was to explore ways to combat aging—and frankly it had been insufferable. Despite all the brainstorming and scientific deliberations, the group had failed to come up with any kind of concrete antiaging plan.

So now he was pacing the room, pulling on his long, brown beard as he habitually did, mystified. How could one open the hood on human biology and tinker intelligently enough to fully stop the aging process? That was the big mystery of the day. This, even though the very next day Francis Collins and Craig Venter would stand with the president of the United States and announce the human genome had, at last, been sequenced. Despite that advance, Craig Venter was still of the opinion that no one knew "shit about biology." And he was right. Everyone was still a long way from understanding how all the gears and switches of the human genome put every one of us six feet under.

Then came the eureka moment: a solution to aging, and it didn't require redesigning the whole evolutionary master-works. Instead, it was only necessary to identify the common damage that aging did to human biology. Once that was done, then one simply had to repair *those* particular elements in the way one repaired a car: Fix the brakes, replace the alternator, rebuild the transmission, and so on. By debugging the system, you could keep the amazing contraption running in top condition . . . indefinitely. After all, weren't we really just these magnificent, if flawed, pieces of organic instrumentation? When you thought about it this way, living forever really was just an engineering problem.

De Grey felt he was a man who could identify these insights better than others. His first degree was in computer science and his second was a Ph.D. in biology. He had only just completed his doctoral thesis on how mitochondria, which power every one of the body's cells, break down and obliterate our cellular works as they age. For years, while working his job computing at a genetics lab in Cambridge, he had pored over books in Trinity Hall's biology libraries, absorbing the intricacies of biomedical gerontology, the study of how the body ages.

So now in his Manhattan Beach hotel, he sat down and furiously scribbled out a list of the ways that humans commonly broke down, and how they might be repaired: cells, neurons, mitochondria, the whole shebang. The key was not to look at aging as something natural, but as a disease, and then to cure it.

Before the sun rose, he had written it all out.

First, there was the mutation of chromosomes, which led to cancer. Then came glycation, the warping and disruption of proteins that glucose (sugar) caused. And there were the so-called "extracellular aggregates"—all the junk that accumulated outside the membranes of the body's trillions of cells that, as we aged, increasingly failed to be properly cleaned up, like a house gone to seed. This included damage like beta-amyloid, which was related to Alzheimer's. Next, de Grey identified *intra*cellular aggregates, the goo that gummed up the works inside of cells over time: substances like lipofuscin, the so-called "wear and tear" pigments that damaged many major organs, eyes, and brains. Cellular senescence was another big problem. This happened when cells aged but didn't entirely break down, creating those zombies that sent out misfired chemical signals and damaged their cellular neighbors. And finally, there was the depletion of the stem cells that drove the development of all humans in the womb and during childhood. De Grey knew the body tapped these cell reservoirs throughout life to renew heart or liver or collagen cells, but he also saw that stem cells aged over time, which made them less than the perfect replacements they were in youth. And of course, their supplies were not unlimited. When they were gone, they were gone. These were the six culprits that aged and unhinged us.

Unlike Kurzweil and Grossman, de Grey's solutions to the problem of mortality imagined science making a series of incremental advancements in drug therapy that would extend the lives of still healthy people who hadn't yet shown symptoms of the cancer, diabetes, Alzheimer's, heart disease, and other illnesses that so often accompanied aging. He was, in effect, proposing to find ways to do what the body does pretty well when it's young, but slowly fails to do as we age.

De Grey didn't pretend that his prescriptions would be perfect; they just had to be good enough to slow and eventually reverse aging so that people who remained healthy at 70 would live youthfully to 150, at which time more advances would allow them to live to 300 until still more came, and so forth. Somewhere along the line, the really Big Breakthroughs would reverse aging altogether. He called this theory "longevity escape velocity." You would die, of course, eventually, because statistically something was going to get you: a bolt of lightning, abduction by aliens, a spouse who simply couldn't stomach the idea of celebrating her 950th wedding anniversary with the same person. But for all intents and purposes, life everlasting *was* possible.

De Grey realized all of this was theoretical, and the remedies were a long way off. But as he sat in the cold dawn light, ransacking all of the research he had done, he was convinced that in the year 2000, scientists working in labs around the world were already making progress. Their efforts just needed to be more properly focused. For now, though, his next step was to work out the details of his insights, and reveal them to others within the biogerontological fold.

He was pretty sure they would conclude he had lost every one of his marbles.

AUBREY DE GREY was a piece of work. In the early 2000s, he seemed to have dropped out of the sky like some John the Baptist, reap-the-whirlwind desert prophet, rattling his staff and railing against traditional medical science. His gaunt face was hidden behind an immense, messianic beard, and a brown ponytail of wavy hair ran thickly down the middle of his back.

His look and style was a 21st-century fusion of Rasputin and the Maharishi Mahesh Yogi—part brooding, part beatific, a man who understood secrets others could only hope to fathom.

And he had wit. When he gave talks, de Grey would open with questions like: "Hands up! Anyone in the audience in favor of malaria? Good! Because there is this characteristic that malaria shares with aging: It kills you!" He had a puckish way with words too, his elongated British elocutions punctuated by little verbal bombs like "It's just bullshit!" or "That's bollocks!" and "Bloody well stupid!"

But no one should be under the impression these lectures were simply out-and-out rants. De Grey *was* a scientist, in two separate fields. His first degree at University of Cambridge in computer science had landed him work with Sinclair Research Ltd., an artificial intelligence software company. His second scientific venture began when he ran into Adelaide Carpenter at a friend's birthday party in Cambridge. Carpenter was a well-respected fruit fly geneticist on sabbatical from the University of California at San Diego. She was 19 years older than de Grey, but they got married anyway. During their long conversations over breakfast and dinner de Grey began to interrogate his new wife about her investigations into the biology of genetics.

"Was anyone working on aging?" he would ask.

"No," she would reply.

"Why not?"

"Because it was wicked hard to study and nobody is going to tackle it. They wouldn't know where to begin."

Well, that was just too delicious a problem. So de Grey forsook his former job and took up gerontology while handling software development and bioinformatics at the Cambridge genetics lab where Adelaide and her students worked. Over the next several years he would harangue Adelaide for information, pore over textbooks and journals, pester biologists with every kind of question, and show up at conferences to interrogate anyone he could find.

Despite becoming a gerontologist, de Grey didn't care much for others in the field. For decades, since the days when gerontology had first emerged in the 1950s, scientists tended to view the aged as some disconnected group of peanut-gallery aliens known as "old people." De Grey likened gerontologists to geologists who thoughtfully reviewed the Richter scale readouts of disastrous earthquakes but did nothing about stopping the destruction itself. *Well, bollocks!* He didn't want to simply *witness* the process of aging. He wanted to halt it!

Nevertheless, de Grey began writing papers in respected journals like *BioEssays* and the *Journal of Anti-Aging Medicine* and *Experimental Gerontology*. He visited conferences and roundtables in Cambridge and Los Angeles and Chicago, and joined scientific societies like the American Aging Association and British Society for Research on Ageing. After all, one had to observe all the appropriate proprieties if one hoped to have an academic hearing.

In 2000, after de Grey completed his Ph.D. and the "eureka" moment had struck, he encapsulated his thinking in his first book, *Ending Aging,* with co-author Michael Rae. When it was published in 2007, he was suddenly everywhere because he was just what mainstream media loved: frank to a fault, articulate, credentialed, and exotic. The *Wall Street Journal* wrote, "If even one of [de Grey's] proposals works, it could mean years of extended healthy living." In 2010, Pulitzer Prize winner Jonathan Weiner was so captured by de Grey's persona that he wrote a whole book, entitled *Long for This World* about the man and his revolutionary quests. De Grey's TED Talks hit numbers that clocked in at the millions. He was even interviewed on *60 Minutes,* sitting under the lights opposite Morley Safer, expostulating on the possibility of immortality, stroking his great beard and explaining how he had worked out his prescriptions for everlasting life—or as he liked to put it, Strategies for Engineered Negligible Senescence, or SENS.

Part of what caught on about de Grey was his straightforward analysis of aging. He was really the first person to come right out and say that it wasn't heart disease or cancer or Alzheimer's that were making us old; it was the opposite. Aging was what broke down hearts, bones, and organs; it accelerated cancer and crippled brains. The diseases that plagued most of us were just aging's side effects. Aging was the mother of *all* diseases. And if that was the case, why were scientists twiddling their academic thumbs solving diseases one by one, when it would be far smarter to get to the root of the problem—or, more accurately, the seven problems he had laid out that morning in Manhattan Beach? Did we not see that every day 100,000 people were dying from age-related diseases? Two-thirds of the human race. At his talks, he would throw his hands up and rail. *We are talking about millions of lives here!*

In 2007, this was a radically different view of aging. Even as Ray Kurzweil was honing his ideas on age prevention with Terry Grossman, even while Art Levinson continued to grow Genentech into a bigger, more successful biotechnology juggernaut than it already was, and even as Craig Venter was figuring out how to create the first artificial form of life, almost no one viewed aging the way de Grey did—as a lethal disability with a mortality rate of 100 percent. Kurzweil himself called de Grey the most energetic and insightful advocate for eliminating aging out there.

AROUND THIS TIME, de Grey became linked, by an unlikely route, with Craig Venter. The editor of *MIT Technology Review,* Jason Pontin, asked Venter if he would sit on a small scientific committee whose job would be to review papers that refuted Aubrey de Grey's claims that aging could be cured. They were calling it the SENS Challenge. *Technology Review* was a magazine read regularly by the geekerati, so the request carried real weight in the scientific world.

Venter had heard of de Grey but wasn't necessarily a fan. He felt the man mostly fulminated, rather than accomplishing any actual science. Nevertheless, the MIT articles that had led to the challenge bothered him. Pontin's pieces in the magazine clearly showed he didn't care for de Grey's views, and to Venter, this felt like the magazine might be railroading the man, or at least trying to marginalize him. Venter didn't care for that. He knew a thing or two about being railroaded and marginalized.

The challenge had its origins in an earlier article Pontin had commissioned about de Grey in 2004, when he dispatched Sherwin Nuland to Cambridge to put de Grey under the microscope. Nuland, Pontin figured, was the perfect man for the job. He was a physician and professor of surgery at Yale's School of Medicine, and an expert on medical history and bioethics. His best-selling book, *How We Die,* had won the National Book Award in 1994. If anyone was capable of disarming de Grey's outlandish views on mortality, Pontin felt it would be Nuland.

Soon Nuland found himself jetting across the Atlantic and spending hours at de Grey's favorite drinking hole, the Eagle, a 350-year-old pub where Francis Crick and James Watson themselves had spent their youthful, pre–Nobel laureate days downing a pint or two as they plumbed the mysteries of deoxyribonucleic acid. De Grey personally preferred drinking Abbot Ale, which he saw as a kind of elixir—the wellspring of his boundless energy and intellectual creativity. That's how he put it.

A thoughtful debate ensued. Nuland wasn't so much interested in the bearded man's remedies for aging as he was concerned with the notion of a planet filled to brimming with humans who never died, never had children, and eventually became all the same age. As he saw it, those would be the inevitable results of a world where radical life extension was common.

De Grey said he understood those concerns, and he could see why people came up with the elaborate rationalizations they did to explain death's inevitability: *Knowing I'll die in the future gives meaning to the present. There is a heaven and eternal life after death. I'll live on in my children or my achievements. I'll come back reincarnated as a better man or woman (but hopefully not a toad or bottle fly).* These thoughts helped people make peace with death, rather than obsessing over the miserable inevitability of The End. What bugged him was the *way* in which all the objections to long life were raised. If science one day came up with a cure for cancer, he said, the world would sing its praises to the rafters. But suggest that we should eliminate aging? That was heresy!

In de Grey's view, staying alive—even indefinitely—was a straightforward extension of the "duty-of-care" concept that went all the way back to common law. This simply meant we should care for others if it was possible to help them avoid harm. If someone lived longer because of a new drug, were you going to take away their diabetes medicine or beta-blockers? Why didn't the same hold true for aging?

That was a good point, but in Nuland's view, not good enough. He said so officially several months later when he wrote his *New Yorker*–style story for *Technology Review*. His assessment was eloquent, and in some ways complimentary, but ultimately dismissive, even chilling.

Personal desires, Nuland said, needed to be balanced with the needs of the rest of humanity—and these were best served by dying when our individual time came. In the end, Nuland concluded that de Grey was dangerous, maybe delusional. It wasn't that he was some insane dictator or rogue menace, humanity's Green Goblin or Lex Luthor. It was more complicated than that. He was a benevolent soul, well meaning and agreeable, who would absolutely immolate the species, all with nothing but our very best interests at heart.

When Nuland's article appeared, something astounding happened: It became one of *Technology Review*'s most popular pieces ever. But the irony was, readers weren't nearly as taken with Nuland's insights as they were fascinated by de Grey's ideas for life everlasting. Pontin hadn't seen that coming.

That was when the SENS Challenge emerged and Craig Venter got involved. Venter had been plenty busy in the years following the completion of the Human Genome Project. By 2008, *Time* had counted him among the 100 most influential people in the world, twice. In June 2005, Venter founded Synthetic Genomics Inc., and then immediately took his newest yacht, *Sorcerer II,* on a globe-encircling expedition to explore the fundamental processes of marine microbes. He felt there were secrets to be revealed in the millions of ancient and invisible creatures that had evolved over billions of years in the world's oceans. Later, in 2010, he and his team would create the very first synthetic life-form at the J. Craig Venter Institute (JCVI), another of his scientific ventures. Up to that day, every form of life that had ever existed on Earth had been honed in the crucibles of natural selection—but Venter's team created an entirely new form of life they would call *Mycoplasma laboratorium.* It was a remarkable feat, and made headlines worldwide.

But again, that would come later. For now, Venter willingly joined the five referees for the SENS Challenge, which included other heavy hitters like Rodney Brooks, the founder of iRobot and Roomba, and Nathan Myhrvold, formerly one of Bill Gates's top advisers. Together, *Technology Review* and de Grey's own Methuselah Foundation agreed to launch a $20,000 prize that would reward any scientist working in the field of biology who could prove that de Grey's thinking was so wrong it was "unworthy of learned" debate.

In the end, Venter and the other judges decided the challengers had not made their cases, and de Grey won. Or at least he didn't lose. Venter, though he was pretty certain de Grey was not the knight errant of everlasting life, felt that supporting de Grey's point of view at least ensured that those who thought outside the box could get a shot at being heard and debated. That's what science needed. Maybe de Grey's prescriptions for longevity escape velocity or engineered negligible senescence made sense; maybe they didn't. But that wasn't the point. The point was to *do the experiment!*

Soon enough, there would be plenty of those to follow.

14 | DON'T F*CK UP

When Art Levinson began considering the remarkable proposition that Larry Page had made to him that October night in 2012, he knew his knowledge of aging and how it worked was just short of zero. Not that he was entirely clueless. He had, after all, picked up a thing or two during those decades at Genentech. He knew that he, and all that company's teams of researchers going back to the 1970s, had been playing in the very same molecular sandbox that made life possible, and death inevitable, even if they hadn't been specifically involved in curing aging. But he also knew that the undertaking was going to be the beast of all beasts.

That's why he couldn't fathom how people could make these wild prognostications about eliminating death when so little was really known about how to do it. Later—though Levinson would never say so outright—these views had to include the thinking of Ray Kurzweil and Aubrey de Grey—and, in December 2015, Harvard genetics professor George Church, who announced at an international summit in Washington, D.C., that he was confident he could reverse aging inside of five or six years.

Now George Church was not some second-rate, white lab coat bumpkin. He was co-founder of Harvard's vaunted Wyss Institute, a member of the National Academy of Sciences, and a key player (along with several others) in the development of the gene-editing system Crispr (Clustered Regularly Interspaced Short Palindromic Repeats). When Church spoke, people listened. Still, this was quite a prediction.

What excited—and frightened—biologists and policymakers about Crispr was its ability to cheaply and easily edit genes; just go into a string of DNA and change them with hardly more difficulty than scissors snipping a bit of ribbon. Gene editing had been around since Boyer and Cohen invented recombinant DNA technology, but Crispr was easier and more accurate, which also made it cheap—and therefore, potentially, dangerous.

But the way Church saw it, Crispr's powerful gene-editing capabilities would soon mean a quick death for dying. Levinson wasn't so sure, and he certainly wasn't willing to make any predictions. In fact, part of him still wondered if the very idea of this company he was getting involved in might not become a monumental waste of time: a big fat lamp without a genie. After all, hadn't the human race been trying to outfox the grim reaper from time in memoriam? Levinson didn't mind if something was difficult, as long as it was possible. Possible could be handled. Complexity was to be expected, even sought out and enjoyed. But just running yourself down some rabbit hole?

But that was only part of the challenge Levinson faced. He had to worry about the business side of things too, the resources: the new company's organization, strategy, total required investment. No one had ever tackled anything like this before. Should the operation be a Big Pharma play à la Genentech, or something utterly different? What manner of human beings should he hire? Biochemists, geneticists, gerontologists, molecular biologists, medical doctors, aging experts, a couple of witch doctors, and a few zombie therapists?

For the better part of three months, Levinson read, researched, and ruminated on these questions in between deliberations with Page and Maris and a few select others. Finally he felt he had all of his ducks in a row. So on January 23, 2013, he and Maris headed to the Googleplex to lay the whole crazy idea out.

GOOGLE'S BOARDROOM WASN'T very fancy, but it was generous enough to seat its 11 directors. Levinson knew most of them from his days on Google's board: Larry Page and Sergey Brin, Google's founders; and John Doerr, one of Google's original board members, chair of Kleiner Perkins Caufield & Byers (KPCB), and the man who had loved Maris's genie-in-a-bottle idea so much. Eric Schmidt, former CEO and now executive chairman of Google, was there too. Between 2006 and 2009, Schmidt and Levinson had both been on the boards of Google and Apple simultaneously, something that placed each in a very exclusive club. The point was, all attendees were pretty comfortable in the room that January day. Google's board respected, even liked Levinson. Hadn't Schmidt himself said when Levinson left the board in 2009 that Art would always have a special place at Google? Well, here he was.

Together, as they sat at the table, the group discussed ideas for creating the company soon to be known as Calico. Laura Melahn, who headed GV's marketing team, had come up with the name, and Levinson liked it—a kind of acronym for the California Life Company, but also a nod to a cat and its nine lives.

The meeting's presentation was simple: no more than seven slides or so, including ideas that Maris had discussed with Doerr several months earlier. Of course, a crucial part of the conversation was confirming that Levinson would run the new company, because all assembled agreed that he had to be part of the deal.

Among the ideas added to the deck were two concepts that Levinson felt were crucial. First was the idea that Calico should be split down the middle, like the two hemispheres of a brain. This helped him solve his "insanity" problem: the one that sometimes got him wondering if the whole idea of curing aging was even feasible. One side of the company would tackle multiple forms of cancer, as well as neurodegenerative diseases like Alzheimer's, dementia, and Parkinson's. These were immense problems among the so-called "diseases of aging." Reducing or, better yet, eliminating them would, all by itself, change the world. But eradicating them wasn't the same as annihilating aging itself. For Levinson, that was an entirely different animal.

Levinson had to admit that this first hemisphere was more in his personal comfort zone, and more in the Genentech model: Find a disease and then find a drug that could eliminate or reduce its damage. Maybe you couldn't guarantee people would live 500 good years, but you could make some serious, if incremental, progress that would improve the overall quality of human life.

In the grand scheme of things, though, incremental progress didn't really eliminate aging. Levinson had explained precisely this insight a few years back, when he was attending a scientific soiree in New York with a tableful of scientists and doctors, including two Nobel laureates. What effect, he asked, did they feel eliminating all cancer would have on the average human life span? Immediately, two of the cancer experts answered they thought 10 years was about right. All at the table nodded. But one of the Nobel Prize winners thought a little longer, and then said, "You know, I don't think it would change things much. Maybe a year or so."

Well, said Levinson, this might amaze you, but if we wiped cancer clean off the map today, we would only increase average life span by 2.8 years. That was it.

The table was stunned.

On the one hand, the improvement seemed almost trifling: a mere 2.8 years. Still, if you cured it, think how many tormented people would be saved. Or think of how much pain and suffering the elimination of Alzheimer's would mean. Alzheimer's was now the fastest growing disease on Earth, and no one had a clue about how it happened, why it happened, or where it came from. Levinson wasn't entirely sure if eliminating all aging would eliminate Alzheimer's, or other forms of dementia. The point was, even if you arrested aging, some diseases might still continue. So why not hedge your bets by developing ways to skin the Calico cat one disease at a time. That was hemisphere number one.

Levinson's second hemisphere took the opposite approach. That division within the company would focus exclusively on the roots of aging itself. This was entirely virgin territory, and who knew if it could be solved—and even if it could, how long it would take? It might happen in small increments, or with one mighty breakthrough. But it wasn't going to happen fast. The time lines and money required were staggering. That was a big reason so few tackled aging—that, and the fact that aging still wasn't considered a disease.

Luckily, Google didn't think along the lines of your average venture fund. The brain trust there had decided to step away from old-fashioned notions of capital investment and instead create a few selected moonshots to see what sort of magic they might turn up. That was a big part of Larry Page's view of the Google way, and a big reason Levinson agreed to come on board. If even one or two of Google's moonshots spun into orbit, there would be more than enough return on investment to cover the losses for those that failed.

Levinson's final variation on Maris's original deck came from his belief that Calico needed to bring in a serious pharmaceutical partner. Levinson suspected this idea might not go over well at the Googleplex, and indeed eyebrows did rise. It could dilute the venture's holdings; such partnerships could be messy and lessen Calico's control. Why not keep everything within the family? But Levinson held to the belief that a Big Pharma player could haul some heavy water when it came to the brutal bench work involved in medicinal chemistry, toxicology, drug development, and testing. The advantages would make the partnership stronger faster, and would outweigh the loss of any downstream dilution of corporate stock. Levinson wanted Calico to focus on solving the biological roots of disease. Let the pharmaceutical partner execute the solutions. The board decided they would have to mull over that idea.

IT WAS A SHORT MEETING, maybe 30 or 40 minutes, including the questions asked by all involved. In due course, it was time to let the board think through the whole presentation, especially Levinson's newest ideas. And so Maris and Levinson departed to await their decision.

As they did, both men felt the meeting had gone pretty well. After enough board meetings, one got a feel for these sorts of things. Yet, decisions *could* go sideways, and not every question had been buttoned up. They hadn't even agreed on the total investment yet! Amazing when you thought about it. And yet the feeling was that those details would be worked out soon enough.

Fifteen minutes or so later, Eric Schmidt walked out of the boardroom, looking very serious. He ambled down the hall where Levinson was standing and grabbed his hand.

"Well," he said, "you got it." Pregnant pause. "Now don't fuck up!" And then they all laughed—the chairman of Apple, the executive chairman of Google, and the CEO of Google Ventures. Such are the little pivots that arise when decisions to change the course of history are made.

15 | CAGE MATCH

On September 8, 2013—a little less than nine months after the January board meeting—Larry Page posted a statement on his blog: "I'm excited to announce Calico, a new company that will focus on health and well-being, in particular the challenge of aging and associated diseases. Art Levinson, Chairman and former CEO of Genentech and Chairman of Apple, will be Chief Executive Officer."

The moment the blog hit the wires, press, pundits, geeks, researchers, venture capitalists—everyone in Silicon Valley—jumped as if they had been shocked with a cattle prod. Phones and emails started lunging around the Valley like great, arcing live wires ripped from the moorings of the main line. Here was one of Silicon Valley's grand pillars of entrepreneurial achievement, and Arthur Levinson, a bona fide Silicon Valley heavyweight, joining forces to run this crazy new operation funded with bushels of Googlebucks. The combination of the two immediately and fundamentally changed the entire landscape of longevity research.

The word on the grapevine was that Page and his colleagues would be writing many checks—upwards of one billion dollars—

focused exclusively on annihilating aging. One rumor had it that when Levinson asked Larry Page how much money Google could ante up, Page simply said, "I'll let you know when we run out."

Though no one outside the inner circle knew it at the time, the initial, ground-floor investment from Google was $250 million. That was the money provided to get the operation on its feet; another $500 million was in the hopper when needed. That was half the money. The other half was coming from the pharmaceutical partner that Levinson had argued at the January board meeting would be so important to the Calico fold: AbbVie, a huge firm that already employed 28,000 people and delivered drugs to 170 different countries. That deal wouldn't be consummated until the fall of 2014, but when it was, AbbVie would kick in up to $250 million more, with another $500 million to come. If Calico could prove its solutions looked reasonably safe and workable, AbbVie would have the option to take the drugs into late-stage FDA trials, and then all the way to market. Still more money for that would come later. So for now, a cool $1.5 billion was guaranteed to be in the bank.

The other big shock, once the press got hold of Page's blog, was the news that Google was getting directly into the health care business. At the time, this surprised those who populated the Valley. After all, wasn't Google a software company that made search engines and such? The very name was synonymous with computing. But Page wanted to assure everyone that computing was beginning to touch all sectors of life, and that included ending aging and death—even if, in Page's words, it appeared "strange or speculative compared with our existing internet businesses."

Barely a few heartbeats after Page's blog posted, *Time* magazine dispatched journalists Harry McCracken and Lev Grossman to get on the job. *"Google vs. Death"—what a story!* Except there wasn't much about Google or death in the article. Instead, the piece mostly focused on explaining Google's moonshots. There was something to be said for moonshots—not so much because Calico, itself, could somehow guarantee longer life, but because Google had decided to back the company in the first place. And who could deny that it was a big deal? That was the underlying, vibrating, unconscious appeal of Calico—Google, Page, Levinson, a billion and a half dollars, life and death.

It was now clear, the best and brightest in the Valley were coming, armed with trainloads of cash tackling the one thing no one in the Valley had yet figured out how to manufacture: time. Hadn't they all recently seen Steve Jobs, supreme scion of the Valley, brought low, just like every other mortal? The man who appeared indomitable, who had said our goal should be to "put a dent in the universe," who had famously written, "Here's to the crazy ones"—hadn't even *he* succumbed, relegated in his last moments to a single, all-encompassing, but inscrutable word, "Wow!"[10]

Yes, death was the great equalizer, but who wanted to be equal? Who wanted to simply *pass away,* be *left behind*? Dying was more than sad; it was an unequivocal cosmic slap-down! A booming message that said who was *really* in charge, and what *really* mattered. And it was not the human race—not even Silicon Valley's anointed, wealthy, driven, and brilliant specimens. It was Death.

But, now, maybe there was hope: for baby boomers, Silicon Valley's denizens, and all those afterward who didn't want to die. Maybe, at last, the human race was rising up. A cage match! The brightest, smartest, and richest facing off with the ultimate serial killer. No more tricks or miracle cures, or declamations and ruminations full of sound and fury signifying, in the end . . . nothing. No, now the human race had its A-Team on the case and woe betide the avenging angel, death's nemesis. In effect, Google and Larry Page were out–*Silicon Valleying* Silicon Valley. Others along the Peninsula might say, "Hey we unveiled a new phone or iPad or car last week. What are you up to?"

"Us? Oh, we killed death."

16 | FIRST PRINCIPLES

The day Larry Page posted his famous blog announcing Calico's arrival, Art Levinson was well into ruminating on who might make up the company's leadership. Hal Barron was one of the candidates. He was a Yale Med School cardiologist who had been Genentech's chief medical officer for 12 years before serving the same role at Roche when the Swiss company bought the remainder of Genentech in 2009. Levinson already considered Barron the best drug developer in the world—so when Barron reached out, Levinson immediately asked him to become Calico's president of research and development.

Another key executive was David Botstein, the selfsame firebrand who 30 years earlier had risen up at the meeting in Cold Spring and harangued the assembled scientists on the injustice of spending billions to sequence the human genome. A "program for unemployed bombmakers" were his exact words. Since then, Botstein had become a believer. The years had transformed him into one of those statesman-scientists whose intellectual capital and political mileage were honored and valued more than his fulminations. He could still be gruff and cantankerous, though, and rarely withheld his opinion if one came to mind, which was often. Like Barron and Levinson, Botstein was also new to the field of aging. Genetics was his wheelhouse, and he was considered one of the world's experts. He had even written a book on the subject, *Decoding the Language of Genetics,* which combined his insights into the history of genetics with efforts to make the arcane language in the field easier to comprehend. Everyone was grateful for that.

Cynthia Kenyon contacted Levinson the minute the news of Calico hit the wires. She was one of the true leading lights in the longevity field, the Herbert Boyer Distinguished Professor of Biochemistry and Biophysics at the University of California at San Francisco. She would head up all of the company's research on aging.

Bob Cohen, an M.D. and oncology specialist, joined the brain trust too. Cohen and Levinson went way back to the early 1990s, where he had helped Genentech and Levinson develop some of their most successful breakthrough cancer drugs. Cohen had a knack for connecting scientific advances that related to human disease. And Levinson knew his opinions and insights would be absolutely honest: something Levinson greatly valued.

Three years later, in 2016, Calico would also bring in Daphne Koller as chief computing officer. Koller's pedigree in AI was undisputed. She had landed her first university degree when she was 17, and then a master's a year later, both at the Hebrew University of Jerusalem. That was 1986. By 1995, she had won her Ph.D. in computer science at Berkeley and was teaching at Stanford's computer science department. In 2004, the MacArthur Foundation awarded her a $500,000 "genius" grant. She used some of the time and money to do research with biologists at UCSF, Levinson and Kenyon's old stomping grounds. While there, she developed a new type of cancer gene map that used Bayesian techniques to help explain why breast tumors in some cancers spread to bone.

For the first several months of the company's existence, the Calico Five—Levinson, Botstein, Barron, Cohen, and Kenyon—wandered between the Googleplex in Mountain View and YouTube's offices in San Bruno, corporately homeless. They were sitting on $1.5 billion of high-grade, high-tech, Big Pharma money, and the company didn't even have a place to hang a shingle! This might seem odd, but for Levinson it was typical. Better to avoid discussions about such things as office space, as well as staff and equipment and all the financial nightmares that go with it, until everyone could bring a little more clarity to the table.

During their itinerant wanderings, the group read and reread paper after scientific paper on aging, peer-reviewed documents in scientific journals like *Nature, Cell,* and *The Proceedings of the National Academy of Sciences.* There were no shortages of hypotheses. The team brought in experts to ask every question they could imagine about longevity and aging and disease. In between, they divvied up the science and made presentations to one another, debated and plotted approaches. They visited research centers throughout the country—all the usual suspects (and a few elsewhere, including Aubrey de Grey, who very much wanted to work with Calico). Then they came back and tore the prevailing wisdom apart some more. Aging was not only poorly understood, they concluded; it was *horribly* understood. It reminded one of Craig Venter's oft quoted insight almost 20 years earlier that "We don't know shit about biology."

If that was true of biology then, it was even truer of aging. The way Levinson and the rest of the Calico Five saw it, this was partly because the field was still so new, and partly because it had a way of attracting quirky, even sloppy, scientific work: the kind that tilted, ever so slightly, toward the less than rigorous side of the equation. As a result, little truly serious research had been devoted to it. People spent billions on vitamins and supplements to avoid aging, yet not a single pharmaceutical company had spent a nickel on developing any antiaging drugs.

Given the garbled state of the research, Levinson decided that Calico should put aside the then accepted lists of "what kills us" for the time being. Maybe those theories were correct. Maybe death was all about telomeres and free radicals and transposons. If so, good luck to those researchers; his hat was off to them. But from where he sat in 2013, it was best that Calico go back to the drawing board. Get it right on your own. Be rigorous. That was the only way to *really* bring the beast to ground.

SOME OF THE RIGOROUS WAYS to bring the beast to ground had roots in Cynthia Kenyon's work. She was a star in the longevity field largely because of a strange and pioneering discovery she had made long before Google and Calico existed—even before Art Levinson rose to become Genentech's CEO and Craig Venter crashed his way through the HGP. It had to do with, of all things, worms—a particular kind of roundworm properly called *Caenorhabditis elegans, C. elegans* for short.

It was 1993, and one of Kenyon's doctoral students was looking at whole bunches of the tiny creatures in petri dishes at her UCSF lab. Kenyon later remembered that her student called what she was witnessing "magical"—not a term you would normally apply to worms. What made them magical was that they kept refusing to die at a time when they should have been long gone. When Kenyon herself peered into the microscope, she remembered thinking. "This can't be possible!"

But it was, and Kenyon felt she knew why: She and her team had modified a key gene in this batch of worms called *Daf-2*, a protein related to sensing insulin glucose. The little creatures consisted of 21,000 genes, a total of 100 million base pairs of DNA. That was a lot of information. And yet when Kenyon and her team changed just those two tiny nucleotides, the worms lived to twice their normal age!

Most *C. elegans* survived about 21 days, and remained youthful until around day 12. That was normal. But after that, they began to slow down. By day 17, they looked like the worm version of folks in the nursing home, and three days later, they were gone. But not these; they were whooping it up like teens on a beach long after day 17, or even day 30. They even stayed sexually active longer. If this were to happen to your average septuagenarians, they would look and act like 35-year-olds, and be living the good life right up to 150.

Kenyon was so surprised by the finding that she went back and double-checked the work. She even repeated the experiment to be sure. It all checked out. And that was good news—because thanks to those magic genes, her career took a 180-degree turn.

NOT LONG BEFORE, Kenyon had found herself in something of a dead end. During her days studying biochemistry at

Georgia Tech, she was invariably polite and soft-spoken—and even now, in her 60s, sometimes spoke like a midwestern teen from the 1950s, using words like "Gee!" and "Cool!" She could even come across as a little ditzy, but that was far from accurate. Kenyon was smart and thoroughly driven. She was valedictorian of her graduating class at Georgia Tech, earned her doctorate at MIT, and did postdoctoral work at University of Cambridge before landing at UCSF.

But Kenyon did have a stubborn streak—or maybe tenacious was a better word. She didn't care if other people said she was wrong, as long as she felt she was right. Her father liked to say, "There's a right way to do things and a wrong way. And then there's Cynthia's way."

Maybe that was why Kenyon decided to explore aging research, even though it did not go over at all well with her colleagues. One told her the field was a backwater for crackpots who couldn't do really *important* science. It was for losers, because nothing could be done about aging, certainly nothing genetic, because genes didn't affect the length of *any* creature's life span; that was set. Didn't she realize that small creatures lived short lives and large ones lived longer ones, and that when it came to life span, genes were not a factor?

Kenyon begged to differ. Because of her background in genetic development, she believed it was clear that genes were the master switches that flipped just about every imaginable biological behavior. So why not aging?

And that was why Kenyon's life-doubling discovery became giant news. When she (and her students) published the first paper in *Nature,* December 1993, researchers suddenly found themselves wondering if maybe there *was* some real science to this aging/longevity thing after all. Maybe there were genes that fundamentally affected how long an organism lived. And maybe those genes could be changed. And if they could . . .

SOME 20 YEARS LATER, when Art Levinson first came across Cynthia Kenyon's idea that it might be possible to genetically toggle the age of a living creature, he too was stunned. Could there really be molecular gears so fundamental that they could double a life span, even a worm's? Then, when he read that another genetic pathway dubbed TOR (target of rapamycin, also related to insulin resistance) doubled the lives of the worms yet again, he was even more amazed. These experiments had now quadrupled the critters' lives, which made them the equivalent of a high-spirited 320-year-old human being. In time, researchers found ways to increase the animals' life spans by a factor of 10! Still later, similar gene manipulation radically increased the life spans of fruit flies.

Now everyone knows that humans aren't worms or fruit flies. But we do share many genetic pathways with seemingly remote creatures, including mice. So researchers tried rearranging the *Daf-2* genes in some mice, and, remarkably, they lived twice as long too. Genetically speaking at least, mice were a lot closer to humans than worms; the two shared 99 percent of their genetic makeup, which suggested results in mice might have serious implications for humans.

Not that Kenyon or Levinson were planning just then to arrange a trial that altered *Daf-2* genes in a lot of human infants to see if they lived for the next 300 years. That would require some sort of longevity pill of its own, and it was why researchers used mice and fruit flies and worms in research trials in the first place: to get quick results. Besides, it was way too early, and because the FDA still didn't consider aging a disease, any such trial would be impossible.

But there might be other ways to go at the problem.

One of the several benefits researchers had found in *Daf-2* mice mutants was a reduction in cancer. The mutated gene seemed to diminish oxidative stress in the animals, which in turn reduced cancer rates. What if Calico were to consider an FDA trial that reduced cancer using insights from the *Daf-2* experiments? That would look like nothing more than an intriguing cancer trial, and if it worked, great. And if an additional side effect was that the same people in the trial slowed their aging as well, even better.

This wasn't an entirely new idea. Others had already attempted similar research. In one trial, scientists attempted to reduce arthritis by using a cancer drug to destroy senescent cells that formed in the joints of aging mice. The idea was that these cells—the kind Aubrey de Grey finds so captivating— increase inflammation in the body. If the drugs reduced senescent cells in painful joints, was it possible your average human would also become generally healthier and younger? It turns out the lab rat trial was right on the money. Human trials were scheduled for 2018, with results expected in 2019.

In the Bronx, at the Institute for Aging Research at Albert Einstein College of Medicine, director Nir Barzilai was working to raise $50 million for an FDA trial he felt could slow aging in one fell swoop, using a drug called metformin. It had been around since the 1950s, and was used to lower insulin resistance in people with diabetes. It turns out that the drug has effects similar to Kenyon's mutated *Daf-2* gene. It reduces insulin resistance, and also lowers cancer rates, oxidative stress, and maybe even Alzheimer's in animals and patients treated for type 2 diabetes.

In general, tweaking genes that lower insulin resistance seems to fake the body into believing it is living in a world where food is scarce. From an evolutionary viewpoint, the genetic processes within the species say, "Okay, listen up! We need to focus on finding food and staying alive, so let's slow the aging process until the situation improves. Later, once we have more food and are sure we can live well enough again to create new offspring, we can do our job, have some babies, and get on with dying." Or put another way, starvation had the effect of slowing aging.

Neither animals nor DNA actually "think" this way, but that was more or less what seemed to happen on a molecular level, and precisely what *Daf-2* seemed to do. These master switches shifted the creatures' evolutionary clocks to ensure the species survived long enough to improve their chances of making more offspring later. The question was: Could scientists perform the same wonders for *Homo sapiens?*

17 | HUMAN LONGEVITY, INC.

During all of those heady years following the completion of the Human Genome Project, during his globe-circling explorations of microorganisms and the creation of the world's first artificial life-form, Craig Venter hadn't really given the problem of aging and death much specific attention outside his brief adventure with Aubrey de Grey. All of that changed, though, the day he got on the phone with Bob Hariri and Peter Diamandis in the fall of 2012, not long after Art Levinson, Bill Maris, and Larry Page had their dinner in Palo Alto. Diamandis and Hariri had a business venture in mind, and they thought Venter might find it intriguing.

Diamandis was one of Silicon Valley's most visible personalities: a dark-haired 51-year-old entrepreneur with backgrounds in molecular biology, medicine, and aeronautics that he had gathered while studying at MIT and Harvard. His father had been one of the most celebrated magazine editors in New York, and at one point owned more than 22 specialty magazines including *Mademoiselle* and *New York*.

Despite earning an M.D., Diamandis turned away from medicine. Space exploration was his personal fascination going back to his childhood, and in the 1990s, after a series of grand entrepreneurial efforts, he finally landed a fitting project when he created his first XPRIZE. It offered $10 million to any company that could privately build and fly a ship carrying three people into space twice within two weeks. It took eight years, but finally, in 2004, SpaceShipOne took the prize. More importantly, it launched a whole series of XPRIZEs that soon came to influence people up and down the Peninsula, from Larry Page to Elon Musk.

These days Diamandis's XPRIZE projects are designed to drive the invention of just about everything from lunar landings to the elimination of poverty. Create "radical breakthroughs for the benefit of humanity" is the phrase Diamandis likes to use. These successes, together with the inception of Singularity University (created with Ray Kurzweil) in 2008, cemented Diamandis's reputation as a mover and shaker in Silicon Valley.

Unlike Diamandis, Bob Hariri was a newcomer to Silicon Valley, although he had known the XPRIZE founder for a decade. Hariri was also a great lover of aviation and an interesting character: big and burly, yet in no way gruff. There could be a boisterous side to him, but when he was talking business, he grew focused and quiet. He had grown up in Queens, raised with his older brother by a single mother, not far from where Ray Kurzweil had lived and wandered during his youth in Jackson Heights. The family wallet had been pretty thin at times, but his mother had always felt that education was a top priority, so he joined the Navy Reserve and got his engineering degree, figuring to become a Navy pilot.

He had wanted to fly for as long as he could remember, but his graduation came right at the end of the Vietnam War, and that left very few opportunities to become a career pilot. So, being good at math, and a self-confessed control freak, he switched to med school and took a commission in the National Guard. What better way, he figured, to keep control over his body and his health than to become an M.D.? Hariri eventually did do some flying in the military, but it wasn't until after he became a neurosurgeon and began building his career that he actually went out and bought his own jet.

Given their common passions for medicine and flying, who could be surprised when Hariri first met Diamandis at an XPRIZE event for doctors fascinated with space and aviation? The two men hit it off right away.

The idea that led to the phone call with Venter originated when Hariri suggested to Diamandis they create a company based on a big breakthrough Hariri had made in the early 2000s: his discovery of placental stem cells. When they first discussed the idea, aging wasn't even on the agenda. Hariri simply felt that placental stem cells held enormous healing and regenerative promise on a whole range of levels. But then one day he and Diamandis found themselves talking with Ray Kurzweil and Bill Maris at GV. *That* was when the idea of tackling aging came up. This was very near the time when Maris was rolling out his own thoughts on longevity with John Doerr and others at Google. Thus, by the time Diamandis and Hariri got on the phone with Venter, they decided to pitch their new company as a play dedicated to a long and healthy life.

Venter's enthusiasm for the business was good news all around. Hariri saw Venter as a true pioneer, a renegade, and visionary—someone who knew how to get it done, whatever "it" was. Hariri had watched Venter manage these sorts of endeavors more than once over the past three decades, not just with the Human Genome Project, but with many of his other undertakings. He knew Venter had hired hundreds of researchers and scientists over the years, and built teams that moved the dial. Nor was it lost on Diamandis and Hariri that Venter's involvement would attract tons of media and venture capital. He was, after all, generally considered the world's foremost genomics expert, and one of the world's highest profile scientists. There could be no doubt, Venter was the Big Dog, and thus his co-founders were perfectly happy to spend whatever time with him he was willing to give.

HARIRI'S VIEWS ON HUMAN HEALTH and aging were different from Venter's, but by no means contrary. Venter believed fervently that all of human health and behavior could be known, if only the mysteries of DNA were unmasked, and that included aging. Hariri saw placental stem cells as "regenerative engines" that could be tapped and then "turned into medicine."

These explorations had begun 25 years earlier, when Hariri was working as a neurosurgeon and trauma doctor at the New York Hospital-Cornell Medical Center. Day after day, he watched patients come into the emergency room with severe brain injuries, and it was a painful thing to witness. He never forgot the case of a woman who had arrived after a senseless automobile accident. She was young, and the injury was bad. Every time he spoke with the family, the big questions they always asked were: "How will she be? Will she come back? Could she be a mother to her children again?" It broke his heart.

Just as the family was asking Hariri these very questions, he was paged for another reason: His wife was being prepped for the first ultrasound of their daughter-to-be. He answered the agonized family as best he could (the prognosis was not promising) and headed to the obstetrics department. But he couldn't stop thinking about that woman. Doctors, it seemed to him, were getting pretty good at saving people from traumatic injuries, but not doing nearly so well at repairing the resulting damage. There had to be a better way.

As he was thinking about this, Hariri walked into his wife's room and saw the ultrasound image of his daughter-to-be. Right above the image he could also see the sonogram of her placenta. Compared to the fetus, it was immense, and that made Hariri think.

At the time, the general view of the placenta was that it was nothing more than a system for shuttling blood from the mother to the growing embryo and fetus: a simple vascular interface. But the engineering side of Hariri told him that didn't make sense. If the placenta was just a vascular interface, it would be small during the early stages of an embryo's development and then grow pretty much at the same rate the fetus did. But this giant organ was way bigger than the fetus, which meant it had to be supplying a lot more than blood. And that was when the lightbulb lit up.

The placenta was—how could Hariri put it—an unappealing structure, big and meaty, shaped like a bloody pizza with something resembling a coaxial cable attached: the umbilical cord. It wasn't something that many researchers were eager to scrutinize. Every obstetrician knew that once a baby was born, the placenta was immediately disposed of. Doctors called it the "afterbirth." But Hariri admitted that in the course of his life, he had been willing more than once to explore a dumpster or two—so why be queasy about probing the placenta for its secrets?

Eventually Hariri's explorations revealed that the organ was a very long way from useless. In fact, it provided everything an embryo needed to develop into a healthy, living, breathing child: It brimmed with pluripotent stem cells, life's purest form of cell, capable of morphing into whatever the body required—liver, muscle, even neurons. This was how living things were made as they developed. Some pluripotent stem cells transformed into skin. Others became bones or hearts or kidneys—all the cellular matter that made a human possible. This also made placentas magnificent stem cell factories. Yet every day nearly all of them were tossed in the rubbish!

A discovery like this might have prompted a lot of scientists to write a paper extolling their findings in a peer-reviewed journal; Hariri had done it himself plenty of times. But this time he didn't write a paper. He wrote a patent. Patent Number 7045148, to be exact, filed in December 2001 and granted the following September.[11] The application explained, in detail, how to collect "embryonic-like stem cells from a placenta" to recharge the stem cells of other humans. The way Hariri saw it, the placenta was a machine, an organic factory designed to create any sort of cell the human body could possibly need, including those that were damaged or dying.

Soon after the patent was created, Hariri founded the Anthrogenesis Corporation and LifeBank, Inc. Later Celgene, a multibillion-dollar pharmaceutical company, bought both companies in 2002, to form Celgene Cellular Therapeutics. Hariri was named chairman, founder, and chief scientific officer.

All that work had gone swimmingly, but by 2012, Hariri felt it was time to more directly explore using placental stem cells to regenerate muscle, bone, and organs. Most of Celgene's work at that time was focused on cancer. As important as that was, Hariri felt broader possibilities lay ahead. That was when he passed his thinking on to Diamandis.

THERE WERE REASONS THE THREE MEN decided to create a company that attacked aging. Like Kurzweil and Levinson, Venter had lost his father early in life, and this affected his belief that it was crucial to get ahead of diseases that kill before, not after, they did their damage. His dad, John Venter, had been one of those men who believed you kept your personal opinions and conditions to yourself. Unfortunately, that hadn't worked out so well. One night, he died of a massive heart attack in his sleep, only a couple of weeks after he had passed a cardiac stress test. Or at least said he had. The autopsy showed his blood vessels were a clogged mess.

Now, Venter was watching his mother grow increasingly frail, and that was also not fun. So at least maybe he could learn from the experience of his parents, and reduce the pain and disease that obliterated the quality of life for millions of people.

When Hariri made his breakthrough placental cell discovery, he saw it as a powerful agent for maintaining health. The cells not only supercharged the fetus during pregnancy, but the mother's body as well. He had seen women horribly sick with autoimmune diseases like multiple sclerosis or Crohn's disease who would often go into complete remission when they became pregnant. The pregnancy seemed to somehow unleash the immune system in miraculous ways to protect both mother and child.

The abiding hope of early researchers had always been that stem cells could somehow be used to repair broken spines, wounded bodies, and ailing organs. As early as the 1960s, stem cells extracted from bone marrow had been successfully used to treat and eliminate certain cancers. But those cells had to be taken from the patients themselves or a genetic match—otherwise they were rejected. That's because they were multipotent, not pluripotent, meaning they could only morph into a relatively small subset of other cells closely related to their origin: blood or bone or kidneys, for example. This made them less flexible than pluripotent cells, which are capable of becoming any cell in the body. But in the early 2000s, pluripotent cells were rare—and, at the time, only available from embryos whose harvest (especially during the Bush administration) raised all sorts of ethical issues.

That was why Hariri found placental stem cells so exciting. They were always pluripotent, but did not come from a human embryo, which made harvesting them less problematic. At Cornell, Hariri had witnessed the power of placental cells during fetal surgery. These were cases in which a fetus might be suffering from a heart or lung problem that could kill or severely injure an infant after it was born. To repair the damage before birth, teams made incisions not only into the mothers, but also into the fetuses themselves. Throughout the procedure, the fetuses would always remain connected to the mothers through the placentas and umbilical cords.

After these procedures, Hariri watched two remarkable things happen. First, the babies that were born almost always fared far better than they would have if the surgeons had waited to operate *after* they were born. And second, the new infants showed no scarring or incisions from the prenatal surgery. The placenta had pumped so many fresh stem cells into the fetus before birth that the body had entirely regenerated!

Another advantage of placental cells was their unusual immunological capabilities. It was well known that when any foreign object entered the body—a cold virus, a bacterial infection, or a simple splinter—the immune system instantly recognized the offending agent and went to work destroying it. This was why rejection was such a struggle after organ transplants, and why stem cells used by other donors had to match. The host body wanted them out, even if the donor wanted the new cells or organs in. But placental cells acted as if they were your very own, preserved at birth and ready to take over for the tired and sick cells that needed replacement.

Hariri had often wondered why a mother's body didn't suffer the same rejection issues when a sperm cell and an egg created a new baby in nine months' time. After all, even a fetus was a foreign body. Yet there was never a problem. Why? Because the placenta actually suppresses several classes of molecules that mask the fetus, the way a chameleon masks itself from the colors around it. Immunologically speaking, the mother never even realizes the baby is there! This was one of the great advances in mammalian evolution: the ability to gestate offspring in a protective womb instead of a pouch like a kangaroo, or the egg of a chicken or salamander.

In Hariri's mind, this meant placental stem cells could deliver an extraordinary biological trifecta: They could be used in any part of the body; they seemed to possess astonishing regenerative powers; and recipients didn't reject them. So wasn't it just a little bit crazy that every year over 129 million human placentas were being tossed into the trash? Hariri wanted to change that. He estimated that for every placenta used, researchers could create some hundred thousand treatments. Maybe some of them could even turn back the biological clock.

VENTER FOUND STEM CELLS fascinating too, but his real interest was in unmasking the mysteries of the human genome. In his mind, that would introduce an era of truly preventative medicine, rather than the current model, the one in which people lurched into their doctors' offices or emergency rooms, in pain or already sick. *Doc, my knees are killing me. I can't seem to see (hear, walk, talk) as well as I used to. I'm exhausted.*

In 2012, what else could a doctor do? Run some tests, figure out what the symptoms meant, *r*eact and try to repair the damage already done. Maybe some drugs could slow the progression. But wouldn't it make more sense to get *ahead* of the trouble before it ran you over?

That was why Venter wanted to unlock the secrets of each patient's genome. Since the days of the Human Genome Project, he had believed that your DNA revealed pretty much everything about you (not counting your personal experience). It wasn't just the way you looked, but the way your body tended to develop and grow strong, and then later, break down. Genes revealed whether you were shy or anxious or aggressive, easygoing or driven, or all of those in some combination. Every bit of information was there, but for now, almost none of it was known. This was why Venter felt it was so important to sequence as many human genes as possible. Once that was accomplished, you could finally know your own personal biological future *in advance,* and repair your body and mind before aging wore them down.

But to make that possible, the cost of sequencing human genes needed to drop, and speeds had to increase. And that was precisely what was happening. The first human genome had cost three billion dollars; in 2013, the price was approaching $2,000, and dropping fast, just as Kurzweil had foreseen.

The three scientists would have a lot more to discuss over the coming months, but once they had met, it became perfectly clear that they should join forces. By fusing two powerful medical technologies—genomics and stem cells—maybe they could pull off a kind of biological hat trick: an enterprise that revolutionized the practice of medicine, seriously extended life, and simultaneously improved its quality. Think of the dividends this might pay to society—not to mention the financial rewards it could reap.

To make money, however, you have to spend money—and that meant large investments would be required. Not millions of dollars, or tens of millions, but hundreds of millions. That was where Diamandis came in. He was the Olympic class fundraiser—or as Venter put it, "quite the man about town." Hariri called him an intellectual cupid. In the course of his many undertakings, he had made friends with just about every big wallet in Silicon Valley. Thus, in mid-2013, Diamandis sat down to brainstorm a board and put together a list of billionaires he thought might invest. Included were Elon Musk, Eric Schmidt, and Larry Page, Peter Thiel of PayPal fame, Microsoft co-founder Paul Allen, and Richard Branson, founder of Virgin Atlantic. That was the short list.

Nine months later, in March 2014, Venter, Hariri, and Diamandis formed their triumvirate and announced the creation of Human Longevity, Inc., tapping the Valley's deep pockets to pool a first round investment of $70 million. It wasn't the kind of money Google could toss at Calico—but it got things rolling, and more would be forthcoming. Almost immediately, HLI's offices sprung to life in San Diego and then Palo Alto. Instantly, the company became a key player. And in typical fashion, Venter began mustering his troops to spawn another breakthrough in genomics.

PART FOUR

SUCCESS

———

The long habit of living,

indisposeth us for dying.

—THOMAS BROWNE

18 | CHEATING DEATH

In the 21st-century world of Silicon Valley, not many people had heard of Benjamin Gompertz, and there was a good reason for it. Born in the 17th century, he was a little known, self-taught mathematician. Because he was a British Jew, he had been barred from a university education, so he took up work at the London Stock Exchange. In his spare time, though, he absorbed all the writings of Isaac Newton and mastered every kind of advanced mathematics. When a couple of his close relatives founded the Alliance Assurance Company in 1824, Gompertz became its head actuary.

Insurance companies like to know when, as a group, people die, and the central duty of an actuary is to figure that out. And that was how the young math whiz came up with an equation known as Gompertz's Law of Mortality. It provided a mathematical indication of when people are most likely to depart the planet.

Art Levinson found this equation fascinating. When he talked about it at Calico, he would leap to the whiteboard to write it out and then rapidly plot its graph, also known as the

Gompertz curve. When expressed, it looked a little like the bottom end of a steep ski slope.

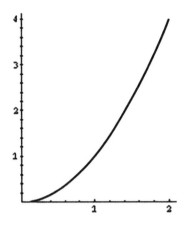

To most people, the equation didn't make a lot of sense. It read: $H(t)=\alpha e^{\beta t}+\lambda$.[12] But to Levinson it was a beautiful thing. He admired its clarity and logic. To take something as powerful and emotionally complex as living and dying and express it in a simple scientific formula—well, that was perfection!

The $H(t)$ in the formula stood for the many deadly hazards humans face over time (t). The variables on the other side of the equal sign together explained how, exactly, all of that dying happens. The really important variables in the equation were alpha, beta, and gamma—the α, β, and λ in the equation.[13]

Levinson had entirely forgotten about Gompertz, until he, Botstein, Kenyon, and the rest got to talking about the mathematics of growing old. Without realizing it, Levinson had seen this same Gompertzian insight back when his uncle Howard had sent him *The World Almanac*. As with those statistics, the Gompertz equation revealed that during the early years of life, the beginning of the curve was pretty flat; death and danger were remote, and health was abundant. Then as the curve began to rise, it showed that each year death marched exponentially closer. The steepness of that curve said something chilling about human life span: The likelihood of dying doubled *every eight and a half years!* Which meant that by the time you got to 70 or 80, you were not going to last much longer.

Levinson explained the workings of the equation like this:

Alpha represented the personal, genetic hand nature dealt you—bad cards or good—together with your own experience: stress, diet, medical treatments, exercise, and economic/social status. Alpha could change from person to person depending on all of those variables. Gamma was a random, but lethal, event: a car accident, drowning, murder—the sorts of tragic occurrences that were completely random. But the third variable, beta, was universal, a force that affects all human beings regardless of their personal experience. No matter how terrific someone's genes and upbringing are, no matter how well one handles stress or how rigorously one might work out and faithfully consume a Mediterranean diet, he or she was not going to live 200 or 300 years. No human lived that long.

Why? Because for one reason or another, evolution long ago set a universal life limit for every animal, including humans. The maximum for *Homo sapiens* appeared to be between 110 and 120 years. No one lived 150 or 200 years. Therefore, if you were really going to radically extend human life, it was clear someone was somehow going to have to change beta. It was the only way you could really solve the Ultimate Problem.

Levinson had come across the equation when he met Larry Norton about 25 years earlier. A physician and cancer biologist at Sloan Kettering, Norton had used the formula to describe how cancer tumors grew. Slow at first with the initial tumor, and then rapidly as tumors spread to other parts of the body. Norton's insight forever changed the way cancer was treated with radiation and drugs. One scientist called the Gompertz curve "one of the greatest quantitative laws of biology."

Among the traits that Levinson found particularly appealing about the equation was that it split the problem of dying into three neat pieces.

There was little anyone could do about gamma. It was impossible to change or eliminate it. As horrible as it is, people sometimes die for no good reason.

Alpha could be improved, but only up to a point; after all, science had already nearly doubled human life span over the past 115 years, at least in the world's wealthiest nations. Continuing advancements in cancer, and a cure for Alzheimer's, would improve alpha even more, and that would be wonderful—but it would not fundamentally change the human ability to pass beyond that maximum limit. That was why alpha was getting tougher and tougher to improve. If nothing else killed you, your chances of dying, on average, still doubled every eight and a half years. Evolution had created an upper limit, and no amount of luck or abundant alphas were ever going to improve beta.

But what if you *could* change beta—actually amend the inborn life span of the human species? That was a different story. Hadn't Cynthia Kenyon found something like this with her *Daf-2* discoveries? Was a solution to beta lurking there, hidden among our three billion genes, that could help the human race make the leap from 80 years past 115 to 200 or even 300, maybe more?

To explore that idea, Levinson asked one of Calico's computational biologists, a researcher named Eugene Melamud, to run some numbers and see exactly what happened if beta could be beat.

Melamud started by reviewing a sample of 100,000 Americans. The statistics showed that by age 50, fewer than 5,000 of those people die: almost 50 percent from poisoning, 18 percent from accidents and other killers. Heart disease dispatched hardly more than 6 percent!

But remember, the average human's chance of dying doubles every eight and a half years, and so after age 50 the decline gathers speed, despite all the beta-blockers and cancer drugs we have thus far applied to our afflictions. By age 60, the number of the deceased reaches 11,000, and by age 72, 25,000 have passed through the veil. At age 100, fewer than 3 percent of those 100,000 will still be living. Melamud's graphs showed that the longer people lived, the longer the list of diseases became: malfunctioning hearts, cancer, and Alzheimer's being the three biggest killers. Whatever slowed those diseases and increased life span occurred thanks only to alpha's whack-a-mole–style medicine.

For fun, Melamud changed the statistical model for beta—the constant 8.5-year number that set the evolutionary life limit for humans at no more than 120 years. When that number was zeroed out, the calculations didn't merely show an improvement; they blew everybody away. If the increase in beta was halted at age 30—a huge *if* to be sure—the median life span of that person would leap to 695 years! That was just the median. Some people might live nearly 1,400 years. If you stopped the clock at age 50, the number dropped to 181 years, still more than twice the average.

Levinson even asked Melamud to run the formula if beta were frozen at age 10, the safest of all ages. The math stunned him: The expected life span for 10-year-olds sans beta was

7,987 years, with 90 percent of them living almost 30,000 years! With beta at zero from age 10, a child's genes were so squeaky clean that almost nothing could kill them. The aging clock would stop, and they would simply continue to repair themselves, pretty much indefinitely.

Of course, this would require accomplishing something that, up until now, only the great gears and wheels of evolution itself had accomplished: resetting life span at the most profound genetic and molecular level. But Levinson's point was, beta was powerful! If you wanted to get a really big bang for your time and energy, *that* was where the magic would be. And if it were accomplished, it would represent the greatest scientific and historic leap in all of human experience. Was it possible?

19 | METHUSELAHS

B y mid-2016, Calico was bustling along. It had 98 employ-ees, with more in the pipeline. The research labs inside of its growing South San Francisco office were strewn with names like the Lily Pond, Northwest Territory, and Mid-dle Earth. Walls of glass were covered with handwritten graphs and computations: the aggregated thoughts and insights of Calico's growing roster of lab cats. And everywhere, researchers were hunkered down, working out the ways to bring death to a halt: some in the microscopy section and others in cell biology or computational science.

Soon Calico was developing arrangements with Ancestry .com to investigate centenarians who seemed, inexplicably, to live so long; the oddities of yeast and the ways they might explain long life; and, perhaps most interesting of all, animals in the biological hinterlands that lived extremely long. The Calico team had found some pretty fascinating examples.

It was obvious that if you compared, say, an elephant and a dung beetle, their life spans would differ. But what if you looked at two very similar animals and found that one survived much longer than its cousins? That was the case of a fish named *Hoplostethus atlanticus,* the orange roughy, which, not long ago, was a popular entrée on menus worldwide.

Orange roughy is very similar to the common pirate perch, which lives in freshwater streams and lakes. Like most fish, they swim around for a few years and then move on to that great pond in the sky. Orange roughy, meanwhile, swim the world's oceans, in cold water, hauling around pretty much the same genes as their perch colleagues. But how long do *they* live? The record is 149 years.

When Levinson, who was an avid consumer of seafood, got that news, he stopped ordering orange roughy on the spot. It made him wonder how many times he had gulped down some poor *Hoplostethus atlanticus* in its youth, robbing it of a century of good times trolling the reefs off the Kamchatka Peninsula or Scotland's North Sea.

But the larger point was that one fish, the perch, was dead and gone in four years; the other stuck around for a century and a half. How did you explain that? This was another example of evolution finding a way to bend beta. And Art Levinson was bound and determined to get to the bottom of it.

It turns out that nature has created all kinds of intriguing examples of this sort. Another was the naked mole rat, an underground-burrowing rodent also known as a hystricomorph that lives in East Africa. It's just about the ugliest creature anyone ever laid eyes on: a mouse-size, pigeon-toed alien with beady, lifeless eyes, clawed feet, and yellow skin so pale and bloodless you'd think it had been sheared off a corpse and draped over its sepulchral body by some amateur taxidermist. At the end of its snout protrude two buck teeth that seem to have been randomly hammered in by some sadistic scientist.

Yet some researchers adore the little beasts, partly because no other rodent lives as long as it does. The hystricomorph record was a male that a physiologist named Shelley Buffenstein brought to the United States from Africa back in 1980, when the little animal was only two years old. After a while, Buffenstein started calling the critter Old Man because he just went on and on. He finally died in 2010, but was still an alpha male in the nest, having a grand old time mating with the queen mole rat right to the end.

Mole rats routinely lived 25 years. Your average mouse might manage to exist three, and your everyday lab rat's life rarely ran to four. And yet those shorter-lived rodents shared a lot of the same genes as the mole rat. So why the big difference in life span?

If anyone knew the answer, it would be Buffenstein. She had been running the largest mole rat colony in the scientific world for years: 2,000 of the brutes at the Barshop Institute for Longevity and Aging Studies in San Antonio. In 2015, she brought her brood to Calico.

Once settled, Buffenstein continued to compare her tribe with a whole herd of other rodents of the lab rat variety: hamsters, the Cactus mouse, the white-footed mouse, gerbils—even other types of blind mole rats. Some of the other mole rats lived up to 20 years, but none lived 30 like the Old Man.

Buffenstein's comparisons, once she had delved into the genetic noise, revealed that mole rats like Old Man enjoyed the benefits of a powerful protein known as Nrf2, which balances the damage oxidation does to cells, including free radicals. It exists in lots of mammals, including humans. Nrf2 in mole rat cells seemed to help improve the way they handled all sorts of perfidious assaults: oxidation, various poisons, inflammation, heat, deteriorating brain cells—pretty much anything that broke the body down.

Nrf2's molecular interactions were incredibly complex: thousands and thousands of bubbling, bouncing, invisible discombobulations across billions of molecules. But in a nutshell, the naked mole rat seemed particularly good at sensing and regulating oxidation in general, and free radicals in particular. If this oxidative stress isn't cleaned up in any living thing, it accumulates a lot of damage. Thus, not unlike Kenyon's mutated *Daf-2* genes, Nrf2 sets in motion a whole domino effect of benefits with nothing more than a single protein that shields the little beasts so well that they live five to six times longer than nearly every other known rodent. One more example of evolution flipping a master switch and stopping the clock!

The more scientists inspected the genomes of the animal world, the stranger their discoveries became. Another was an immense creature that the indigenous Inupiat people haul out of the Arctic Ocean onto the packed, hardtack beach of Barrow, Alaska, every fall and spring. Barrow (now known as Utqiaġvik) is the northernmost city in the United States: the last slip of the planet that North America has to offer before giving up nothing more than wind, snow, and the harsh gale-swept waters of the Beaufort Sea.

When John "Craig" George arrived in Barrow in 1977 to take up work as a young lab assistant and wildlife biologist for the Naval Arctic Research Laboratory (NARL), he told his boss he wasn't sure he would last very long. It wasn't that he minded shoveling animal dung, or keeping track of elk and bear and walrus out on the tundra. But where was the stately beauty of Alaska? Certainly not here!

Barrow, you see, was a little like the mole rat of Alaska. Even today, the place looks like some wind-whipped, gold rush settlement out of a 1950s B movie, an architect's nightmare pocked with World War II-era Quonset huts and their drab descendants: ramshackle, prefab metal and pressed-wood buildings with an occasional geodesic dome here or there, each sitting on pylons hammered into the ice-hard permafrost to keep it from listing into the tundra when summer briefly makes its way to what the locals call "the top of the world." Here, the streets don't even require paving; they stay *that* cold.

Nevertheless, 40 years after George's arrival, he had grown to love the place, and was still living there when he made a remarkable discovery about life span inside the body of the great creature in question: a bowhead whale.

Although most whaling has been outlawed worldwide, under a special relationship with the federal government and the Alaska Eskimo Whaling Commission (AEWC), the Inupiat people of Utqiaġvik are allowed to harvest bowheads for a few weeks a year. The deal was arranged because the whales are central to the native culture in the way buffalo once were for the tribes of the American Plains and West. Only so many whales can be harvested, and their meat, under the agreement, must be freely distributed to the natives of the village. Nothing can be sold either at a restaurant or store.

George was a great fan of bowheads, and knew just about everything about them. They were immense, among the largest animals on Earth, often as long as an 18-wheeler and weighing 45 to 65 tons. Largely because of their gargantuan dimensions, they had been revered by the Inupiats for more than 2,500 years. During the vast majority of those years, Inupiat whalers hunted the immense animals using long wooden harpoons, hafted with broad, flint blades. But beginning around 1890, those harpoons were replaced when Yankee whalers from New England started heading north. The Inupiat worked with the white whalers and took up the new technology that came with them: metal harpoons called Temple toggles, which were catapulted from a kind of cannon on deck.

One spring day in 1992, George arrived with one of his colleagues, Billy Adams, just as one of the whales was being hauled on shore. The whale was mature: 50, maybe 60 years old. Everyone figured he was getting pretty long in the tooth, because the consensus then was that all whales lived about the same length of time: no more than 75 years.

As the two biologists were looking the whale over, Adams noticed a divot in its back. It appeared strange enough that George asked if he could see that section of the whale as they were preparing to butcher and distribute it to the villagers. That was part of George's job at NARL, keeping tabs on all animals in the region.

So George cuts his way into the 18 inches or so of blubber to see if he can get his hand into the divot, and he feels a harpoon. Normally, that wouldn't be very unusual. Harpoons were sometimes found in the great animals. But when he pulled the harpoon out, the hair on George's neck stood on end. In his hand, he held a large blade of slate that had been carefully hafted into the end of a long pike of bone or ivory: beautifully crafted and shaved to a razor's edge in the shape of a triangle five inches long and four inches wide. Stone Age technology. Nothing like it had been created since the Yankee whalers had arrived with their Temple toggles 120 years earlier!

George knew enough about whale craft and history to understand what this meant. Some Inupiat hunter, coming in for the kill, riding in a whaling boat made of wood and sealskin no larger than the whale itself, had stood up in the frigid, open sea and thrust the harpoon into its back more than 120 years ago. That was when Ulysses S. Grant was president, and Jules Verne wrote *Around the World in Eighty Days!*

It wasn't until 2015 that scientists got around to sequencing the genome of bowhead whales. The news revealed what everyone had come to expect: Bowheads were by far the longest lived mammals on Earth. It wasn't unusual for them to survive 215 years! Right now, some of those out there beyond Utqiaġvik might have been swimming the Beaufort Sea when Napoleon was marching to Moscow.

Other animals, like the quahog clam (the one used in clam chowder), were known to live 400 years. And the well-known ancient tortoises of the Galápagos Islands poked along for upwards of 100 years. And in 2016, scientists had confirmed that some Greenland sharks might swim the cold waters of the North Atlantic for 500 years. But those were fish and amphibians and mollusks. Bowhead whales were mammals— large and complex—and they routinely lived almost three times longer than your average, healthy human. Once again, evolution had set a different clock, a different beta. But why? And how?

Over the years, Craig George developed some theories. For one thing, new studies revealed that bowheads didn't even begin to mate until they were 25 years old. There was a direct correlation between the time a mammal grew sexually active and how long it lived. Another factor was that like humans, bowheads usually had only one calf at a time, and took 14 months to gestate. And like humans, they required a lot of care after birth. So, over time, evolution tended to select bowheads that would live longer: the better to ensure the species' off-spring survived and had time to continue breeding.

And then there was that old issue related to calorie restriction. Bowheads were the only whales in the world that lived in cold water year-round. While all of the world's other whales swam to warm waters to bear their children, bowheads spent every last minute of their existence among the frigid seas of the Arctic. That made food scarce, which meant evolution would select for bowheads that could survive longer without food.

This, in turn, would slow the rate of reproduction. Research had shown bowheads could go 18 months without eating a single plankton or shrimp, and still go strong. (This was one reason their blubber was, by far, the thickest among all mammals.) The animals simply needed longer life spans and reproductive cycles to survive, and the evolutionary lottery had allowed them to manage it.

Rabbits and rats, on the other hand, are good examples of species that live in a world where they rapidly proliferate in climates where food is plentiful. They have no reason to survive especially long. They can procreate like, well, bunnies, and then pass on to make room for their offspring. In more ways than one, this paralleled the *Daf-2* gene mutations in worms, fruit flies, and mice, which also slowed their aging, or the effect of the drug metformin as it changes the insulin pathways in humans. On a molecular/cellular level, all of these actions cause the creatures to react as though they are living in an environment where food is scarce.

George had no particular opinions on that insight, but he knew one thing: Bowheads were astonishingly tough—strong and healthy to the end. The powers of their DNA repair were stunning. Throughout their lives, they seemed to continually repair the huge numbers of cells needed to keep them alive and swimming millions of miles. Never once, after a good thousand of his investigations over the years, had George found evidence of any cancer or dementia in a bowhead.

Whatever was going on, all the evidence indicated that evolution could somehow change key genetic pathways that lengthened the life of a species. And that begged the bigger question: If evolution could find a way to do this, could science do it too?

20 | THE STARS WERE REMARKABLE

The stars were remarkable! It was one of those nights when the whole spine of the Milky Way rises up like diamond dust and you can feel the great wheel of the cosmos hold you in its galactic hand.

Nevertheless, Riccardo Sabatini's girlfriend was not happy. Here they were in one of the most beautiful places in the world: Tomales Bay, overlooking the Pacific Ocean up past San Francisco. And in a hot tub, no less, alcohol within easy reach . . . and what's *he* doing? Checking his phone.

But Sabatini couldn't help himself; he was a nervous wreck because he was in charge of the "Face Project"—the one Craig Venter put him on at Human Longevity, Inc., almost the moment the company had hired its first computer science team. Now, Sabatini's group was on the cusp of knowing whether the whole manifold undertaking was going to succeed or go down like a bad WWE match. Very soon, the project's first human face would reveal itself, downloaded in a great burst of digits from the Cloud, a little like stardust. Or at least that was what Sabatini was hoping.

He knew it was silly to be gawking at a smartphone, rather than beckoning the stars with the love of his life. But the Face Project was a big deal—a remarkable challenge. Venter had put the team—specifically Sabatini and Franz Ochs, who had created the first version of Google Translate, plus a whole passel of other brilliant Silicon Valley computer scientists—to a test: Predict what someone's face would look like based on their DNA, *and only their DNA. No pictures, no video. Nothing but the information in their genes.*[14]

When Venter first laid out the idea, HLI's software wizards told him it was insane. Couldn't be done. At least not in any reasonable length of time—maybe 10 years. Venter looked at them all like a saddened rector who had caught the altar boys sipping the church wine. "Of course you can do this," he said. "If I were doing it, I could probably get it done in a couple of weeks."

Venter knew that wasn't true, of course, not if he were given a strapping dose of Kurzweilian augmented intelligence. But that was one of Venter's ways of motivating the teams that worked with him, and they knew it. The whole crew was a bunch of type A, utterly geeked-out programmers; otherwise, Venter wouldn't have hired them. So all he had to do was toss a challenge their way, tell them they couldn't do it, and wait for them to prove him wrong.

Now, in October 2015, they had run the numbers, tweaked the great batches of machine-learning algorithms, thrashed the Cloud with data, and were furiously crunching the artificially intelligent numbers, waiting for the first models to emerge. The immensity of the data was shocking. The team had spent months sequencing thousands of genomes at 300 gigabytes each, plus all of the medical, biological, and historical information on each patient: age, weight, skin color, eyes, personal medical histories. Next, they applied boatloads of computer algorithms to shuffle the trillions of possibilities into facial models that made sense. Word at one point was that the project had so burdened Amazon's cloud computing systems that they crashed. "We broke the Cloud!" Venter told me. But the really big question was: Would the idea work?

And that was why Sabatini was eyeing his phone. Then, at last, the answer came. There, with the Big Dipper twinkling brightly above him, Sabatini saw . . . success! The team had created something most people in the genetic field had believed utterly impossible: a full-on human face that looked almost precisely like images of the originals, each one made possible by extracting nothing more than specific bits of a particular human's deoxyribonucleic acid.

It was a beautiful thing.

Of course, if you simply looked at the science, it all made perfect sense; after all, the genetic artifacts of a face had to be buried in the genome somewhere. Where else would they be? It was the genome that *made* one's face possible, did it not? But it was one thing to know there was a needle in the haystack, and quite another to actually find it. Sabatini and his wizards had done that. Did someone say this would take 10 years? The team did it in eight months! They had extracted precisely the right nuggets of data from the double helix needed to form the picture of a real and accurate face. And they had done it by turning molecules into digits.

That was really the purpose of Venter's Face Project: to provide a test case that revealed how artificial intelligence—or, as some put it, machine learning—could extract the revelations hidden within every human genome. If one could accurately predict what a person looked like based on his or her genes, it demonstrated that in time all of that other information could be extracted, too: every molecule that constituted a "self," including how you might die.

21 | HERE BE DRAGONS

By the time Human Longevity, Inc.'s Face Project was under way, the company's business plan had been well set. The idea wasn't to simply aggregate genetic information; these days, anyone could do that. No, HLI would gather genetic information with an accuracy and depth that would reveal nothing less than how the great gears of evolution constructed both the human species and the individual known as "you."

The Face Project was only one of many undertakings that Venter had simmering throughout the corridors at HLI. Also included were a series of research collaborations with Genentech, the J. Craig Venter Institute (JCVI), and King's College London. The King's College connection allowed HLI to get its hands on the genomes and microbiomes of 2,000 twins. Deals were made with cancer institutes and insurance companies from the United Kingdom to South Africa. Within two years, the company had grown to 200 employees in San Diego and Silicon Valley. Venter hired an assortment of top-rung executives, including Brad Perkins, former chief strategy and innovations officer at the Centers for Disease Control and

Prevention as chief medical officer; Bill Biggs to handle genomic sequencing; and, eventually, Ken Bloom as president.

Biggs had been setting up sequencing labs for 20 years, basically since they existed. His name befitted him. He was a big man with graying blond hair that flopped over his high forehead, partial to loose slacks and Hawaiian shirts. Bloom had originally come into HLI to head its immunotherapy division, but took on the role of president in early 2016. He was an affable, articulate man who had spent years in the academic world, then created a health care company later bought by GE Healthcare, where he had spent several years as chief medical officer.

Biggs's work would be especially important, because Venter had immediately bought two Illumina HiSeq X Ten Sequencing Systems (the grandchildren of Hunkapiller's DNA sequencers from the HGP days), with three more in the pipeline. Venter's goal was to initially sequence 2,000 human genomes a month, but accelerate to 40,000 by the end of the first year. By 2016, Biggs had installed 26 Illumina sequencers with the company knocking out over 700 human genomes a week: 60 terabytes of raw information and 240 terabytes after the information was analyzed. That was the equivalent content contained in 3,120,000 full-length movies a year.

Venter eventually crammed the place so full of sequencers that Biggs had to start giving them names like Obi-Wan, Leia, and R2-D2. It turned out that the staff found it easier to track mythical names for the contraptions than use random numbers. Generating these many genomes a week was what Brad Perkins liked to call "getting to scale."

Bloom agreed. By his reckoning, HLI would need to analyze a good one million integrated genomes before it could hope to gain a really solid idea of what any human double helix could reveal. All of this was entirely consistent with Venter's goal for HLI, but different from Calico and the SENS Research Foundation. He wasn't shooting to attain immortality or radically extend human life—certainly not in the ways Kurzweil and de Grey had been talking about. Venter's focus was on "extending health span" (or, as some of the gerontology wonks liked to put it, "compressing morbidity"). The goal was to get the maximum number of years of life that evolution had worked out for *Homo sapiens,* and to make them good ones rather than the painful, long goodbyes that marked the ends of so many lives.

Not that he was opposed to radical life extension. If Art Levinson and the researchers over at Calico could manage to create a pill that jumped human life span to a healthy few hundred years, fine by him: He'd be the first to gulp it down. On the other hand, there might be consequences if everyone did that. Venter was halfway serious when he said men might have to be castrated to ensure long-lived humans didn't cram the planet full of people.

Either way, there was plenty of work to be done. More deals and hardware followed at HLI: high-end imaging equipment, deeper machine learning expertise, more computing power, the sequencing of the microbiome, cancer cells, and tumors— whatever Venter could get his hands on to begin peeling away the obstreperous riddles the human genome held close. Then, he would apply all of that data to tackle whatever life-killing diseases he could before they took an early hold.

At its simplest, Venter saw the enterprise as a database company faced with solving the most complex translational challenge humans had ever looked in the eye. It really was like trying to decipher an incredibly complex foreign language. If such a mystery could be unmasked, the practice of medicine would change profoundly. Doctors would stop treating symptoms and start using patients' personal genetic information to head off disease. Every human being might not live forever, but because their ailments would be treated before symptoms emerged, they would live far better, and, therefore, far longer.

And think what an improvement that would be! After all, nearly every cancer is curable at Stage I, often at Stage II. Early detection might be *the* simplest cancer treatment: far easier and less painful than radiation or chemotherapy or surgery. Or what if you knew in your 20s that you were genetically predisposed to heart disease? Maybe you would change your lifestyle. Or take some preventative drug. Or, very possibly, thanks to all of those new insights about the genome, use Crispr to rearrange a few of your genes to eliminate the problem entirely, *before* it became a problem. With technology like this, science could have saved the lives of people like John Venter, Fredric Kurzweil, and Sol Levinson.

This was all easier said than done, of course. Back in the early, euphoric days of the Human Genome Project, scientists had become so excited about the huge advance it represented that everyone forgot that *sequencing* the genome was not the same as *comprehending* it. Right now, science understood 2 percent of all those laddered spirals. Of the 33,000 specific genes that did the work of creating a human being, 32,340 were then unknown: pregnant with information, but a black hole bigger than the Messier 87 galaxy (and that was the biggest one in the known universe). You could imagine it was something like an old-world map from the age of discovery where some frustrated cartographer had scratched out a few outlines of continental coasts and then, inside of large white spaces beyond, scribbled the words "Here be dragons."

But if Human Longevity, Inc., could fill in the blanks, then the bald spots on the great genomic map would disappear, and every bit of that information would be available for license to anyone who wanted it. And if HLI also chose to develop any new drugs or treatments of its own, then there was that possibility too. Alliances could always be arranged. But first things first: Gather hundreds of thousands of human genomes, and then ransack the mountains of data to decipher what it all meant. That was the ticket.

TO ACCOMPLISH IMPRESSIVE FEATS such as this, HLI needed two kinds of information: high-resolution sequencing of people's individual genomes, as well as deep dives into each patient's personal and medical history. Collectively, this is known as phenotypic data.

Phenotypic data synced a patient's genome with the real world of his or her health and background. Was the person 20 years old or 60? Were they Olympic specimens, or did they have heart problems and arthritis? How tall were they? What did they eat? Were they obese or slim? Where did they come from and what was the health of their parents and siblings like? Did they have any diseases? Did their parents? Combining genomic and phenotypic information created what was known as an "integrated genome," because it revealed both sides of the same human coin, and helped to match what you experienced in life with the details of your DNA.

HLI's massive, integrated genome enterprise was Sabatini's Face Project all over again, writ large. That project had taken eight mind-searing months of unremitting machine learning. *We broke the Cloud!* And now Venter wanted to do the same thing, top to bottom, with hundreds of thousands of human genomes.

This idea went way back with Venter. One day, when we were talking in his HLI office, he told me in his inimitable way that it wasn't as though creating the company had been "some kind of brain fart." As far back as 18 years earlier, he had told the science journalist James Shreeve, "We're going to be on the forefront of everything. We're going to need to build the fastest computer in the world, with data production orders of magnitude bigger than anything else. We're thinking on a different scale. Just doing the human genome and stopping there is way short of what can be accomplished."

In the Venterian mind, health, aging, disease, and the genome were all variations on the same theme. Each revealed the other. It was just that it had taken a decade and a half for the world's computing software to catch up. The need and the will had been there, but not certain resources—the technology and money. At last these had emerged too, so now it was time to succeed. And in his mind, the genome was the key: the wellspring of all human insight.

And so HLI's machines had begun cranking out the trillions and trillions of bits of data that had for so long been hiding up evolution's long and hoary sleeves. And, at last, they were unmasking more than a few of its stubborn secrets.

22 | EVERYONE HAS SEEN THE ADS

Everyone has seen the ads. Pharmaceuticals with names like Plavix, Lexapro, and Humira that seemed to be the cure for every possible ailment—rheumatoid arthritis, erectile dysfunction, high blood pressure, Crohn's disease, hepatitis, depression—the ads brimming with smiling, happy people romping with their dogs, hugging their children, embracing their spouses as the sun sets and the joys of a healthy life reveal themselves in all their glory.

Yet, no matter how sublime the images, no matter how thick they were with remedies, it was also impossible to miss the alarming ways each drug might maim or destroy a part of your brain or anatomy with some side effect: serious liver problems, suicidal thoughts, high blood pressure, blindness, cancer, autoimmune diseases, loss of muscle control, incontinence, even death itself. The lists seem to go on longer than the remedies! Why all of these *disclaimers* describing the many ways your cure could also be the end of you? The answer was simple: It was because so much of the pharmaceutical industry is a high-stakes, genetic crapshoot.

That became all too clear one summer day in 2016 when Ken Bloom, HLI's president, was holding forth with a small group that included then Vice President Joe Biden and a cluster of Big Pharma executives. Biden soon began berating the group for gouging patients and insurers with the outrageous prices they charged for their drugs.

Now, the minions of the pharmaceutical industry were hardly pure as the new driven snow when it came to charges like this. But those in the room nevertheless felt compelled to speak up. One of the heads of Merck looked at Biden and said, more or less, "Hell, we'd love to reduce the cost of drugs. Inside our labs we have the ability to synthesize just about any compound you can think up, but that's not the problem. The problem is *we don't understand the chemistry*." If Merck could sit down and tell the federal government which specific molecules might actually solve cancer or Alzheimer's or name-your-ailment, the company would happily run to synthesize busloads of cheap and perfect drugs. But who knew the answer to that? Nobody.

Nobody walked into a lab with a perfect solution, because no one truly understood how the human body worked—which was another way of saying nobody knew how the human genome worked. The best they could hope for right now was promising research that would lead to a series of FDA trials that would become, after years and many millions of dollars, either functional enough to pass muster or flamed-out disasters.

It was as if drug companies were playing a vast game of seven-card Texas hold 'em, just hoping their researchers could pull the cards for a royal flush or full house out of the deck. They had 52 cards, which meant winning *was* possible, but by no means a slam dunk. Most every pharmaceutical company gave developing an effective drug their best shot. Sometimes you won, and sometimes you lost. Whatever the case, it always cost boatloads of money—and frankly, it was usually messy, which meant no drug out there could truly tailor itself to each and every human being.

That was the rub, and that was why the FDA required all of those *disclaimers*. Because if some poor soul used a drug that damaged rather than helped him, and didn't know about it, all sorts of biological and legal hell would break loose, and that would not be a good thing for anyone. The point was: Costs for drugs, and for those lengthy examples of their side effects, were not going to disappear until medicine got a far better handle on what the human genome was trying to tell everyone!

Bloom had other examples of how insights into the human genome could kill you or save your life, depending. Take the infamous H1N1 flu epidemic of 2009. H1N1 killed 203,000 people worldwide—one of the worst pandemics in recent history. The first known outbreak was in Veracruz, Mexico. In analyzing the epidemic's genomic data, HLI's chief data scientist Amalio Telenti found that for every 40,000 children, one died of the disease. That wasn't a lot (unless you were the child who died), but the statistics had a "genomic" ring, as if something in the genes made some children more susceptible to the virus than others.

When Telenti looked at the records of the children that died, he noticed about 60 percent had preexisting lung illnesses like asthma or cystic fibrosis. It was easy enough to see how those diseases could make the flu deadly for them—but what about the other 40 percent? Before they got the flu, they appeared to be perfectly healthy. Then the next thing you knew they were gone, wiped out by the virus.

It turned out that the thing killing those children was in their genes. They simply didn't have the specific DNA that enabled them to fight off the H1N1 virus. But who would have known it? Normally the virus wouldn't kill most people, because no one got it in the first place. And if none of those children had come across that particular strain of flu, they would have been just fine.

The point for HLI was that the best way to drop medical costs, improve health, and ensure that a killer disease didn't get you was to understand what secrets your genome held. But again, that would only be possible when huge amounts of the genetic and phenotypic information could be assembled.

Now, at the end of 2016, almost three years after HLI's founding, Venter had upped the stakes and officially set one million integrated human genomes as the company's goal. Why a million? When Bloom would embark upon his meetings with pharmaceutical companies or insurance conglomerates or federal agencies, he had a nice analogy he liked to use to explain the idea.

Imagine you plan a trip from the United States to Japan. You know some basic Japanese and have a little book with some helpful phrases. That's great, if you only need to get from the airport to your hotel, or maybe buy some sushi at the local *katsupōten*. But if anyone starts asking you where you're from, or what you do for a living or your thoughts on Japanese politics, pretty soon you're lost.

But it could be worse: What if someone decided to engage you in insights about Zen Buddhism or Sartre's views on existentialism or even an ounce of biology? That would require a very deep vocabulary, as well as subtle grammar and syntax— which meant, to use the vernacular, you were screwed.

The same held true for the genome. Without lots and lots of genomes synced with integrated phenotypic information, good luck comprehending what the strangely linked nucleotides are trying to tell you. You need, in effect, to improve your vocabulary, upgrade your Japanese dictionary. So the Data *were* important. And HLI had been making progress in those first three years after its founding growing the dictionary: It had gone from zero integrated genomes to 40,000, which was about 37,000 more than anyone else in the world had at the time. Along the way, it had managed to peel back a few layers of the genomic onion. For example, everyone knew they inherited 50 percent of their genes from their mother, and the other half from their father, right? Well, no. HLI's initial findings indicated that most humans introduced at least 50,000 entirely fresh and unknown rungs into their personal DNA, about 8,500 of which had never been seen in any other individual thus far sequenced.

Bloom called this the Wheel of Fortune, because the new genes were utterly new and random mutations. True, they constituted only a small percentage of your total DNA—nevertheless, the shift could introduce entirely new proteins. Maybe they would throw a wrench in your genes, or maybe they would make you smarter or stronger. There was no way of knowing. That was how the evolutionary lottery worked; that was why species evolved slowly, and why each of us is as different as a newly fallen snowflake.

HLI's findings revealed other surprises too. The company had continued work at the Venter Institute, analyzing the genes of thousands of centenarians. For decades, gerontologists and quacks and everyone in between had been looking to the Exceptionally Long-Lived for insight into their extended existence.

Everyone has read, at one time or another, the story in their local newspaper about "Pearl," the 110-year-old who was still as spry as a sapling. When asked the inevitable question about her secret to such a long life, she would say with a wizened grin, "Cigarettes, chocolate, and a shot of whiskey every day. And all the sex you can get!" Some funny bon mots like that. Well, scientists, too, wanted to know why the world's 316,000 centenarians were still drawing breath.

In 2011, author Dan Buettner had come across an extraordinary story when updating his book *The Blue Zones: 9 Lessons for Living Longer*. "Blue Zones" are areas of the world where Buettner noticed that people seem to live an unusually long time. One was the Greek island of Ikaria, located in the Aegean Sea not far off the coast of Turkey.

According to Greek myth, Ikaria was the place where Icarus had plummeted to the sea when he flew too close to the sun, thus the name of the island. According to the legend, Icarus's father Daedalus was considered the greatest inventor and scientist of his day, and so he was summoned by King Minos of Crete to create a labyrinth to imprison the Minotaur, a beast with the head of a bull and the body of a man. After Daedalus dutifully built the labyrinth, Minos trapped him and his son inside to protect its secret. But Daedalus, being the clever inventor that he was, fashioned magnificent wings made of feathers and wax for him and his son, and together they made their escape from death and the labyrinth.

Daedalus cautioned his son not to fly too close to the sun, because its heat would melt his newly constructed wings. But during the flight, Icarus was so overcome with the joy and pride of flying that he disobeyed his father and flew too high. His wings melted and he plunged helplessly into the Aegean.

More recently, Ikaria has become famous for something else. As Buettner found, many Ikarians *are* unusually long-lived, routinely reaching ages beyond 80, 90, or 100, strong and healthy until the end with their morbidity seriously compressed. I visited the island to see for myself. At local cemeteries, I found tiny plots festooned with flowers and pictures of those who had passed, but not before they had lived long lives: ΒΑΕΙΛΙΚΗ ΛΕΡΙΑΛΗ 1920 to 2014; ΕΥΑΓΓΕΛΙΑ ΚΑΡΝΑΒΑ, died April 21, 2015, age 99; ΕΛΕΝΗ ΚΟΥΡΑΚΗ, 1910 to 2008.

One of Buettner's more fascinating discoveries was a dark-haired, bowling ball of a man named Stamatis Moraitis. Stamatis had emigrated from Ikaria to the United States after World War II. He moved to Port Jefferson, New York, where he married, built a painting business, and raised a nice family with three kids. All was well until he was diagnosed with advanced lung cancer in his early 60s. His prognosis was six to nine months.

Doctors recommended that Moraitis undergo aggressive cancer treatment, but he decided instead to return to Ikaria, where he could pass his final days among its peaceful hills. So off he went, planning to enjoy time with his parents (who were still alive and healthy) and live out his last days in their little whitewashed cottage on the north side of the island.

But after several weeks of lying in bed waiting to die, nothing happened. In fact, Moraitis started to feel better. He began sipping a little local wine and spending time with his friends. Soon he began to plant a few vegetables in the garden. Still he didn't die. Instead he grew stronger, built a vineyard, and made 400 gallons of wine a year. He expanded the house so his kids could visit, and lived 35 more years, utterly cancer free. No drugs. No treatments. Just the sun, clean air, and good vibrations of Ikaria.[15]

The media loved this story, and so did readers of Buettner's *Blue Zones* books. Clearly, this place delivered some sort of elixir that fortified the bones and blood, and laid disease to waste. At least that seemed to be the headline.

But the idea of a longevity elixir was not Buettner's take-away. Moraitis's story was a fine yarn that helped reveal the joys of Blue Zone living, but he knew there weren't any magic potions. Mostly the reasons Ikarians lived so long (especially those who were born in the early 1900s) had to do with their lifestyle: walking for miles up and down the island's high hills, eating fresh, organic food from their own gardens, imbibing healthy herbal teas, living by the sea with very little stress, and spending lots of quality time with their family and good friends. No one worried about time, or the stress that came with it. Of course, the occasional glass of local wine might not have hurt either.

The truth was, nearly anyone would do pretty well this way. Except then, they would actually have to live in a relatively stress-free Blue Zone. And that would be difficult, because most people do not settle down in small Greek islands where anxiety is low and the food is local and fresh. Buettner knew better than most that Ikarians didn't actively try to live exceptionally long lives; it was simply a natural side effect of how they went about their business. Still, there had to be some way to bottle all of this vitality, didn't there? Sure enough, after the publication of Buettner's book, people from all over started coming to places like Thea's Inn in Ikaria to get their proper doses of longevity.

Buettner had met Thea Parikos during one of his research trips to the island. Later, I met her too, because her appearances in *Blue Zones* books had made her a celebrity of sorts. Thea loved people coming to visit her little inn. But did they have to be so obsessed with long life? Travelers would show up at her place in the tiny village of Nas (population 90), and after spending some time eating the food and breathing the bracing Aegean air, head back to America or Sweden or Germany or England, figuring they would soon emerge as healthy as the gods themselves. Of course, it didn't work that way. Life was good if you lived there, but leave and all the benefits disappeared. Kind of like Shangri-la.

The desire for quick longevity fixes was understandable. Why not hope that people like Pearl and Stamatis possessed some sort of ambrosia that made living and dying more bearable? This was precisely why Venter and Human Longevity, Inc., had wondered if some people had specialized genes the rest of the human race had been deprived of: little bundled proteins that acted as microscopic Fountains of Youth. And if they did have them, wouldn't it be nice to find them, and learn to swap them into the rest of us so that everyone could live long and prosper?

However, as HLI mined its growing reservoir of genomes, it found no such fountain. At least not so far, and probably never. The analysis of the company's first round of 30,000 to 40,000 genomes showed that people who lived to a hundred didn't have supergenes that bequeathed long life; they simply had fewer frail ones. Later, researcher Graham Ruby and his team at Calico found pretty much the same thing based on the millions of Ancestry.com records they tabulated and analyzed. It seems centenarians aren't blessed with any genetic silver bullets. They're dealt the equivalent of a full house: terrific genetic cards in all the right combinations. If you happen to live a Blue Zones lifestyle, all the better; you might live even longer. But in the end, no matter how well you live, no matter how many colonics you try or heaps of kale you eat, the degradations of your genes will still get you. It wasn't just Blue Zone living or Pearl's whisky and cigarettes that kept centenarians going. It was the absence of lousy genes.

After all of HLI's thousands of genomes were compiled, and after the machine-learning algorithms had done their work, this meant the company was getting a ringside view of what unraveled human youth. The deterioration was so common that based on the way the average genome changed over time, Venter's team actually could see, within a couple of years one way or another, how old a person was! That's how precisely the damage was built into the human system. HLI also found that the genes of some people were falling apart faster than usual. Maybe they had been dealt crappy cards; maybe they might personally have damaged their body in other ways (stress, alcohol, obesity). But one way or another, some people were aging faster than others—and that was valuable information.

Generally speaking, scientists had known for a long time that healthy genes meant a healthy body, and vice versa. The difference with HLI's findings was that now, specific genes (or combinations of them) were being revealed, genome by genome. This was making it increasingly clear where the frailty genes hid themselves, as well as how and why genes fall apart in general. As more and more of these were discovered, the next step would be to create drugs that could slow the damage, or go in and repair the battered genes themselves. That was the long-term goal.

This was, of course, exactly what Venter had hoped for, and precisely what he wanted HLI to deliver: the aggregation and analysis of massive amounts of data. Even at this early stage, the process was proving to be an excellent way to decipher the specific ways the human body shuffled down the road to perdition. And by 2016, Venter was just getting started.

He wasn't alone though. Others were also now seeing the potential of eliminating aging, and fresh resources were beginning to flow in from—where else?—Silicon Valley. With a little help from Hollywood.

23 | WOBBLING WEEBLES

mmmm . . . mmmmm. The Moroccan phyllo chicken puffs were *soooo* tasty. Just the right combination of shredded chicken, perfectly spiced and then rolled *b'stilla* style with that contra-mix of ginger and cumin, cinnamon and coriander. And the way the egg was made: Superb! It made one wonder why no one was eating them.

Perhaps because they were too enthralled? It *was* quiet. But that wasn't unusual among the homes in Mandeville Canyon, where, out there beyond L.A.'s fevered highways, the living was good. Certainly no one was *dying,* at least not in the acute sense. Nevertheless, dying was on the minds of the assembled. This included Goldie Hawn, who sat, stately and erect, on a comfortable couch with her tumble of blond hair. She had a question for Nobel laureate and microbiologist Elizabeth Blackburn about "the mitochondria."

Hawn had been told about a molecule called glutathione, a brawny antioxidant that boosted mitochondria: the organelles that powered every cell in the human body. Glutathione was sometimes called "the God molecule" (which made scientists cringe because, of course, there was no single molecule that could rewind aging). It also didn't work very well as an oral supplement. But if anyone *did* overindulge, by injecting it, for example, they might find they would soon be dissolving their livers and kidneys. Blackburn suggested the best approach might be to simply eat a varied and healthy diet.

The reason for this particular evening's soiree was the kickoff in early 2016 for the National Academy of Medicine's Grand Challenge for Healthy Longevity. When raising funds for ventures of these sorts, a cocktail of science, money, and the desire for long life could have a way of creating a nice snow-ball effect.

The goal of the challenge was to pool $25 million to sponsor breakthroughs in the field of aging science. The challenge itself hadn't yet been entirely defined, except insofar as it was similar to Peter Diamandis's XPRIZE endeavors. Diamandis, in fact, had consulted on other prizes with the man who was behind the evening's challenge in collaboration with Victor Dzau, the august head of the National Academy of Medicine. That man was Dr. Joon Yun.

In 2014, Yun, an M.D. and hedge fund founder, had launched the Palo Alto Longevity Prize. Yun saw human biology as a complex machine encoded with DNA, and liked to say it was time the human race "hacked the code." Life was, after all, nothing more than programmable software; therefore, all science had to do was start debugging the suboptimal system. Of course, knowing which code to debug was the crucial issue, and that was the reason for the grand prize and why the scientific teams that signed on had bought in.

Yun's family had been farmers in Korea for generations, but he grew up in the United States where he graduated from Harvard, earned his medical degree at Duke, and then undertook his clinical training at Stanford. Finding himself in Silicon Valley, Yun switched from medicine to hedge funds, where he was the president and managing partner of Palo Alto Investors, LLC, a company that specialized in health care investments. In 2017, the fund's assets topped one billion dollars.

Being an M.D., Yun was bothered enough by death and dying that he gave away one million dollars of his own money to get the Palo Alto Longevity Prize rolling. In 2014, two goals were set: First, take any wild animal and, by some acceptable intervention, increase that animal's life span by 50 percent. Second, using the heart as a baseline, improve an aging mammal's "homeostatic capacity" so effectively that it acted young again. In other words, turn back the clock. Prize Number One had to come before Prize Number Two, and the award for both was to be split down the middle: $500,000 each.

Yun had a marvelously simple way of explaining what he meant by "homeostatic capacity." Imagine a Weeble, the little toys with the round bottoms that refuse to fall over. That was what good homeostasis did in any living thing: enabled it to bounce back, just like a Weeble, or a healthy 20-year-old. Neither fatigue nor soreness keeps a young healthy human down for long, because the genetics of the creature is optimized to ensure all the biological mechanisms operate at top homeostatic capacity. Youth and health were synonymous.

But, alas, humans do, in time, wobble as aging sets in, and they eventually fall down. Life's abuses—radiation, loathsome chemicals, inflammatory and damaging foods, stress, and all the other ongoing deoxyribonucleic pilferings of the cells and stem cells of living things—batter genes unremittingly.

The goal of the prize was to find a hack that boosted homeostatic capacity.

Despite Yun's Weeble analogy, the Palo Alto Longevity Prize had so far struggled to meet its challenge. Initially, Prize Number One was scheduled to be completed by the summer of 2016, two years following its inception. But by early 2019, despite several comers, no prizes had yet been awarded. Prize Number Two was "yet to be determined."

The $25 million National Academy of Medicine's Grand Challenge for Healthy Longevity also remained a work in progress. But Yun never felt that any of these efforts was about the prize itself. In his mind, they were beacons: ways to draw attention to the complications of aging so that more of the right kind of people would develop the resources needed to change the world. It was time to rethink the conduct of the medical system. The National Academy of Medicine seemed a good place to start.

Prizes like the Grand Challenge were only a small part of an ever accelerating drive for death-defying endeavors. In 2017, suddenly and everywhere, the media were again alight with discussions of radical life extension, just as they had been three and four years earlier. Except now there was a twist: It was all about Silicon Valley. Longevity venture funds and startups had begun popping up like little brown mushrooms. Companies with high-tech names like Verily (founded by Bill Maris's friend Andy Conrad), Unity Biotechnology, Navitor, United Therapeutics (Ray Kurzweil was on the board), Alkahest, ZeroCater, Stemcentrx, Nootrobox, and Bulletproof, all now existed on California's corporate rolls. These also included Venter's Human Longevity, Inc., and Aubrey de Grey's SENS Research Foundation.

Many of these were included in a *New Yorker* article published in April 2017 entitled, "Silicon Valley's Quest to Live Forever." Similar pieces quickly followed. Articles in *Time, Smithsonian,* even *Town and Country* of all places, began popping up with titles like "How Silicon Valley Is Trying to Hack Its Way Into a Longer Life," and "Can Human Mortality Really Be Hacked?" The subjects of Silicon Valley and immortality seemed to be suddenly joined at the hip.

All the emerging ventures were happy to meet with the media to explain the progress they were making. The articles revealed how advancements in genomics, genetics, stem cells, proteomics, something called a Bod Pod, DNA repair, advanced supplements, pig placentas—all of them—would soon have death on the run. There were explorations of senescent cells, "young blood" transfusions, also known as parabiosis, and a raft of others. But the science mostly felt shallow, and there were still no big breakthroughs.

None of these ventures had the financing of Calico or HLI, although interest in them was growing. Some efforts had the support of Aubrey de Grey's SENS Research Foundation, the Buck Institute, or the occasional angel investor like Amazon CEO Jeff Bezos or PayPal's Peter Thiel. But these fell into the categories of mere millions, not hundreds of millions. Nevertheless, the new enterprises happily set out to spread the word to the media. All except one: Calico.

Since its inception in 2013, Calico seemed to have vanished. Sure, there was the obligatory press release now and then, and clearly the company existed. But was it getting anywhere? It had been more than three years, and yet Art Levinson, the seer of biotech, the chair of Apple, the man who was running the show, had offered nothing—not the day Calico announced its existence, and not any days, months, or years afterward. None of the talk that had taken place at the Google board meeting in early 2013 had been revealed—none of the mysterious funding details, none of the dinner conversations in Palo Alto or anywhere else. Every Silicon Valley reporter from the *New York Times, Washington Post, Fortune, Forbes, Wall Street Journal,* and more yearned for some morsel of information that explained why Google was funding this remarkable undertaking. And yet Levinson was as silent as a Buddhist monk. Which, of course, only made its secrets all the more tantalizing.

TO BE BLUNT, Art Levinson didn't feel that what he, or Calico, was up to was anyone's business. This was vexing—not only to journalists, but also to Levinson's peers. Ray Kurzweil was listed as an adviser to Levinson, through his connections with Larry Page and Alphabet, but Kurzweil knew only that Art seemed to be playing things "very close to the vest."

Venter also wondered what all the secrecy was about. In separate conversations, he and Kurzweil and de Grey each mentioned to me that if all parties in the scientific world shared their insights, everyone in the field would benefit—and that included Calico.

Naturally, theories about how the company came to be and where it was headed abounded. Nir Barzilai, the director of the Institute for Aging Research at the Albert Einstein College of Medicine, and the scientist who was working to raise $50 million for an FDA trial using metformin, said he didn't know what the company was doing, but whatever it was, it didn't seem to be attacking the problem.

Another scientist who claimed to be familiar with Calico said the company began as a vanity project, "as self-serving as the Medici [family] building a Renaissance chapel in Italy, but with a little extra Silicon Valley narcissism thrown in." And then just a few weeks after the *New Yorker* piece came out, the news and opinion website *Vox* published a piece entitled "Google Is Super Secretive About Its Anti-Aging Research. No One Knows Why." Julia Belluz, the reporter, decided to poke around the Valley and get to the bottom of it. The piece ranged far and wide, from scientists who continually offered comments on how perplexed or frustrated they were, to theories that Levinson had learned to be secretive from none other than Steve Jobs himself. Remarks like these really chapped Levinson's hide; nevertheless, he kept his tongue and never responded publicly.

There was one other theory about Levinson's silence: Being a product of the highly competitive world of biotechnology, maybe he preferred to keep his mouth shut to maintain a competitive edge. There was something to that. But Levinson told me the main reason he was being so quiet was because he abhorred overpromising. Overpromise and all you do is create unfulfilled expectations. He hated that; it undermined the credibility of the whole enterprise. Science was hard and humbling, and it was pitiful how little we understood the human organism. So best to simply stand silently before the immensity of thing and gird your loins—because you were in for a battle, and handing out headlines was just a waste of valuable time.

THIS APPROACH REVEALED some of the basic differences between Craig Venter and Art Levinson. Both believed deeply in the power of knowledge, but how they went about *gathering* knowledge and executing on it was another story. One was the tortoise, and the other the hare. Levinson was patient; Venter, aggressive and swift. Levinson valued focus and effectiveness. He tended to stand back, survey the landscape, search out chinks in the armor of whatever problem he was trying to solve, and then attack where he saw promise: Drill deep.

In Venter's case, it was no accident that his big break-through for speeding up the sequencing of the human genome had been called "shotgunning." *Do the experiment! Onward!* This did not mean that he was foolhardy, although he had been accused of that more than once in his life. He may have shot himself in the foot here and there, but nowadays he made a distinction between risky behavior and flat-out stupidity. Yes, a venture might look risky to those unwilling to try something new. But if you did your homework, weighed the risks against the rewards, there were reasons to take the plunge. In fact, in his mind the whole problem with the scientific community was that it was way too soft on risk. Risks made the world go round. Mistakes *created* knowledge! And that was why he planned to ensure that HLI fundamentally change the way medicine was practiced.

None of this made Levinson the total opposite of Venter, timid and risk-averse. Far from it. But he liked to chew on problems, and he liked the idea of spreading his bets with moves like the two-hemisphere approach. And he *was* still going after the Ultimate Problem: aging itself. Don't just disrupt the old-fashioned practice of medicine; disrupt the killer at its root, period.

Luckily, Levinson had been handed the opportunity for a moonshot. Venter did not have that luxury. But did that really matter? What was the alternative? Stop doing the experiment? *That* wasn't going to happen. No, Venter's goal was to develop a *new* approach to medicine, one that got ahead of death and dying, rather than waiting until it was too late and already shoving you out the door.

24 | REVOLUTIONIZING MEDICINE

E ven before the Human Genome Project marked its completion way back in 2000, Craig Venter used to carry a holo-
graphic information-bearing silicon chip around in his
wallet—the kind that you sometimes saw on credit cards—
with the photo of a regular-looking guy. This card, Venter would
proudly tell people, contained every bit of the man's genetic
code. It could tell you that if he smoked, or that his chances of
developing cancer before age 60 were almost 4 out of 10. It
revealed whether he might have a genetic tendency toward some
mental or emotional illnesses, and explained that he was among
the 30 percent of the population that benefited from taking
aspirin to fight heart disease (which was good news, because he
was carrying the *APOE* gene—DNA that made him more likely
to suffer from strokes and heart disease). Armed with this information, the man could decide what sort of diet might be best for
him, explore the time of day he was most productive, maybe even
improve his chances of finding a compatible mate.

Where did this font of biological data come from? How
could anybody, even Craig Venter, have information like this in

his back pocket in 1999? Well, he couldn't. It was just a mock-up Venter used during lectures, a fake illustration. But back then, he assured people, once genomes were cheap enough to be sequenced, once all the nitty-gritty details of *selfness* were properly nailed down, the day would come when people would have that card in their hands and could take control of their lives—because the vast genomic database at their disposal would allow each and every person to know all there was to know about their medical future.

It took 15 years, but in October 2015, Venter finally envisioned a service at Human Longevity, Inc., that could begin to deliver the very insights that faux chip had only pretended to provide. At last, the technology was catching up with the concept. Venter even had a name for it. He called it the Health Nucleus. For an eye-watering $25,000, it guaranteed that whoever cared to come to HLI's San Diego offices could be as biologically scrutinized as any human on the planet.

In the corporate world, companies often examined the health of potential CEOs or other corner-office executives. But Health Nucleus made those checkups look like the diagnostic equivalent of a grade school nurse asking little boys to turn their heads and cough. Several of the tests were so advanced that under FDA rules, HLI had to characterize the service as part of a study. This essentially made the patient a complicit lab rat in a large experiment designed to accumulate the highest quality genotypic and phenotypic information HLI could gather, while generating some income along the way. Whoever signed on to Health Nucleus would not only have their genomes inspected, but also their bodies, brains, gaits, and bone density—even their metabolites and microbiomes—all the better to delay the inevitable date of their particular demise.

To anyone not checking beneath the surface, Health Nucleus might look like a money grab; an innovative way to rob as many members of the One Percent of their excess cash as possible. But the service was absolutely legitimate. It also promised that as new information emerged, participating customers would be updated on an ongoing basis.

Besides, Venter had to make *some* money. By July 2016, HLI had raised north of $300 million. But the investment had come from traditional investors who (because they didn't include Larry Page and the generous people on the Alphabet board) required, if not profit, then at least revenue, some return on investment. This meant Venter had to generate income *and* get actual research done at the same time, and that sometimes made life a royal pain. After all, who wouldn't prefer to do pure research and wrestle with the sublime mysteries of human biology without having investors breathing down one's neck? But how had Mick Jagger once put it? "You can't always get what you want."

Not that it was in Venter's nature to bide his time anyway. He relished concrete, preferably spectacular, results, just as he had with Celera during his battles over the Human Genome Project, his creation of the first synthetic life-form, and the Face Project. That was why it was so important to not simply tweak the medical arts, but to revolutionize them. Thus came HLI's Health Nucleus, a doorway to reinvention.

FOR ANYONE WHO WANTS to take advantage of HLI's Health Nucleus service, there are certain protocols. They aren't the Final Protocols, like the ones practiced at Alcor—the opposite, really—all about *avoiding* the requirements of Alcor's

Chill Chamber. Before arriving, each client is politely asked to fill out all manner of online questionnaires about their health, and to submit every bit of medical information possible to the assigned Health Nucleus physician: recent blood tests, brain scans or MRIs, histories of surgery or illness—as much phenotypic information as possible.

On the surface this seems reasonable enough, but occasionally the questionnaires could cause dark thoughts to arise in a patient's mind. Take the section on magnetic resonance imaging (MRI). "The MRI . . . produces detailed pictures of organs, soft tissues, bones, and virtually all other internal body structures . . . [and helps] researchers quantify volumes of different parts of the brain . . . to understand your risk of certain neurological conditions that are associated with aging."

When reading passages like this, the reasonable part of a client's brain thinks, *Well, sure, this makes sense. Why wouldn't I want to know if I have a brain aneurysm waiting to happen, or that I'm losing neurons at an alarming rate, or my bones are brittle, or cancers that have not yet begun to reveal themselves are lurking within? Knowing these clearly gives me advanced warning, an upper hand.*

But then, some of the more *un*reasonable parts of the brain kick in, like the amygdala, the little fear center lodged in the middle of the brain behind the eyes: *But do I really have to know everything about the density of my bones? Or the total content of my body fat, or the discovery that soon my marbles will start trickling south?*

When people balked at partaking in the Health Nucleus like this, it confounded Venter. Why wouldn't they want to know that they had medical problems *before* they got out of hand, rather than die an early death like his father had? Venter told me about a woman who had read an article about him and the Health Nucleus in *Forbes*. She tweeted him to say he was evil because he wanted to use the tools to change God's will. "So cheating death means you're trying to cheat God?" Venter responded. "He *wants* you to die of prostate cancer so you better just get on with it?"

For those who partake in the Health Nucleus experience, the scrutiny begins even as the client rolls up to the facility to be greeted by Virgil, the security guard at HLI's San Diego offices. He's there with a big smile as patients are escorted into the futuristic confines of a suite. The service is entirely first class. No refrigerator-white walls, no gurneys or saline bags hanging from rolling poles, no beeping and gurgling machines as one waits interminably for the medical amenities. Here, the atmosphere is more spa-like, with bright and engaging staff who provide visitors with spiffy, loose clothing, healthy snacks, both breakfast and lunch to order, even selected reading—simply pick any book on the shelves in your suite, and peruse it while comfortably awaiting the next battery of tests. Take it home afterward, if you like.

Nevertheless, the day of testing itself lasts eight full hours. Shortly upon arrival, the phlebotomist siphons off 20 or so vials of blood. These are needed to entirely sequence the subject's genome, all three billion base pairs. Companies like Ancestry.com and 23andMe might say they are analyzing your DNA, but the truth is they only look at snippets of it: the parts science already largely understands, like how much Neanderthal DNA you can claim, or what part of the world various members of your family hailed from, and, more recently, in 23andMe's case, insights into whether you have the genes associated with heart disease or Parkinson's or Alzheimer's.

These make up a few drops in the oceans of information contained in any human genome.

The Health Nucleus, on the other hand, sequences *all* the patients' DNA. They may not understand much of what it means right now, but only by gathering the information in the first place can the great AI algorithms hope to unpeel their secrets. It's part of the big biomedical feedback loop.

In addition to the genome, the service gathers two other "omes" as well: the metabolome and microbiome. Sampling the metabolome allows scientists to analyze the trillions upon trillions of small molecules roaming within and among the cells of the body that drive millions of yet unknown pathways within. One of the joys of sequencing the microbiome is that it requires a stool sample to get a look at what is going on in your gut.

If science still remains in the dark about the genome, the metabolome and microbiome are even more confounding, like strange hieroglyphs from an ancient culture: undeniably real, but mystifying beyond any sensible ciphering. The metabolome takes science into the wild world of proteins and the marvelous ways they fold, pucker, and build out the hardware that drives every one of the 100 trillion cells within your body. The microbiome is an altogether different system that includes the ranks of invisible symbiotic organisms, mostly bacteria, that live within each member of the human race—usually in the stomach and intestines, but in several other sectors too, including the skin, hair, and eyes.

Amazingly, the microbiome consists of 10 times the genetic information the human genome itself does, and is as much a part of what keeps us alive as our own DNA. It affects diet, health, disease—even emotion. But the details of how all these high-speed transactions take place remain almost entirely mysterious, because only recently did we really learn they existed or had meaning at all. The only sure thing any scientist can say right now is that, together, all of these "omes" somehow communicate with and profoundly affect each person's life.

In addition to these tests, Health Nucleus patients spend an hour and a half having every centimeter of their brains and bodies scanned. HLI promises the highest resolution MRI scans in the world. Resolutions fine enough to pick out sticky beta-amyloids in the brain or signs of neuronal shrinkage, or cancer tumors the size of a pea. Later, electrocardiograms— movies of a subject's heart as it goes about its quotidian labors (42 million beats a year)—are administered.

Next comes the DEXA bone density scan, which reveals not only how much muscle a subject has in comparison with body fat, but where the muscle and fat themselves reside—a key indicator of health, or lack of it. Gait tests also assess how subjects move. Telltale signs of a shaky gait can reveal the earliest signs of dementia.

Finally, cognitive tests end the day, monitoring how quickly the brain reacts, as well as how it handles logic, spatial problems, and decision making.

It is difficult to imagine the Health Nucleus running a more thorough examination of your "self," and by 2016 it was working. Two years in, 500 brains and bodies had been run through HLI's hardware, thoroughly analyzed and tabulated. Venter had found that fully 30 percent of the clients had discovered some serious problem that they had otherwise been unaware of. Venter was careful to point out that these were not people who had been heading to the hospital because their doctors had found something wrong with them, or because some *symptom* had made it clear they needed to be treated. These were people who had assumed they were perfectly healthy!

Revelations like that could be sobering. Research suggests that Health Nucleus has been able to detect diseases related to aging that were serious enough to warrant treatment within the next month in 8 percent of its 209 participants. In 2 percent of these participants, early stage cancers were detected.[16]

Venter told the story of one woman, just 27, who had her brain scanned by Health Nucleus. Deep inside, the doctors found an aneurism: a damaged vessel that looks like a bubble in a tire. Thanks to the discovery, she arranged immediately for a neurosurgeon to remove it. It is possible she could have lived a long life with the aneurism in there waiting to explode, said Venter. But chances are that one day, the vessel would have blown out. "Her first, and last, symptom would have been bleeding to death through her nose."

Then there was the story of an older couple all prepared to go on an overseas vacation the day after their Health Nucleus visit. They were in good health, they thought, and figured the battery of tests would be a little something they could revisit after they returned. Except the machines found a cancer tumor beneath the breastbone of the husband that had been missed in previous exams. Not long after the surgery, the man contacted Venter to say the exam ruined their vacation, but saved his life. So, thanks.

VENTER LOVED TO TELL STORIES like these. Not that he wanted anyone to be ill, but because the illnesses were discovered early. That was the point. They provided the most dramatic possible examples of the direction he felt medicine should take the human race. You *thought* you were okay, but you really weren't. Your body found you out. But that's a good thing, because now we have predicted the weather of your medical future. Now the trouble can be repaired. Maybe not every time, but far more than if you had remained clueless.

Venter admitted that for now, HLI was mostly using Health Nucleus's scanners, MRIs, sound waves, and needles to make these discoveries. Maybe that was still a bit reactive in the old-fashioned way, but was that so bad? Already, Health Nucleus was uncovering cancers early enough to cure them. Once the omes—the genome, metabolome, and microbiome—got cranking and the artificial intelligence algorithms began making sense of all that data, then science could get down to creating a new kind of Precision Medicine. At least the current version of the Health Nucleus was a start.

Health Nucleus's high costs were still a problem, though. After all, who but the wealthy could use such a service? But Venter was working on that, and like the cost of sequencing the genome itself, he was certain the prices would plummet. Brad Perkins, HLI's chief medical officer, predicted that in 10 years everyone would have his genome sequenced. It would be as normal as checking your ears, and the cost would be zero. But first, gather the data and crunch the numbers. That was the ticket.

Well, one of them, anyhow.

25 | SUPER CELLS

n the summer of 2016, Bob Hariri was sitting in the Palo Alto offices of Human Longevity, Inc., listening to Riccardo Sabatini tell him all about the company's Face Project. Hariri's adolescent son was with him, and in about half an hour they would be hopping onto his Bombardier Challenger 604 jet before heading to San Diego, and then off to Asia for a couple of weeks of family R & R.

As an HLI founder, Hariri had heard of Sabatini's work and was fascinated by it, but he also knew his role at HLI was soon likely to change. There was talk among the triumvirate—Hariri, Venter, and Diamandis—that it might be best to split off the stem cell work to create an entirely new business. It wasn't that there was any ill will among the three. But Venter, as CEO, had pretty much focused HLI on genomics and Health Nucleus. Hariri's investigations of stem cell therapy were undeniably interesting, and related to longevity and health span, but were a little out of the orbit of HLI's current plans. For his part, Hariri really wanted to focus on placental stem cells, and felt he was making serious progress.

Sure enough, in early 2017, the stem cell side of HLI split off, and Hariri and Diamandis, with a fresh supply of Silicon Valley investors, formed a new company called Celularity, designed exclusively "to turn stem cells into medicine." This did not diminish anyone's belief that stem cell therapy could be a powerful ally in the fight against aging, not to mention a whole flock of other ailments. The shift merely meant the two operations could move forward faster and more independently. Later, when the time came, they could reconvene as collaborators. That was the plan anyhow.

DURING THE COURSE of his long explorations at Celgene, HLI, and Celularity, Hariri had continued to develop some unusual views on aging. He saw three very good reasons to make the affliction go away: It robbed people of their health, mind, and looks. Clearly, the use of the brain and body were pretty useful, but looks? Wasn't that egotistical, the stuff of Hollywood and *those* kind of people? No, said Hariri. He held that the older, more frail and haggard people appeared, the more society marginalized them. Aged faces and bodies became a signal for all to see that it was time to move on. So even if your brain and body were strong, if you *looked* old, you were ushered into the societal dust heap. But what if you had access to medicines created by placental stem cells? Those, at least theoretically, could solve all three problems: regenerating body, mind, and appearance.

This was not an entirely new idea. Before Diamandis and Hariri had begun brainstorming their longevity play, scientists outside the United States had undertaken stem cell research more aggressively than the FDA in the United States. Among them was the Karolinska Institutet in Stockholm, Sweden, unequivocally regarded as one of Europe's best medical establishments. At Karolinska, scientists had injected stem cells into patients with blood, brain, eye, bone, and liver disorders, including cancer. The studies were ongoing, but so far the new treatments seemed to be working. Stem cells were simply injected into damaged organs and soon began to regenerate stronger, fresher cells. No petri dishes or complex pharmaceuticals required.

Stem cells were being put to novel uses elsewhere too. In 2016, researchers at another of Venter's companies, Synthetic Genomics, began collaborating with Martine Rothblatt, founder of United Therapeutics (and before that, creator of Sirius XM Satellite Radio).[17] In one project, the two companies genetically modified the hearts and lungs of pigs. Next, they planned to transplant those organs directly into humans who needed them: something called xenotransplantation.

Pig valves and other assorted porcine organs had been used for decades to bide time for people suffering from failing hearts, but using whole hearts and lungs from pigs creates huge problems because the body rejects them. Venter's plan was to use genomic sequencers to compare the genomes of pigs and humans, precisely identify the genes that created rejection problems between the two species, use Crispr technology to snip out the offending genes, and then insert the edited versions into pluripotent pigs' ovaries to create brand-new pigs carrying "humanized" lungs and hearts. It turns out the organs of the average pig are about the same size as the average human, and the genetics are remarkably similar too.

If transplants of this kind happen someday, they will essentially transform recipients into chimeras: part pig, part human.

Of course, if the pig's genes were changed too much, their stem cells might not survive. "It's not like by changing a couple genes you've got it solved," Venter said. Nevertheless, so far the experiments had been promising, if not perfect.

But maybe none of this would be necessary if placental cells could perform their magic. Imagine an aging baby boomer whose cells are giving out from all of the damage that his DNA hasn't been repairing as well as it did back at age 25. Sore knees or, worse, a heart or spine or pancreas or brain starting to sputter.

Now, rather than a heart transplant (pig or otherwise), or great buckets of drugs to keep the body clattering along, doctors could inject Hariri's placental medicines. As the old stem cells give out, the pristine, new ones step in. Later, when another part of the body begins to run down, a new, fresh batch could be supplied, and so on, until boomers everywhere were being youthfully topped off and their cells reset—not only healthier, but actually younger, and therefore not marginalized! Ken Bloom, HLI's president, had said himself that stem cells might someday find a way to push the length of human life beyond 120 years—maybe way past that.

But as compelling as placental stem cells might appear, they weren't perfect. At least, not yet. For one thing, the fresh stem cells that one receives from their own body will always adhere to whatever genetic ailments that body's DNA already carries. If someone is genetically prone to arthritis or heart problems, or even addictions or depression, those problems are going to reappear eventually. Cancer could also be an issue. Introducing new stem cells into the body of someone with a predisposition to various cancers might actually encourage tumors rather than eliminate them. In some ways, cancer cells were like pluripotent stem cells in that they can replicate indefinitely.

Down the road, Crispr technology might fix problems like these with a couple of nicks of the Crispr scissors. But Crispr had its own problems. It could easily change and swap cells, but once the DNA of a pluripotent stem cell is rearranged, that change remains forever and is even passed along to the next generation, just as if evolution and your own parents had provided the DNA. One would want to be very careful that there were no unintended consequences when swapping these genes.

Already the impossible had happened in 2018, when the scientific world learned that Chinese scientist He Jiankui had used Crispr to alter embryos that were then implanted in a woman who later bore twin girls. He did this entirely on his own. His goal, he said, was to eliminate genes that could cause the newborns to get HIV, because the children's father is HIV-positive. But the fact that the scientist had independently and forever changed the DNA of living humans appalled scientists and bioethicists.[18] If one gene like this could be edited, what would stop rogue scientists from creating someone's idea of a superbaby? Or unwittingly developing a baby with a new and unknown disease?

The fear was that this kind of gene editing was moving too fast. Scientists were still trying to suss out the ways stem cells reacted to the different bone or liver or heart cells they might replace. How long were they effective? Which cells triggered what signals? These explorations took time, and they were complicated. It wasn't like changing a carburetor. And of course, there was the problem of the Big Black Box, the brain, which, for reasons only evolution could fathom, did not generate large reservoirs of stem cells like many other parts of the anatomy.

And what if older neurons *were* replaced wholesale with new stem cells? They might scramble different sectors of the brain by destroying the new connections between the originals. Fiddle with those, and who knew what mayhem might follow? Memories, learning, and other cerebral functions that the brain had grown accustomed to might simply vanish. On the other hand, in the case of a disease like Alzheimer's, maybe new memories would be better than no memories at all.

One age-related affliction particularly intrigued Hariri, and he suspected curing it could slow death's march pretty quickly: sarcopenia. Sarcopenia was a disease that accelerated the loss of muscle in some people before their time. Since the FDA defined it as a disease, clinical trials were possible. Furthermore, anyone who was aging—and that was everyone—suffered from a form of sarcopenia. It was simply what happened as time passed. Hariri had found that by the time the average *Homo sapiens* turns 25, muscle mass begins to drop off at the rate of 1 to 2 percent a year. By age 60, half of it is gone.

One might think that this loss would only affect a body's strength and steadiness, and that would be true. But there are other factors as well. It turns out that most of the blood in the body resides in muscle. Its high venous capacitance is essential to long-term health, because venous capacitance is what delivers the goods to your immune system. So now a 60-year-old human hasn't only lost half of his muscle mass, but also half of his venous capacity *and* immune system. This means that anyone over 25 has begun suffering from a chronic form of sarcopenia—and though you can slow the process with proper diet and exercise, it inevitably continues. There's no way around it. In Hariri's mind, placental stem cells offered a perfect cure, because the cells could regenerate muscle. That would, in turn, reduce fat, renovate the vascular and immune systems, and generally reverse aging. One 2009 study even disclosed that increasing muscle lowered the likelihood of cancer.[19]

Would a world brimming with baby boomers find a treatment for sarcopenia appealing? Forget worrying about ageism or flabby arms, compromised immune systems, or the sad smiles of people as they gazed at the elderly couple over there with their walkers, thinking, Aw, isn't that sweet? Because that couple, even with lots of years in the bank, would not need walkers anymore. They would be vigorous, healthy, upright, and perfectly capable of pulling their weight in the real world. One hundred could become the new 60! That, at least, was how Hariri and Diamandis saw it playing out.

But right now, all of that was still science fiction. No one was going to be biologically "topped off" with stem cells and rejuvenated just yet. Nevertheless, Hariri and Diamandis—the two Celularity founders—had high hopes. The company was already developing several clinical trials to move as quickly as possible toward FDA approval. Maybe stem cells would become the holy grail of radical longevity, and thousand-year life spans would abide as the human race broke its evolutionary bonds. Who could say? All you could do was try. As one scientist put it, "The science will go where the science will go."

26 | THE SEED OF THE SINGULARITY

f the science necessary to solve aging was going to go anywhere, one last remarkable and ironic piece of the longevity puzzle would have to fall into place. Smart machines would need to arise in defense of the human race. Already machine learning was embedding itself in the medical arts, and digital technology had long ago become science's handmaiden. Venter's work with the Human Genome Project had marked a milestone. But now, as the search for immortality deepened, much more digital muscle would be necessary.

Art Levinson himself had put the facts concisely: When it came to flipping the genetic switches needed to evade aging, there was no way any human at a lab bench —no matter how gifted, how insightful, or how hardworking—could possibly locate and comprehend their magical pathways. And without that, curing the Ultimate Problem was simply not going to happen. *Homo sapiens* required a tool that was faster, smarter, and more tireless than humans themselves. The kind that Riccardo Sabatini had used in the Face Project made a good example. "Machine learning" was one term that Sabatini and other computer scientists used to describe this brand of work, but there was another more common name that nearly everyone had heard of—artificial intelligence (AI).

AI is different from other forms of computer code. It consists of legions of algorithms that are eerily similar to the human mind itself: AI can learn to solve problems without being explicitly told what to do ahead of time. It can, in some ways, think for itself, at high speed. It's the stuff of *Terminator*-style invasions and countless dystopian futures. Ironic, then, that such capabilities should now emerge as our saviors. It's doubly ironic that those same tools have been the source of so much of Silicon Valley's wealth. It's almost as if evolution itself had somehow anointed the Valley—with all its computing power and money—as the chosen instrument for immunizing death. This creates, in the machines and their algorithms, a kind of symbiosis: digits and molecules, biology and technology coming together in a strange and unexpected harmony.

RAY KURZWEIL COULD HAVE told you this was going to happen. More than 50 years ago, when he was 14 years old, he wrote a paper that outlined how a machine might somehow become as intelligent as a human. That was even before he had landed a spot in the Westinghouse Science Talent Search and shaken the hand of President Johnson. He hadn't yet divined a direct connection between artificial intelligence and longevity just yet, but he always fervently believed that truly intelligent machines could solve nearly any problem.

The essentials of that thinking hadn't really changed since Kurzweil's paper. In fact, he used much of it as the basis for his best-selling 2012 book, *How to Create a Mind*. The book argued that human-level intelligence could be created in computers by reverse engineering the human brain. Figure out how the neocortex worked, employ pioneering software and hardware to do the same in a computer, and voilà! A fully humanlike, but entirely artificial, machine.

Just after the book came out, Larry Page suggested that Kurzweil join Google to "bring natural language understanding" to the company—figure out, in other words, how computers might someday talk and communicate just like humans. Initially, Kurzweil had only planned to ask Page if Google, or Bill Maris's Google Ventures, might like to invest in the business he wanted to create based on the book. But, Page said, just come into the Google fold. This way, Kurzweil could work with the canny computer scientists at Google and tap into its bountiful digital resources—not to mention free office space and all the hardware and software cycles a big thinker could ask for.

So in December 2012, Kurzweil, for the first time in his life, joined a company that didn't have his own name on the corporate logo. But that was okay. The dream of creating something as remarkable as a virtual mind—the holy grail of artificial intelligence—was deep in the man's DNA. If he had to become an employee to solve the world's problems, including death, he could live with that.

The team's first endeavor under Kurzweil's tutelage as a director of engineering was to create machine-learning algorithms that could understand users' emails and then provide short but sensible answers, all on their own. This turned out to be tougher than almost anyone thought.

It took nearly five years of work with a group of 35 scientists before Team Kurzweil created its first Google product: Smart Reply, a Gmail mobile app. The initial version, launched in

May 2017, listened to the email you received, and then Smart Reply provided three possible answers, short responses like "Let's do Monday," or "Yay! Awesome!"

Smart Reply wasn't anything that was going to give Skynet or the *Terminator* a run for its money, nor was it going to solve aging—not immediately. But in Kurzweil's view, it made a good first example of artificially intelligent software comprehending a human thought and then providing a response that made sense. On the surface, it might appear trivial, but it really wasn't. And in the end it would lead to life everlasting. How?

Building on Smart Reply, Kurzweil planned to ratchet up his project to the point where machines could, on the fly and in context, speak as fluently in any language as he, or anyone else, could. The new version would be able to pull all the right words in all the right order out of thin air, and carry on an entirely sensible, humanlike conversation. Once that was possible, he figured the machines would be pretty much as smart as we were, which also made them the seed of the Singularity he felt would arrive in the mid-21st century.

The seminal concept behind Kurzweil's work was something he called intelligent pattern recognizers—layers and layers of them that reside in the brain. In his view, these modules were what had made the *Homo sapiens* neocortex—the most recently evolved sector of the human brain—such a ringing success. Kurzweil estimated the cerebral cortex houses about 300 million of them, each consisting of clusters of neurons. Placed in context, he held that these modules rapidly bootstrap simple concepts in an increasingly complex human hierarchy that, layer by layer, delivers remarkable insights like art, mathematics, and language. The modules manage this by quickly identifying a few low-level cues, then sensibly pull in more modules to generate still more boot-strapped knowledge.

For example, a module that sees the visual image of a hori-zontal bar and then sees two sides of a pyramid would, in the general context of a sentence, immediately recognize it as an A. Other related modules would see additional letters related to A, to piece together the word "Apple," rather than, say, "Pear." More modules would attach additional words and then tastes: maybe the smell of pies, memories, a location that the modules then figure out is a kitchen—until the next thing you know, you're craving a piece of your grandmother's apple pie, just out of the oven. This, in turn might trigger all sorts of other thoughts, feel-ings, memories, and insights. All of this happens in a blink, pow-ered by the brain's hundred billion interconnected neurons.

This might seem an exceedingly simple example, and a long way from Shakespeare's "Tomorrow, and tomorrow, and tomorrow / creeps in this petty pace from day to day . . ." But for Kurzweil, the point was that this network of interwoven, highly flexible modules supplied the wellspring of human intel-ligence. And his goal was to develop the artificially intelligent software that could reverse engineer this unique human trait.

If such an advance were possible, it might not be immedi-ately obvious how artificial intelligence would lead to immor-tality. But to Kurzweil, it was all of a piece. With the advent of AI, he foresaw the evolution of a newer, far more powerful version of the human body and mind: one that wasn't strictly biological, but instead employed nanotechnology, cell-size nanobots, that could clean out arteries, strengthen muscle, and boost organs while simultaneously allowing the brains of mere mortals to access the vast cerebral spaces of the Cloud. But not in the way we do now, with clunky phones and iPads, but with invisible, cell-size machines injected like serums into the cerebral cortex, essentially becoming enhanced, artificial brain cells, something I found myself calling neurobots.

Within decades, Kurzweil predicts, millions of people will be physically invincible, supplied with trillions of neurobots capable of linking directly to the ubiquitous Cloud. Anyone thus augmented will not require stem cell rejuvenation, or even revamped genetics. They wouldn't need to ask Google which Michael Keaton movie won an Academy Award nomination in 2014; the answer would simply *be* there, available like every other memory. The average human would not *watch* a movie; she would be immersed, imagining it more completely than our own recollections currently do. One would not hum a song; the music would come into the mind, full-blown, in the highest possible fidelity. In a blink, neurobots will even be able to shift your reality from wherever your body is currently located into any other place you might like: Kathmandu, ancient Rome, or a beach in the Seychelles, complete with warm sun and crystal clear water lapping your toes, every sensation as real as real. It wouldn't *be* real, but it would *feel* that way, thanks to a seamless, sensory melding of the neurobots rearranging the chemistry in your brain.

Best of all, this new human hybrid could be digitally backed up and then downloaded to create a cloned copy containing all of the information in your mind and body, so that even if your "self" suddenly died, you would have a perfect backup available to resume life as if nothing at all had happened—true immortality that would, once and for all, absolutely obliterate Gompertz's beta.

Kurzweil considered this a fourth and final bridge beyond his previous three, the ones he and Terry Grossman had envisioned together in the early years of the 21st century. With it, his ultimate view of everlasting life would at last emerge at a time and place that didn't simply upgrade old-fashioned biology—the kind Calico and HLI were working on—but upgraded it with nanotechnology that made you immortal and incredibly intelligent, almost godlike. Kurzweil, of course, would never use the term "godlike." To him, entwining humans and machines so thoroughly that they became indistinguishable was simply the next natural course of human evolution.

ONE MIGHT FEEL that Kurzweil's Bridge Four thinking was *just* a touch outside the views of the average *Homo sapiens*. Some, however, felt it was a very real threat. Elon Musk and, prior to his death in 2018, Stephen Hawking, had warned that superintelligent AIs could take over the planet—partly thanks to the work Musk's friend Larry Page was supporting. "I have exposure to very cutting-edge AI," Musk told attendees at the National Governors Association in July 2017, "and I think people should be really concerned about it."

Earlier, Hawking had written in an open letter with Musk and a few dozen other artificial intelligence experts that the emergence of AI would lead to creatures so smart and swift they would leave us looking like the cerebral equivalent of an amoeba. It could, he said, become the "worst event in the history of our civilization."

Remarks like these aggravated the Kurzweilian brain. More and more, he grew peevish with media cries that repeatedly told the world that in no time, we'd all be living in a dystopian future where our overlords transformed Siri into some menacing version of George Orwell's *1984*. But look how technology had advanced the human race! Despite the horrors of the last century, the rate of death caused by war over the past 600 years had dropped several hundred fold. Murder rates were rapidly declining. FBI statistics showed that between 1993 and 2015, the U.S. murder rate had plummeted 50 percent. The same was true of property crime. Despite media reports of our collective demise, Kurzweil believed, the world was a better, safer, happier, and smarter place, mostly thanks to the advances that the keepers of science and innovation made possible.

For Kurzweil, the smart thing was to let technology march ahead, Tom Swift-style, because that was where we were headed. It was all right there in LOAR (the Law of Accelerating Returns). Yes, one had to be vigilant and control the power of smart machines. He had been saying that for years. But no need to hit the panic button. Machines wouldn't match human intelligence for another 10 years, and the Singularity itself wouldn't arrive until 2045, a date with destiny that he planned to keep, when he celebrated his 97th birthday. The best approach would be to put safety measures into place along the lines of Isaac Asimov's "Three Laws of Robotics."[20] Like the first stone knives, created over two million years ago, all technologies could be used for good or ill. But if properly managed, artificial intelligence would surely be our saviors, not our terminators—our partners, not our competitors. Just watch: AI was going to save our skins. Kurzweil could see it. Levinson and Venter saw it too, each in their own way. There could be no doubt: Smart machines was where the end of The End lay.

27 | THE NEW ORACLES

n early 2016, when she became Calico Labs' chief computing officer, the views and aspirations of Raymond Kurzweil did not inhabit the mind of Daphne Koller. This wasn't because she shunned Kurzweil, or digits, algorithms, or computer code; far from it. She loved them all. It was just that Kurzweil wasn't her favorite when it came to the stratagems of machine learning and artificial intelligence. Bridge Four wasn't her thing. Her inspiration was Thomas Bayes, an 18th-century mathematician and Presbyterian minister. She had explored his work and theories in the 1990s, and then used them to develop some of the most advanced artificial intelligence algorithms in the world.

Before joining Calico, Koller knew she could write her own ticket at any of Silicon Valley's great Cloud makers: Google, Facebook, Apple. But did she really want to create software that made better Twitter feeds, or cool faces on Snapchat, or yet another product that piled up more of the planet's digital ad revenues? In the sprawling world of Google, she would be a blip: one more very smart human in a sea of geeks. But Calico was different. She had never forgotten Steve Jobs's grand goal: "Make a dent in the universe." At Calico, maybe she *could* make a dent—save lives, perhaps millions—even her own.

Thomas Bayes would have appreciated Koller's interest in saving lives, being both a Presbyterian minister and a devoted supporter of the humanist philosophies that called for the rational improvement of the human race—also the foundation of transhumanism. The mathematician's work had been largely forgotten when Koller first began exploring it. But she liked the way he thought. It delivered a human flexibility unusual in mathematics. Instead of using set rules and cold logic, it was designed to adapt.

A simple example was the big urn problem. Imagine a large urn filled with balls. Half are black, the other half white. What was the likelihood that when one of the balls was pulled from the urn, it would be black? Well, obviously, 50-50. But what were the odds of pulling the very *next* black ball from the urn? Now the situation had changed; every time a ball was retrieved it would change again, and again, depending on the situation. Bayesian probability took these differing possibilities into account, or tried to. In the jargon of computer scientists, it both *explored* information and then *exploited* it—not unlike a human mind.

Good news, too, when it came to computer science, because Koller knew the world was becoming an increasingly noisy and confusing place. The rigid rules created by most computer code simply would not get the job done. Not where biology was concerned, and especially not molecular biology, which was about as messy as it got. No algorithm written by the human mind—no matter how fast or logical—could resolve the complex and rapid molecular pathways at work in a genome or a biome or any "ome." Not that humans were *completely* useless; the initial coding had to be set up correctly. But after that, the algorithms were cut loose do their stuff, independently, like a living thing solving each problem it faced *as it faced it* without constantly coming back for human instruction. This was the only way that the billions of genetic communications could be unsnarled.

When Koller developed her cancer gene-mapping techniques at UCSF after receiving her MacArthur grant, the program blasted through data on thousands of genes, and then tested the likelihood that changes created by one gene could be teased out by locating changes in the others. She also developed code that examined the rates at which specific genes within a cell created its corresponding protein, and how that creation depended on signals from proteins encoded by still more genes.

All of this sounded a lot like Kurzweil's pattern-recognition nodes. Both needed to understand context and then react on their own in real time. Kurzweil's AI nodes were meant to solve a broad range of problems that could eventually lead to immortality. Koller's algorithms were more specific, delving way, way down into the noisy, and entirely invisible world of organic chemistry by letting the algorithms come up with their own solutions. But in this way, they too were thinking, artificially.

David Botstein, Calico's chief scientific officer, was of the opinion that understanding these pathways was central to Calico's hopes for success. He and Levinson agreed that crunching lots of numbers to figure out what the human genome was trying to say was crucial—but Botstein wanted to know more. What the hell were all of those molecules *inside* the genes actually doing? How did a gene turn some proteins on and some off? How did one gene affect others? If only you could rummage among them all, look them in the eye, and say, "Ah-hah! *Now* I

understand what you're up to." That was the only real way anyone could hope to begin undoing all the damage that took the
human body apart.

To achieve this, Botstein was having custom-made sequencers developed for Calico, and Calico alone, by two companies
collaborating in California: Pacific Biosciences and Bionano
Genomics.[21] These hand-built sequencers, and these only, he
felt, would provide the kind of resolution that revealed the
invisible machinations of proteins and molecules.

ONE OF THE PROJECTS Calico began exploring when
Koller arrived in 2016 illustrated just how numbingly complex
the problems were that the company faced. Between 2006 and
2010, an organization called the UK BioBank recruited 500,000
subjects between the ages of 40 and 69 years old and tested the
living daylights out of them. BioBank's researchers could tell
you just about everything about the project's recruits: their
inflammatory markers, cholesterol and hormone levels, saliva
samples, urine and blood results. They could tally up grip
strength, the volume of the recruits' brains—even how quickly
they could walk 100 meters. The genes of 100,000 participants
had already been sequenced, and then those people were asked
to wear 24-hour activity monitors for a week. Recently, fMRI
machines had begun scanning a fresh batch of 100,000 people.
All of this in addition to the vast database BioBank was already
developing about recruits' diet, cognitive function, work history, and digestive health.

Venter and the researchers at Human Longevity, Inc.,
had been gathering information at a blistering clip too, but it
was hard to imagine a more robust aggregation of human

biology than the findings the UK Biobank was compiling. In addition, the bank had also begun following up with those in the studies, plotting their progress as they marched forward. Already they had tabulated 9,000 phenotypes correlated with their unique DNA.

The numbers were mind paralyzing: trillions of cells, each interacting with billions of genes performing untold numbers of biological interactions. All of them unveiling the two faces of humanity. One that could reveal you and you alone; the other that represented the great biological database that made all humans possible. The questions were endless—and who could say which genetic alterations provided the final answers? Koller felt pretty sure Calico would find more than one, but less than 5,000. She wondered if maybe five major genetic pathways could eliminate aging. If so, perhaps Calico could then come up with five drug regimens that would intervene and repair the killing. That would solve beta outright.

One fact was clear: The ultimate answers weren't going to come from a "who." They would come from a "what." Maybe not from Kurzweil's neurobots, or human-machine hybrids. Not yet. But from increasingly intelligent machines that were thinking up new ways to think. Their very *own* ways. That made them the new oracles: software reading the burnt offerings of all that massive data accumulating at exponential speed as the contraptions taught themselves to mend humanity, rather than terminate it. Imagine: Machines solving the ultimate *human* problem.

The irony was almost cosmic.

28 | WOULD IT ALL WORK?

Mortality stalks us all. In the fall of 2016, Craig Venter got word that he was diagnosed with prostate cancer. Stage III. I saw him the day he sent the email out to HLI's staff. He had made a routine visit to the Health Nucleus, and there his biology found him out. No one ever wanted to get news like that—especially a man who intended to live out the full allotment of his 120 years. It was ironic. Here was all of that information in the genome that he himself had worked so hard to uncover, and now it had come home to roost.

But for him, that was a good thing. A glorious thing! He still had vivid memories of that rat-shack-Quonset-hut excuse for a hospital in Da Nang where he laced up those shredded and blasted 18-year-olds while the life poured out of them. But now HLI could help millions dodge the bullets of their own death. He himself was the proof. The Health Nucleus had found the cancer, the surgeons quickly plucked out the offending prostate, and now he was free of the disease. The 10-year survival rate was 99 percent. He'd be 80 by then. But the technology would be 10 years better too.

To keep pushing that technology, Venter announced in 2017 that HLI would meet his threshold of a million genomes by 2020. The company was already rolling out its latest, top-of-the-line Illumina sequencers to accelerate the work.

In the meantime HLI's machine-learning algorithms kept chewing up the data to make more sense out of the massive, genetic dictionary it was trying to decode. Researchers there had developed a new algorithm to sequence one of the most important regions on the human chromosome: chromosome 6, responsible for the regulation of the immune system, central to understanding autoimmune diseases, cancer, organ transplant compatibility, and allergies. That discovery could speed the creation of new drugs that touched on all of those diseases.

By early 2018, Human Longevity, Inc., also revamped its Health Nucleus services to create two basic memberships: HNX and HNX Platinum. Platinum was still priced at the full $25,000, plus $6,000 a year after two years if you wanted continuing access to the higher-end package. That included updated tests that might reveal bladder cancer or congestive heart problems or atrial fibrillation. Also included were total-body MRIs, comprehensive lab work, full screening of your body's chemical composition and health, neurocognitive testing—even a gait and balance tracker, among several other medical analyses. These were clearly for the very wealthy.

Plain old HNX was considerably less expensive at $4,950 for a onetime membership. It delivered whole genome sequencing, complete MRI, and about half of the other platinum-level services. After that initial cost, patients would continue to pay $2,950 annually for four ongoing services designed to reveal trouble before it could do too much damage.

The really big plan, though, was for HLI to launch 50 Health Nucleus sites around the world. Venter saw these at last bringing his medical revolution into the mainstream. The new centers would roll out within the next year in places like Asia, Europe, and the United States. If Venter had his way, the prices would continue to drop.

Would it all work? Venter looked around his office and smiled. "It has to," he said. How else could HLI hope to acquire one million integrated genomes, and how else would the world's medical practitioners come to understand that the time to prevent disease was now, rather than by playing catch-up with the Dreaded Symptoms *after the fact?*

From the outside, everything at HLI seemed to be humming along. But on the inside, it wasn't. Venter's goals were ambitious, and costly. Multiple executives had departed, and the company was burning cash at a furious rate. Finally one day in May 2018, a majority of the investors and board at Human Longevity, Inc., made it clear in a conference call that it had to stop. Venter didn't agree, and when others on the board held fast, it was a Mexican stand-off. Venter decided he had no other choice but to walk out of HLI's sunny San Diego headquarters. It was over that fast.

The departure had the eerie echo of Venter's removal from Celera, the company he ran that had accelerated the sequencing of the Human Genome Project. He had departed there a mere 18 months after standing before all the world to announce the great endeavor's completion in the summer of 2000. Back then, he said he faced severe pressure "from the people who put up the money . . . so I was walking a tightrope, though at times it felt like sliding along a razor blade."[22]

The end of that relationship had been bitter enough, but this time HLI also sued the J. Craig Venter Institute (JCVI) for stealing HLI's trade secrets. Venter denied the charges. JCVI attorney Steven Strauss said the claims were "baseless, without merit, and contain numerous factual errors," adding that JCVI planned to "vigorously defend against these allegations as the legal process advances." One way or another, though, Venter was off the board and no longer HLI's CEO. The triumvirate—Venter, Hariri, and Diamandis—was dissolved.

In July 2018, HLI promoted Dr. David Karow as its interim CEO, Scott Sorensen as interim chief operating officer, and Noah Nasser as chief financial officer. Both Karow and Sorensen had been hired as executives under Venter's watch. Nasser arrived shortly afterward.

Karow was a physician and researcher who had been working at the University of California at San Diego when he joined the company. His specialty was combining genomics and magnetic resonance imaging to find new ways to expose very early stage cancers throughout the body. Ironically, one of his pioneering finds was the early detection of prostate cancer.

Sorensen had joined HLI as chief technology officer after 16 years at Ancestry.com, a company that had worked with Calico. His focus was the integration of genomics and technology, as well as more effective and user-friendly ways to leverage HLI's Health Nucleus software platform.

After Venter's departure, it was unclear what, precisely, the next move would be. Outright dissolution of the company was one possibility. That, or come up with a less costly way to deliver on HLI's big promise to revolutionize medicine. A 30-day deadline was set.

By midsummer 2018 the new team worked out a different approach: HLI would continue to focus on preventing disease early, a goal that Venter had all along considered a bedrock concept. The Health Nucleus approach would also remain central, integrating the use of MRI and other advanced scanning technologies while continuing to expand its database of omes: genome, metabolome, microbiome.

The major change came in shifting the scale and speed at which the company would now begin to move. The plan to open 50 Health Nucleus centers around the world was no more. Those centers were expensive and burdened by foreign regulatory issues. The way the board saw it, scaling them was not sustainable. Nor would Human Longevity seek any longer to aggressively gather a million integrated genomes—certainly not by 2020.

HLI's new strategy was to disintermediate traditional medicine in the way that Airbnb and Uber had disrupted the hospitality and transportation industries. The current Health Nucleus center in San Diego would remain. But instead of the costly rollout of its own facilities worldwide, HLI began planning partnerships with a variety of institutions: physicians interested in longevity medicine, hospitals and clinics that wanted to prevent or slow the diseases of aging. HLI's partners would gather participating patients' blood tests, gather their omes, and provide imaging to HLI while the Health Nucleus service—now called Core Reports—would provide an online interface, as well as available experts to explain what all the data revealed. The key to the new approach was the software platform and database analyses that HLI proposed to deliver without the cost of brick-and-mortar HNX centers spread around the globe.

This model was similar to the back-end software platform and front-end interface that Airbnb uses to make it so easy for its partners to service millions of overnight guests around the world. Except in this case, the same sort of artificial intelligence that had the seer-like potential to reveal a customer's future health would now power HLI's platform.

Karow called this "democratizing precision health analytics," which was another way of saying that HLI could still create a better medical mousetrap while simultaneously generating income and enlarging its all-important genomic database. After all, no one doubted that the Health Nucleus approach was working; by the end of 2016, after 500 clients had passed through the San Diego office, 30 percent discovered ailments they didn't know they had, and another 14 percent learned of entirely new health issues that were potentially lethal. Now, almost two years later, 3,000 participants had used Health Nucleus, and the numbers had jumped to 40 and 14 percent, respectively. Obviously the preventative approach was getting results—and, again, these were people who thought they were in excellent health.

Given these successes, Karow wondered what HLI would find as prices dropped and partner organizations joined its more mainstream ranks. Theoretically, as prices decreased further, the database and analytics would grow richer; at least, that was the plan and hope. Today the cost of sequencing a human genome stands at roughly $1,000—$700 less than it was only three years earlier—and full-body MRIs are being completed in 45 minutes, rather than the one to two hours that most HNX scans initially took. By 2020, Karow predicts, services will drop from $5,000 an HNX patient to $1,500 or less, and full-body MRIs will be completed in 30 minutes. The main thing was to build on past successes and focus on what Karow called a workable "commercial strategy."

Still, by early 2019, the new HLI had yet to nail down even one Health Nucleus business partner. But Karow insisted the company's finances were solid and partnerships would soon materialize. After all, who would have thought, when Airbnb was launched in 2008, it would be booking a million rooms a night within five years?

Given Venter's past, you could almost have predicted the events that unfolded at Human Longevity, Inc. The man attracted drama like mass attracts gravity. He was the hare, not the tortoise. *Do the experiment!* But HLI's pockets weren't as deep as Calico's, and even Silicon Valley investors have their limits. As one member of the genomic community put it, Venter was complicated. He lived by the idea that you stake out big goals and then try to live up to them. Sometimes it works; sometimes you crash.

Not that any of this was likely to stop Venter. He had been down roads like these before—in Vietnam, in Buffalo, at NIH, at Celera, and now at HLI. His passion for arresting aging remained strong. In the lawsuit that HLI filed, the company alleged that Venter, immediately after his departure, had begun planning to create a new company that would explore the "preventative medicine space." Whether that was on the docket, or even true, remained to be seen, and Venter couldn't say much while dealing with a lawsuit. As the summer of 2018 progressed, he and his wife, Heather Kowalski, said they had taken some time to "regroup, reassess, and de-stress." By the fall, Venter had gotten back into the swing of things at JCVI and was continuing his ongoing organ transplant work with Martine Rothblatt at United Therapeutics. Was he giving up? It didn't seem likely. It just wasn't in his DNA.

29 | PLAN A

After all the conversations, queries, and explorations into the complicated ways death might be arrested; after I had traveled 50,000 miles from here to there and back again, meditating on what The End really meant, Hugh Hixon kept edging into my mind. I decided to go back for a visit and walk among Alcor's shiny canisters and patients as they mutely awaited resurrection. There, Hixon—the constant gardener—remained, devotedly shuffling among his stainless steel dewars, topping them off, and, now and again, tipping the people who hoped never to die into their frigid cocoons.

Professor Laurence Pilgeram was still there, in one of the neuro cans. But his family wasn't happy about that. They are suing Alcor for one million dollars, arguing that Pilgeram didn't want to be a neuro after all.

But that wasn't stopping other Alcor members from using the foundation's services. When I last checked, neuro member A-1547 had passed through the veil, Norma Peterson. She was living near Alcor in a memory care nursing home. Then one February morning her heart gave out. The FCP team was right there. They performed the Final Protocols and, soon after, her vitrified body was placed in its appointed canister.

Hixon's words echoed in my mind. *Time is our enemy. I can't stop it, but I sure as hell can slow it down.* And he was doing just that. Counting Norma Peterson, 31 more patients had arrived at Alcor's Chill Chamber since the day Laurence Pilgeram's heart stopped in April 2015. Diane Cremeens, Alcor's patient coordinator, said that in just those four years, people's views of cryonics were changing. Interest was up, significantly. The calls she received about Alcor's services were now arriving daily, and the foundation was adding roughly one new member a month. A few years ago that would have been unthinkable.

But again, Alcor was plan B. Where was plan A?

CALICO WAS WORKING ON THAT. The proof came just before and just after the beginning of 2018, when Art Levinson told me about two remarkable discoveries made at the lab. Each revealed that science might outwit aging after all, and finally turn Gompertz's rising curve into the long, flat line of unending youth the company was built to create.

The first discovery came from Shelley Buffenstein's preposterous mole rats. The findings revealed beyond a shadow of doubt that the critters simply refused to age.[23] Even as the years passed, their hearts remained strong, females kept breeding even after 30 years, and their body compositions, bone quality, and metabolism functioned as well as they did when they were pups.

This was not simply surviving to a ripe old age, like Ikaria's centenarians. This was as if a 100-year-old was romping around in the body and mind of a teenager. The little animals did die, eventually, of course, but not from aging; maybe a fight, or because of a genetic problem with a faulty organ or gland. But not from growing old. For Levinson, this proved that it was possible for a mammal to defy beta: the intrinsic, unstoppable killer. Now, Calico hoped to pass the same secrets on to *Homo sapiens*. Figuring that out might take some time, but at least now it looked as if science had at last proven that somehow aging could be stopped.

Calico's second discovery unveiled the opposite side of the coin: the creation of youth. This research had to do with the way eggs and sperm talk to one another.

In any living organism, eggs sit dormant in the female, ready to be fertilized. But during that time, like every other cell in the body, the eggs also age, accumulating small clumps: the evidence of time's damage. Given that damage, how can an older animal create a brand-new offspring, the epitome of youth?

Cynthia Kenyon's group found the answer as they watched *C. elegans* sperm approach the creatures' eggs. (Worms have sperm and eggs too.) In real time, they could see the sperm sending a chemical signal that awakened tiny membranes called lysosomes within the egg. These then reached out like long fingers to snatch the damaged clumps and obliterate them. That meant that by the time the sperm arrived for the happy moment, the egg was perfectly rejuvenated, ready to begin fresh and new.

So far, Kenyon and her fellow researcher K. Adam Bohnert had only seen this happen in worms and, later, frogs. But maybe the mechanism worked in all living creatures, including humans. It made sense that it would. Why, after all, would evolution toss aside a system that worked so well?

This opened the possibility that a drug for humans could be developed that might trigger similar lysosomes to happily go about shredding damaged cells found throughout aging bodies—rejuvenating hearts, livers, muscle, skin, brain, and bone. Was this possible? "Maybe," said Kenyon, "maybe, maybe . . . with a little help from genetic engineering."

30 | UNBOUNDING THE FUTURE

By now, the last of the four forces that drive great endeavors was undeniably in the wind: Success. In May 2018, Japan's Ministry of Health gave researchers at Osaka University permission to begin injecting 100 million stem cells into three patients with advanced heart failure in 2019.[24] If a second trial involving 10 patients succeeds after that, scientists plan to roll the treatment out commercially.

Another 2018 study at the University of Washington revealed that when monkeys with damaged hearts were injected with stem cells from human hearts, their hearts regained up to two-thirds of their normal capacity. Essentially, the procedure turned their biological clocks backward. If these approaches work, they could slow or repair millions of damaged hearts. Stroke and heart disease continue to decline, but they are still the world's number one killers.

Meanwhile, Silicon Valley's millionaires and billionaires continue to transform their high-technology plays into longevity plays, investing money in venture funds like Proteus, and start-ups with names like Halcyon Molecular and Butterfly

Sciences. Some analysts reckon the market for regenerative medicine will hit $20 billion by 2025.

Aubrey de Grey was still funding multiple longevity research projects including one at the University of Arizona and another at Yale. His SENS Research Foundation was doing so well that by early 2018 the foundation had closed five million dollars in donations when it was only asking for $250,000.

In 2018 Celularity, Inc., the company Bob Hariri and Peter Diamandis founded, landed another $250 million from investors and a board of directors that included life coach guru Tony Robbins; Andrew von Eschenbach, former commissioner of the U.S. Food and Drug Administration; and John Sculley, ex-CEO of Pepsi and Apple (and the man who had ousted Steve Jobs in 1985). Celularity researchers were developing reconstructive and orthopedic treatments, as well as cures for wounds and burns. More than 12 preclinical trials were in the works. Hariri predicted that placental stem cell therapies would soon go mainstream. If they did, it would mark the first wave of biotech advancement—Kurzweil's Bridge Two arriving not on schedule but ahead of it.

One of Celularity's early investors, and a board member, turned out to be Bill Maris. Maris had surprised almost everyone in Silicon Valley with his departure from Google Ventures in 2016. He went on to create a new venture firm called Section 32, and by 2018, it had raised $350 million. The investments so far were going into life sciences, health care, and high technology. One of the largest investments ($133 million) was in a Silicon Valley start-up called Alector, which focuses on combining antibody technology and new discoveries in human genetics to develop novel therapies for Alzheimer's disease and other forms of dementia.

Peter Thiel, an Alcor board member, was busy too, having recently invested in more than 14 health and biotech companies. His fascination with parabiosis, the transfusion of young blood into older people, seemed to be gaining traction. Ambrosia, a start-up in Monterey, California, was selling transfusions of human plasma drawn from young donors to its 600 clients (average age 60) at $8,000 per 1.5 liters. Although the promise was to deliver a ready-made injection of youth, the jury was still out as to how effective that approach was.[25]

In addition to Celularity, Peter Diamandis had become involved in two more longevity ventures. One, founded by a team of Harvard researchers, is called Elevian and focuses on the same blood-based therapeutics Peter Thiel found so fascinating. It promises to "target root-cause aging processes" and "develop new medicines to restore regenerative capacity." One of the diseases now on their radar: sarcopenia. Diamandis's other venture is called Fountain, another partnership with Tony Robbins that involves a worldwide network of regenerative and longevity medical clinics linked to Celularity that sounded something like Venter's old HNX idea. As of early 2019, though, there had been no formal announcements.[26]

In the midst of these endeavors, Amazon CEO Jeff Bezos, now the world's richest human, had begun injecting tens of millions of dollars into longevity ventures—including Unity Biotechnology, the company backed by the Mayo Clinic that is working on ways to eliminate senescent cells in the body.

Even Bill Gates—the man who once remarked, "It seems pretty egocentric while we still have malaria and TB, for rich people to fund things so they can live longer"—was jumping on the longevity bandwagon. The cost of treating Alzheimer's in 2017, he said, was skyrocketing: $259 billion in the United States alone. Unchecked, it could rise to $1.1 trillion by 2050. During the past two years, Gates announced donations of $100 million of his own money for Alzheimer's and dementia research.[27]

My, how things had changed. In 2012, during that October dinner at Larry Page's house in Palo Alto, it had all sounded so crazy: the idea of stopping the world's most successful serial killer. But now it was happening. In early 2019 Art Levinson told me that Calico had begun early stage work with its pharmaceutical partner, AbbVie, to develop new drugs to treat cancer and neurodegeneration. He felt the progress was promising. Meanwhile, the company had expanded into new quarters next door, and the number of Calico employees was pushing 200. The need, the will, the money, and the science were all flowing. The death of dying was going mainstream.

Now what?

CAN DEATH BE CHEATED? Are we there yet? Do we even want to be?

I knew plenty of people who said they couldn't imagine living forever. It was wrongheaded, selfish, unnatural. Sometimes they just laughed. I didn't push it, but I had to wonder: When exactly was anyone ready to die? Really. What would any of us be thinking the day we gazed into the abyss knowing that this was *the moment?* Unless we were in unbearable pain, I was pretty sure we would all say, "Wait!"

The desire to avoid death is powerful. The very purpose of our genes is to keep us up and running so we can make more versions of ourselves. It's in the DNA, literally. Maybe that's why we spin the endless tales we do, imagining ways to outmatch death, generating explanations for heaven or reincarnation, Elysium or Nirvana. It may even be the reason for Ray Kurzweil's vision of a time and place where everyone is rejuvenated and their minds expanded, like angels on the Last Day—a nice sci-fi fairy tale to give death the runaround.

Yet, despite those drives, every one of us *is* dying, at least so far. It has always been that way—which can only mean that if we somehow eliminate our march to the grave, it is not simply going to bend the great river of human history. It's going to twist it in ways that will be difficult for us to wrap our currently mortal minds around.

When historians someday look over their shoulders at the early decades of the 21st century, they will not find that aging had been cured and the grim reaper put to ground. Not yet, because it hasn't happened. No one has resuscitated an Alcor patient. There are no stories of Celularity giving 90-year-olds an elixir that makes them suddenly look 30. And Calico has yet to hand out a pill that guarantees a healthy life beyond 300.

Nevertheless, something remarkable *has* happened. Science *is* going to cheat death. That line was crossed the day Art Levinson and Google hopped on board Bill Maris's genie-in-a-bottle idea—and the day Craig Venter, Peter Diamandis, and Bob Hariri launched Human Longevity, Inc. And those ventures emerged—whether or not anyone believes it—because decades earlier Ray Kurzweil began ardently plowing the longevity road, with some serious help from Aubrey de Grey. They were the catalysts that set the grand endeavor into motion and attracted billions of dollars to the immortality business.

The first breakthroughs are already in front of us, and a series of profound advancements will follow in the next five to ten years. At first the improvements will be small: stem cells for treating arthritis, battered knees, and organ disease. Next, we will see new and increasingly specific treatments for cancer and deteriorating brains, driven mostly by insights into human genomics. After that, further discoveries will arrest, and even reverse, the aging that evolution long ago foisted upon us.

All of this will happen as artificial intelligence comes increasingly to grips with the stubborn intricacies of human biology, using codes so elaborate that even their makers don't fully comprehend how they do what they do. Each insight will build as a growing generation of entrepreneurs, doctors, researchers, and computer scientists come to realize that what once looked like snake oil no longer is.

How will the world look when we are all living hundreds of years? Scenarios like that can go in a lot of directions. Scientists might decide they've pulled another Manhattan Project, and find themselves horrified at what their work has wrought. Maybe there will be so many of us that we'll burn the planet down, making immortality moot. Or perhaps Elon Musk will find ways, after all, to off-load millions of humans from Earth to set up shop on Mars.

As the wealth gap broadens, will the rich grow richer, and younger, while the less fortunate grow old, unable to pay for their personal rejuvenation? Maybe we will we stop having babies? That could happen. In the world's so-called developed countries, the longer people live, the fewer children they have. A recent *New York Times* poll revealed that Americans were having fewer children, mostly because the cost of having them was so high. But if we become a childless species, who would experience their first kiss? Their first swim? Their first Big Idea? And come to think of it, what would the world look like on Thanksgiving with 100 descendants on hand, and every one of them apparently the same age? Could marriages survive

400 years? Would there really be a difference between a mother who was 300 and a daughter who was 270, assuming there *was* a daughter?

One doctor I know suggested that in this brave new future, when we reach age 21, we'll have to make a choice: Either have children and die a normal death, or live extremely long, but childless. Maybe we will remain young, but grow emotionally withered and ossified, rocking in our chairs, endlessly checking our Twitter feeds. Or will we, now blessed with unlimited amounts of time, at last find the work that each of us truly loves? With our clocks stopped, we might discover more time to enjoy our families and closest friends, learn from our mistakes, and get our lives right: fulfilled and happy at last.

It may even happen that the heavenly future Ray Kurzweil imagines will abide, with the human race not only upgraded like flights of angels but released to live in whatever amplified mind we can imagine.

It's a lot to think about, the capsizing of the human condition. And any or all of these possibilities may soon unfold before us like some great and intricate tapestry. It's hard to say. The only certainty is that the unbounded future, when it comes, will mark a paradigm shift unlike any the world has ever seen: right up there with the arrival of hurtling asteroids, the appearance of extraterrestrials, and the emergence of machines as intelligent as we are.

Whatever happens, it's not going to be boring.

EPILOGUE: THE END OF THE END

was sitting with Ray Kurzweil one Friday afternoon when I asked him how he felt about the passage of time . . . and the idea of running out of it. He didn't like to talk about it much these days, but in 2008 he had made a pilgrimage to Mount Auburn Hospital in Boston to have his chest cracked open, and his mitral heart valve repaired. It was a genetic shortcoming, lifelong, and it needed to be taken care of. A leaky heart valve is never a recipe for immortality.

The procedure didn't require new valves from pigs, only some suturing. Doctors felt the valve would be just fine for the foreseeable future. So when I brought up the question of mortality, he just grinned that same big kid grin he showed everyone on *I've Got a Secret*. "I worry about that a lot less," he said, "now that I know I'm not going to die."

And why should he think otherwise? The Bridges were advancing. Nanotechnology was evolving, and artificially intelligent algorithms were devotedly undoing the mysteries of *Homo sapiens'* demise every day. For Kurzweil, it was only a matter of time, and time's acceleration.

After all these years, there could be little doubt that Kurzweil had indeed accomplished the promise he had made during his childhood days in Jackson Heights. He *had* changed the world—less with his inventions than his ideas. Others may have explored the notion of living forever, but no one had driven the message into the mainstream with the unrepentant fervor of Raymond Kurzweil. And no one hammered away harder at the importance of exponential growth than he— science driven by the irresistible fusion of human and artificial intelligence. More than ever, he, like Levinson and Venter, Hariri and even de Grey, had come to believe that any problem could be solved—even the one that, so far, had killed every living thing on Earth.

Venter had clearly faced a few rocky years since the creation of Human Longevity, Inc. There was the prostate cancer, then his departure from HLI. In August 2017, his mother, Elizabeth, passed away at age 94. Venter always said that the last mortal barrier each of us faces is the one between our parents and us. Now she was gone, and so was the barrier.

Not that he was embracing the idea of stepping into the grave. When I put the question of his personal mortality to him during one of our meetings, he mentioned he had recently turned 70 and had to admit some days he was feeling the deterioration of his genes. But that didn't mean he planned to roll over. In fact, one of the things that really ticked him off that 70th year was a letter from the federal government saying he was required to begin taking his Social Security benefits. When you hit age 70½ that was the law, whether you wanted to collect the checks or not. But, dammit, Social Security checks were for old people, not him. Even worse, this made a statement about the way the world saw age 70—that it was just a matter of time before you hopped into the funeral casket while the dearly beloved nodded and murmured over what a fine person you were. He still planned on living nicely past 100, and racing sailboats and riding his motorcycle at age 87, the way he had in his pre-Vietnam days. In the meantime, prostate or not, HLI or no HLI, a lot of work remained to be done, and he planned to keep at it.

Art Levinson had neither developed cancer nor had his heart opened for inspection. But he was as lucky to be alive as either Craig Venter or Ray Kurzweil. Two different diseases had killed his mother in her 30s and father in his 60s, but so far he had managed to elude those particular genes.

More than once Levinson told me he didn't spend a lot of time trying to improve his personal health span—or, for that matter, count on life everlasting at all, even though it was Calico's stock-in-trade. No supplements. No MRIs. No genetic tests. Nor had he signed up for Alcor. A little tennis pretty much summed up his days burning calories, unless you wanted to count the pacing. Levinson was a world-class pacer. His Apple Watch routinely recorded walks of four miles a day: 10,000 steps, almost all of them as he walked Calico's corridors and labs, peeking in on the Lily Pond or Middle Earth. He ate a lot of fish (but never orange roughy anymore), and loved his latest gadget, an app paired with a digital strip of sensors that told him whether or not he was getting in some good, quality sleep. So far, his efficiency was first-rate: a sleeping heart rate between 44 and 49 beats per minute, and a respiration of 11 per.

When I asked Levinson about the idea of growing older, his answer surprised me, mainly because I expected him to skirt the question. Among the ironies in his life was that he was both fascinated with death, and in complete denial about it. But that day he answered the question straight out. His biggest concern was the loss of the people he cared about, but he tried not to dwell on that. He preferred to focus on how lucky he was. People underestimated the importance of luck, good or bad. Never think you were better than anyone else, he said, because luck could lift you up or slam you down in a heartbeat. If anybody felt he had made it big solely because he was brilliant or creative, or somehow superior—well, that made him a fatuous ass. For him, denial of death was best. Never mind The End. Just keep feeling like an 11-year-old and have at it.

IT WASN'T LONG AFTER those conversations that I made one final journey: this one back to Ikaria, the place where old Stamatis Moraitis had returned with terminal cancer and then lived another 35 years. And the place where Icarus, or the myth of him, plunged to death on fluttering wings.

Ikarians kindly pointed out the exact location of their namesake's death for me, and off I went to track it down. It took some work to get there. Even for Ikaria, it's an out-of-the-way place, located at the base of a steep cliff on the west side of the island. An immense slab of flat granite marks it: a good acre of slanted rock that looked as if it had been tossed at the Aegean by an angry god.

I stood upon it, feeling tiny, and looked up at the perfect cobalt sky. I could imagine Icarus floating high, riding the trade winds, and then suddenly plummeting toward me—a boy frantically screaming and flapping, the bright orb of the hot sun above him and his great wings now melted and useless when just a moment ago they had been lifting him high above the sea, so free and powerful, attaining the impossible.

There was a metaphor here about death and science, desire and pride, and messing with Mother Nature. It was as old as humanity itself. The boy had thought he was invincible, above the laws of nature. And then he had flown too close to the sun. His father, Daedalus—the greatest scientist and inventor of his time—had warned him not to fly too high, but he couldn't help himself. The impossible can be intoxicating that way.

Which path will humanity take? Will we fly too close to the sun? Or take the advice Daedalus gave Icarus: *By all means, boy, fly, but not too high.* It's hard to say; humans are unpredictable that way. But maybe, I thought, gazing up at the wide and brilliant sky, these questions only begged the next, even larger, question: When forever comes, will we be able to survive it?

ACKNOWLEDGMENTS

Not a word of thanks can be written on this page until it is written first for Cyndy, my wife, best friend, and the core of our family. Without her, none of this manuscript would have been possible. Cyn sometimes told me, "You know this book about immortality is going to kill you." But I suspect it was harder on her than me. She had to put up with my insane travel, my antics, the incessant barrage of this idea or that problem or the latest finding tossed at her daily. And yet she always willingly peeled her eyelids when I asked her, once again, to read another version of the manuscript. Cyndy is one of the best reasons why living 300 or 400 years would be a good thing. She is positive proof that there is hope for the human race if we can just be like her—insightful, warm, intelligent, patient, and loving. The same goes for our children, Molly, Steven, Hannah, and Annie, all four of whom have supported me from the first kernel of this idea to its completion.

Many others, of course, helped bring *Immortality, Inc.* to fruition. My deepest thanks to the National Geographic Society and the Society's director of expeditions, Rebecca Martin, whose grant supported this project from the start, even though it didn't stack up as a "classic" National Geographic expedition. Without this backing, I would never have been able research this book as deeply as I did. To Rob McQuilkin, my agent, I am profoundly grateful. The word "calm" should be in Rob's middle name, or maybe "intelligent" or "insightful." His personal and editorial support have been invaluable, and this book would not exist if not for his help. I am also deeply indebted to the editors at National Geographic Partners who backed the idea for this book and its many tangled themes rather than forcing it to become a straight-out science or how-to book. Susan Hitchcock, *Immortality*'s editor, has been extraordinarily strong and dedicated. Throughout, she held fast to the book's story and core goals, and never gave up helping to make the book better right up to the final manuscript. The same goes for Hilary Black, an insightful supporter from start to finish, and Bill Strachan, who helped advance the book's overall arc.

I also want to thank Sanjana Bendi, University of Pittsburgh student and doctor-to-be, for managing to accurately transcribe hours upon hours of interviews. No matter how complex the material or how garbled the conversations, she always managed to deliver excellent transcriptions of my stumbling efforts. To my friends and trusted readers, I will always be grateful. Reading is incredibly time consuming. Reading more than one version of a manuscript is doubly so (or worse), yet Eric Ruben, Fran Johns, Cheryl Pierce, Wendy Roberts, and my daughters Molly and Hannah Walter all took the time to provide me honest and insightful feedback.

Finally, thank you to all of the people I harangued and pestered and tracked down for the interviews needed to write this book. These include many hours of meetings, phone calls, and emails with Ray Kurzweil, Arthur Levinson, Craig Venter, Aubrey de Grey, Robert Hariri, as well as long sessions with Bill Maris, David Botstein, Hal Barron, Cynthia Kenyon, Daphne Koller, Amalio Telenti, Riccardo Sabatini, Ken Bloom, Brad Perkins, Heather Kowalski, Max More, Natasha Vita-More, and many others. A special thanks to Aimee Markey at Calico Labs for arranging so many meetings. In the earliest days of this quest, Ray Kurzweil was especially helpful, not only in making himself available, but by providing initial access to Art Levinson and Craig Venter.

All of these people helped me create the book I set out to write. If anything good came of it, you have them to thank. But if you find any mistakes, that's on me.

NOTES

CHAPTER 1

1. UPMC is now in trials to use these procedures on humans suffering from massive blood loss caused by gunshot wounds, traumatic automobile accidents, or other lethal damage.

CHAPTER 2

2. Heaven's Gate was an American UFO religious cult founded in 1974 and based in San Diego, California. On March 26, 1997, police discovered the bodies of 39 members of the group who had participated in a mass suicide to reach what they believed was an extraterrestrial spacecraft following comet Hale–Bopp.

CHAPTER 3

3. In 1899, cancer ranked as the nation's seventh most lethal disease.
4. Additional details about this can be found at the American Cancer Institute here: https://www.cancer.org/latest-news/cancer-statistics-report-death-rate-down-23-percent-in-21-years.html.

CHAPTER 4

5. For more information see: https://www.who.int/media centre/news/releases/2012/dementia_20120411/en.

CHAPTER 8

6. Frank Rosenblatt created the famous perceptron algorithm in 1957, the first computer that could learn new skills by trial and error, using a type of neural network that simulated human thought processes. Among his many other insights, Marvin Minsky's strong suit was artificial neural networks. Both scientists believed it was ultimately possible to create machines that acted human.

7. Kleiner later became Kurzweil's longtime business partner, and the chief financial officer of many of his companies.

CHAPTER 10

8. The story of why Rosalind Franklin was not awarded the Nobel Prize is complicated. Her death in 1958 precluded her winning a Nobel Prize since the prizes are not awarded posthumously, and the Nobel committees had not completed their research nor made their final decisions before her death. Also, no more than three scientists could be awarded any one prize. But there are indications that Watson and Crick underplayed the importance of her role in revealing the first x-ray image of the DNA molecule that was so crucial to their work. In 1962, Watson suggested that he and Crick should have been awarded the Nobel in physiology or medicine (as they were), and Wilkins and Franklin should have been awarded the prize in chemistry. Later, much more information came out about the importance of Franklin's work. And in 1982 Aaron Klug, Franklin's colleague and the principal beneficiary in her will, was awarded the Nobel Prize in chemistry for the very research Franklin had initiated and that she introduced to Klug before her death. Had she survived, it's very likely she would have won the prize in 1982.

CHAPTER 12

9. This has turned out not to be true. In fact, for the first time since the early part of the 20th century, life expectancy dropped in 2015, 2016, and 2017 in the United States. The major culprits: opioid overdoses and rising suicide rates. More recently, Kurzweil has predicted that by 2029 we will be increasing our life span by a year every year going into the future.

CHAPTER 15

10. There is some doubt as to whether Steve Jobs actually said "dent in the universe." During a 1985 *Playboy* interview, Jobs did use a very similar phrase, but instead said "ding in the universe." You can find the entire interview at reprints .longform.org/playboy-interview-steve-jobs.

CHAPTER 17

11. You can read a description of Hariri's original patent at: patents.justia.com/patent/7045148.

CHAPTER 18

12. Precisely speaking, this formula is known as the Gompertz-Makeham Law of Mortality. Gompertz's original formula did not include "λ" or gamma. William Makeham, another English actuary and mathematician, added it in the mid-1800s. For more details on Gompertz's law, explore "A Simple Derivation of the Gompertz Law for Human Mortality" by B. I. Shklovskii. A PDF is available at arxiv.org/PS_cache/q-bio/pdf/0411/0411019v3.pdf.

13. The "e" or epsilon in the formula is a variable commonly used in mathematics that has negligible effect, but is often included.

CHAPTER 20

14. You can also see examples of the Face Project's results in Sabatini's 2016 TED Talk here: ted.com/talks/riccardo_ sabatini_how_to_read_the_genome_and_build_a_human_ being.

CHAPTER 22

15. Stamatis passed away February 3, 2013, 35 years after he was diagnosed with cancer. He was either 98 or 102. He was never sure of his exact birth date. For more, read pappaspost.com/ remembering-stamatis-moraitis-man-almost-forgot-die.

CHAPTER 24

16. For more details on findings from Health Nucleus, see Human Longevity, Inc.'s paper, "Precision Medicine Screening Using Whole-Genome Sequencing and Advanced Imaging to Identify Disease Risk in Adults," biorxiv.org/content/ early/2017/05/03/133538, also subsequently published in *Proceedings of the National Academy of Sciences (PNAS),* doi: 10.1073/pnas.1706096114. Also, see Ryan Cross's article "This $25,000 Physical Has Found Some 'Serious' Health Problems. Others Say It Has Serious Problems," *Science* magazine, sciencemag.org/news/2017/05/25000-physical -has-found-some-serious-health-problems-others-say-it -has-serious.

CHAPTER 25

17. Martine Rothblatt was also former president of Geostar and the world's highest paid transgender person. In 2013, she made $38 million. washingtonpost.com/lifestyle/magazine/ martine-rothblatt-she-founded-siriusxm-a-religion-and

-a-biotech-for-starters/2014/12/11/5a8a4866-71ab-11e4
-ad12-3734c461eab6_story.html.

18. For more about this remarkable event, read Pam Belluck, "Chinese Scientist Who Says He Edited Babies' Genes Defends His Work," *New York Times,* November 28, 2018; and Rob Stein, "Chinese Scientist Says He's First to Create Genetically Modified Babies Using Crispr," National Public Radio *(Morning Edition),* November 26, 2018, npr.org/ sections/health-shots/2018/11/26/670752865/chinese -scientist-says-hes-first-to-genetically-edit-babies.

19. Two studies link aging and reduced muscle mass. This study showed that an increase in muscle mass and exercise seemed to reduce the likelihood of cancer. See J. R. Ruiz, X. Sui, F. Lobelo, et al., "Muscular Strength and Adiposity as Predictors of Adulthood Cancer Mortality in Men," *Cancer Epidemiology Biomarkers and Prevention* 18, no. 5 (2009): 1468–76, doi:10.1158/1055-9965.EPI-08-1075, ncbi.nlm.nih.gov/pmc/ articles/PMC2885882. For another study that indicates a correlation between increased muscular strength and longer life, see Jonatan R. Ruiz, Xuemei Sui, Felipe Lobelo, James R. Morrow, Allen W. Jackson, Michael Sjöström, et al., "Association Between Muscular Strength and Mortality in Men: Prospective Cohort Study," *BMJ* 337 (2008): doi.org/ 10.1136/bmj.a439.

CHAPTER 26

20. Though foreshadowed in earlier short stories, Isaac Asimov originally introduced his elegant Three Laws of Robots in his 1942 short story "Runaround," which was later included in his 1950 landmark collection of short stories *I, Robot.* The laws read: "One, a robot may not injure a human being or, through

inaction, allow a human being to come to harm . . . Two, a robot must obey orders given it by human beings except where such orders would conflict with the First Law . . . And law three, a robot must protect its own existence as long as such protection does not conflict with the First or Second Law."

CHAPTER 27

21. Ironically, Illumina, Inc., the DNA sequencing company used by Craig Venter and HLI, agreed to buy Pacific Biosciences in 2018 for $1.2 billion.

CHAPTER 28

22. From Nicholas Wade, "Thrown Aside, Genome Pioneer Plots a Rebound," *New York Times,* April 30, 2002, nytimes .com/2002/04/30/health/thrown-aside-genome-pioneer -plots-a-rebound.html.

CHAPTER 29

23. Calico's scientific paper published in *Mammalian Genome* can be viewed at ncbi.nlm.nih.gov/pmc/articles/PMC 4935753.

CHAPTER 30

24. This marks one of the first clinical applications of induced pluripotent stem (iPS) cells. See Katarina Zimmer's "First iPS Cell Trial for Heart Disease Raises Excitement, Concern" at the-scientist.com/news-opinion/first-ips-cell-trial-for -heart-disease-raises-excitement-concern-64743.

25. So far it seems there is little evidence that patients suffering from Alzheimer's can be treated effectively with blood

plasma from young donors. See Jocelyn Kaiser's "Blood From Young People Does Little to Reverse Alzheimer's in First Test" at sciencemag.org/news/2017/11/blood-young -people-does-little-reverse-alzheimer-s-first-test. However, scientists aren't giving up, and studies are ongoing: sanfrancisco.cbslocal.com/2017/11/06/could-blood-plasma -be-the-fountain-of-youth.

26. In spring 2018, Tony Robbins posted on Facebook that he had just completed a stem cell procedure that "saved my shoulder after struggling with excruciating pain from spinal stenosis and, more recently, a torn rotator cuff" (facebook .com/TonyRobbins/posts/10156548872894060). This was at the Stem Cell Institute in Panama City, Panama.

27. Gates made two announcements in November 2017: He donated $50 million to the Dementia Discovery Fund in the United Kingdom, and $50 million more for start-ups focused on Alzheimer's research. See Deniz Cam's "Bill Gates Is Investing $100 Million in Alzheimer's Research, Citing Family History," forbes.com/sites/denizcam/2017/11/13/ microsoft-billionaire-bill-gates-is-investing-100-million -in-alzheimers-research/#145c8c57328f.

SELECTED SOURCES
AND SUGGESTED READING

The great bulk of the research for this book was conducted over more than three years during long face-to-face interviews with many of the people featured herein.

All of these discussions, and the many phone conversations and emails that followed, were also supplemented by stacks of books, magazines, and websites as I attempted to complete my research. The following list is by no mean exhaustive, but I hope it will be helpful to any readers who are interested in investigating the subject further.

SELECTED SOURCES AND SUGGESTED READING

INTERVIEWS

Arthur Levinson, Calico Labs

Raymond Kurzweil, Alphabet, Inc.

J. Craig Venter, Human Longevity, Inc./The J. Craig
    Venter Institute

Robert Hariri, Human Longevity, Inc./Celularity

Peter Diamandis, Human Longevity, Inc./Celularity

Aubrey de Grey, SENS Research Foundation

Bill Maris, Section 32

Hal Barron, Calico Labs

David Botstein, Calico Labs

Cynthia Kenyon, Calico Labs

Daphne Koller, Calico Labs

Bob Cohen, Calico Labs

Ken Bloom, Human Longevity, Inc.

Brad Perkins, Human Longevity, Inc.

William Briggs, Human Longevity, Inc.

Amalio Telenti, Human Longevity, Inc.

Riccardo Sabatini, Human Longevity, Inc.

David Karow, Human Longevity, Inc.

Heather Kowalski, Human Longevity, Inc./The J. Craig
    Venter Institute

Max More, Alcor Life Extension Foundation

Hugh Hixon, Alcor Life Extension Foundation

Aaron Drake, Alcor Life Extension Foundation

Diane Cremeens, Alcor Life Extension Foundation

J. Craig George, North Slope Borough Department of
    Wildlife Management

Joon Yun, Palo Alto Investors, LLC

Jason Pontin, *MIT Technology Review*

Herbert Boyer, Genentech, Inc.

David Masci, Pew Research Center

Carolyn Funk, Pew Research Center

BOOKS

Botstein, David. *Decoding the Language of Genetics*. Cold Spring Harbor Laboratory Press, 2015.

Buettner, Dan. *The Blue Zones: 9 Lessons for Living Longer From the People Who Have Lived the Longest*. National Geographic, 2012.

———. *The Blue Zones Solution: Eating and Living Like the World's Healthiest People*. National Geographic, 2015.

Dawkins, Richard. *The Blind Watchmaker*. Penguin, 1986.

———. *The Selfish Gene*. Oxford University Press, 1989.

De Grey, Aubrey D. N. J. *The Mitochondrial Free Radical Theory of Aging* (Molecular Biology Intelligence series). R. G. Landis Co., 1999.

De Grey, Aubrey D. N. J. with Michael Rae. *Ending Aging—The Rejuvenation Breakthroughs That Could Reverse Human Aging in Our Lifetime*. St. Martin's Press, 2007.

"Dementia Cases Set to Triple by 2050 but Still Largely Ignored" (news release). The World Health Organization, April 11, 2012. www.who.int/mediacentre/news/releases/2012/dementia_20120411/en.

Friedman, Howard S., and Leslie R. Martin. *The Longevity Project*. Hudson Street Press, 2011.

Gertner, Jon. *The Idea Factory: Bell Labs and the Great Age of American Innovation*. Penguin Press, 2012.

Kurzweil, Raymond. *The Age of Spiritual Machines: When Computers Exceed Human Intelligence*. Penguin Books, 2000.

———. *How to Create a Mind: The Secret of Human Thought Revealed*. Viking Press, 2013.

——. *The Singularity Is Near: When Humans Transcend Biology.* Viking Press, 2005.

——. *The 10% Solution for a Healthy Life: How to Reduce Fat in Your Diet and Eliminate Virtually All Risk of Heart Disease.* Crown Publishers, 1993.

Kurzweil, Raymond, and Terry Grossman. *Fantastic Voyage: Live Long Enough to Live Forever.* Rodale Press, 2005.

——. *Transcend: Nine Steps to Living Well Forever.* Rodale, 2011.

Moravec, Hans P. *Mind Children: The Future of Robot and Human Intelligence.* Harvard University Press, 1988.

——. *Robot: Mere Machine to Transcendent Mind.* Oxford University Press, 1999.

More, Max, and Natasha Vita-More. *The Transhumanist Reader: Classical and Contemporary Essays on the Science, Technology, and Philosophy of the Human Future.* Oxford: John Wiley & Sons, 2013.

Mukherjee, Siddhartha. *The Emperor of All Maladies: A Biography of Cancer.* Scribner, 2010.

Nuland, Sherwin, B. *How We Die: Reflections on Life's Final Chapter.* Alfred A. Knopf, Inc., 1994.

Shreeve, James. *The Genome War: How Craig Venter Tried to Capture the Code of Life and Save the World.* Alfred A. Knopf, 2004.

Smith Hughes, Sally. *Genentech: The Beginnings of Biotech.* University of Chicago Press, 2011.

Venter, J. Craig. *A Life Decoded: My Genome: My Life*, Penguin Books, 2008.

——. *Life at the Speed of Light: From the Double Helix to the Dawn of Digital Life.* Penguin Books, 2014.

Watson, James D. *The Double Helix: A Personal Account of the Discovery of the Structure of DNA.* Atheneum, 1968.

Watson, James D., Andrew James Berry, and Kevin Davies. *DNA: The Story of the Genetic Revolution*. Alfred A. Knopf, 2017.

Weiner, Jonathan. *Long for This World: The Strange Science of Immortality*. Ecco, 2011.

MAGAZINES AND WEBSITES

Abdelgadir, Elamin, Razan Ali, Fauzia Rashid, and Alaaeldin Bashier. "Effect of Metformin on Different Non-Diabetes Related Conditions, a Special Focus on Malignant Conditions." *Journal of Clinical Medicine Research* 9, no. 5 (2017). www.ncbi.nlm.nih.gov/pmc/articles/PMC5380171.

Aberlin, Mary Beth. "Age-Old Questions: How Do We Age, and Can We Slow It Down?" *The Scientist,* March 1, 2015.

Achenbach, Joel. "Harvard Professor Says He Can Cure Aging, But Is That a Good Idea." *Washington Post* (Achenblog), December 2, 2015. washingtonpost.com/news/achenblog/wp/2015/12/02/professor-george-church-says-he-can-reverse-the-aging-process.

Asian Scientist Newsroom. "Removing Old Cells Could Prevent Arthritis." *Asian Scientist,* June 14, 2017.

Baer, Drake. "5 Amazing Predictions by Futurist Ray Kurzweil That Came True—and 4 That Haven't." *Business Insider,* October 20, 2015. www.businessinsider.com.au/15-startling-incredible-and-provactive-predictions-from-googles-genius-futurist-2015-9.

Bansal, Ankita, and Heidi A. Tissenbaum. "Quantity or Quality? Living Longer Doesn't Necessarily Mean Living Healthier." *The Scientist,* March 1, 2015.

Bohnert, K. Adam, and Cynthia Kenyon. "A Lysosomal Switch Triggers Proteostasis Renewal in the Immortal *C. elegans* Germ Lineage." *Nature,* November 30, 2017.

Brooker, Katrina. "Google Wants You to Live Forever." *Bloomberg Markets,* April 2015.

Buettner, Dan. "The Island Where People Forget to Die." *New York Times,* October 24, 2012. www.nytimes.com/2012/10/28/magazine/the-island-where-people-forget-to-die.html.

Buhr, Sarah. "With $250 Million, Peter Diamandis' New Startup Is All About Taking Stem Cells From Placentas." *TechCrunch,* February 15, 2018.

"Cancer Progress Report 2011: Transforming Patient Care Through Innovation." The American Association for Cancer Research, 2011. www.cancerprogressreport.org/Pages/cpr11-contents.aspx.

Connor, Steve. "The Miracle Cure: Scientists Turn Human Skin Into Stem Cells." *The Independent,* February 9, 2014.

Cross, Ryan. "This $25,000 Physical Has Found Some 'Serious' Health Problems. Others Say It Has Serious Problems." *Science,* May 12, 2017. sciencemag.org/news/2017/05/25000-physical-has-found-some-serious-health-problems-others-say-it-has-serious.

Cutas, D. E. "Life Extension, Overpopulation and the Right to Life: Against Lethal Ethics." *The Journal of Medical Ethics,* August 29, 2008.

De Grey, Aubrey. 1997. "A Proposed Refinement of the Mitochondrial Free Radical Theory of Aging." *Bioessays,* February 1997.

———. "Life Span Extension Research and Public Debate: Societal Considerations." Methuselah Foundation, August 7, 2011. www.sens.org/files/pdf/ENHANCE-PP.pdf.

De Magalhães, João Pedro. "The Big, the Bad and the Ugly: Extreme Animals as Inspiration for Biomedical Research." *EMBO Reports,* July 3, 2015.

Di Iulio, Julia, Istvan Bartha, Emily H. M. Wong, Hung-Chun Yu, Victor Lavrenko, Dongchan Yang, Inkyung Jung, Michael A. Hicks, Naisha Shah, Ewen F. Kirkness, Martin M. Fabani, William H. Biggs, Bing Ren, J. Craig Venter, and Amalio Telenti. "The Human Noncoding Genome Defined by Genetic Diversity." *Nature Genetics* 50 (2018): 333–37. nature.com/articles/s41588-018-0062-7.

Friend, Tad. "The God Pill." *The New Yorker,* April 3, 2017.

Golden, Frederick, and Michael D. Lemonick. 2000. "The Race Is Over." *Time,* July 3, 2000.

"Google Announces Calico, a New Company Focused on Health and Well-Being." News from Google, September 18, 2013. googlepress.blogspot.com/2013/09/calico-announcement .html.

Gump, Jacob M., and Andrew Thorburn. "Autophagy and Apoptosis—What's the Connection?" *Trends in Cell Biology* 21, no. 7 (2011): 387–92. www.ncbi.nlm.nih.gov/pmc/articles/ PMC3539742.

Hariri, Robert J. "Method of Collecting Placental Stem Cells." U.S. Patent No. 7045148; Filed: December 5, 2001. patents .justia.com/patent/20020123141#history.

Herships, Sally. "There Are More Adult Diapers Sold in Japan Than Baby Diapers." Marketplace, August 29, 2016. market place.org/2016/08/09/world/japans-changing-culture.

Highfield, Roger. "What's Wrong With Craig Venter?: Multi-Millionaire Maverick, Says He Can Help You Live a Better, Longer Life." *New Republic,* February 2, 2016.

Hou, Yujun, Sofie Lautrup, Stephanie Cordonnier, Yue Wang, Deborah L. Croteau, Eduardo Zavala, Yongqing Zhang, et al. "NAD+ Supplementation Normalizes Key Alzheimer's Features and DNA Damage Responses in a New AD Mouse

Model With Introduced DNA Repair Deficiency." *PNAS* 115, no. 8 (2018): E1876–85. www.pnas.org/content/115/8/E1876.

Ingraham, Christopher. "Americans Are Dying Younger Than People in Other Rich Nations." *Washington Post,* December 27, 2017. washingtonpost.com/news/wonk/wp/2017/12/27/americans-are-dying-younger-than-people-in-other-rich-nations.

Jeon, Ok Hee, Chaekyu Kim, Remi-Martin Laberge, Marco Demaria, Sona Rathod, Alain P. Vasserot, Jae Wook Chung, et al. "Local Clearance of Senescent Cells Attenuates the Development of Post-Traumatic Osteoarthritis and Creates a Pro-Regenerative Environment." *Nature Medicine* 23 (2017): 775–81.

Jones, Brad. "A Breakthrough Initiative Has Been Announced to Manufacture Human Organs." Futurism (Health & Medicine), November 11, 2017.

Joseph, Nancy. "Leading Biotechnology Into the 21st Century." *Perspectives Newsletter,* College of Arts and Sciences: University of Washington, June 1, 2000.

Keane, Michael, Jeremy Semeiks, Bo Thomsen, and Joao Pedro De Magalhaes. "Insights Into the Evolution of Longevity From the Bowhead Whale Genome." *Cell Reports,* January 6, 2015. cell.com/cell-reports/pdf/S2211-1247(14)01019-5.pdf.

Keep, Elmo. "Can Human Mortality Really Be Hacked?" *Smithsonian,* June 2017.

Kirkwood, Thomas. "Why Can't We Live Forever?" *Scientific American,* September 2010.

Kurzweil, Ray. "How My Predictions Are Faring: An Update by Ray Kurzweil." Kurzweil Accelerating Intelligence (blog),

October 1, 2010. www.kurzweilai.net/images/How-My
-Predictions-Are-Faring.pdf.

Lamming, Dudley W., and Sabatini, David M. "A Radical
Role for TOR in Longevity." *Cell Metabolism* 13, no. 6
(2011): 617–18. cell.com/cell-metabolism/fulltext/S1550
-4131(11)00186-0.

Lewis, Kaitlyn N., Ilya Soifer, Eugene Melamud, Margaret Roy,
R. Scott McIsaac, Matthew Hibbs, and Rochelle Buffenstein. "Unraveling the Message: Insights Into Comparative
Genomics of the Naked Mole-Rat." *Mammalian Genome* 27,
no. 7–8 (2016): 259–78. www.ncbi.nlm.nih.gov/pmc/
articles/PMC4935753.

López-Otin, Carlos, Maria A. Blasco, Linda Partidge, Manuel
Serrano, and Guido Kroemer. "The Hallmarks of Aging."
Cell, June 6, 2013.

Masci, David, and Funk, Carolyn. "Living to 120 and Beyond:
Americans' Views on Aging, Medical Advances and Radical
Life Extension." Pew Research Center, August 6, 2013.
pewforum.org/2013/08/06/living-to-120-and-beyond
-americans-views-on-aging-medical-advances-and-radical
-life-extension.

——. "To Count Our Days: The Scientific and Ethical Dimensions of Radical Life Extension." Pew Research Center,
August 6, 2013. pewforum.org/2013/08/06/to-count-our
-days-the-scientific-and-ethical-dimensions-of-radical-life
-extension.

McCracken, Harry, and Lev Grossman. "Google vs. Death: How
CEO Larry Page Has Transformed the Search Giant Into a
Factory for Moonshots." *Time,* September 30, 2013.
doi.org/10.1038/s41588-018-0062-7.

Miller, Claire Cain, and Pollack, Andrew. "Tech Titans Form

Biotechnology Company." *New York Times,* September 18, 2013.

Moustafa, Ahmed, Chao Xie, Ewen Kirkness, William Biggs, Emily Wong, Yaron Turpaz, Kenneth Bloom, Eric Delwart, Karen E. Nelson, J. Craig Venter, and Amalio Telenti. "The Blood DNA Virome in 8,000 Humans." *PLOS/Pathogens* 13, no. 3 (2017): e1006292. doi.org/10.1371/journal.ppat.1006292.

Ocampo, Alejandro, Pradeep Reddy, Paloma Martinez-Redondo, Aida Platero-Luengo, Fumiyuki Hatanaka, Tomoaki Hishida, Mo Li, David Lam, et al. "In Vivo Amelioration of Age-Associated Hallmarks by Partial Reprogramming." *Cell,* December 15, 2016.

O'Keefe, Brian. "Ray Kurzweil—The Smartest (or the Nuttiest) Futurist on Earth." *Fortune,* May 14, 2007.

Park, Alice. "Alzheimer's from a New Angle." *Time,* February 11, 2016.

———. "In 40 Years of Cancer Research, How Far Have We Come?" *Time,* September 21, 2011.

Pringle, Heather. "Long Live the Humans." *Scientific American,* October 2013.

Rosa, Cheryl, Judith Zeh, J. Craig George, Oliver Botta, Melanie Zauscher, Jeffrey Bada, and Todd M. O'Hara. "Age Estimates Based on Aspartic Acid Racemization for Bowhead Whales *(Balaena mysticetus)* Harvested in 1998–2000 and the Relationship Between Racemization Rate and Body Temperature." *Marine Mammal Science,* July 2013.

Rosenthal, Elizabeth. "Bird Flu Going to East Africa, United Nations Officials Fear." *New York Times International,* October 20, 2005.

Ruby, J. Graham, Megan Smith, and Rochelle Buffenstein. "Naked Mole-Rat Mortality Rates Defy Gompertzian

Laws by Not Increasing With Age." *eLife* 7 (2018): e31157. elifesciences.org/articles/31157.

Shermer, Michael. "Radical Life-Extension Is Not Around the Corner-Can Science and Silicon Valley Defeat Death?" *Scientific American,* October 1, 2016. scientificamerican.com/article/radical-life-extension-is-not-around-the-corner.

Sifferlin, Alexandra. "How Silicon Valley Is Trying to Hack Its Way Into a Longer Life." *Time,* February 16, 2017.

Simon, Stacy. "Cancer Statistics Report: Death Rate Down 23% in 21 Years." The American Cancer Society, January 7, 2016. cancer.org/latest-news/cancer-statistics-report-death-rate-down-23-percent-in-21-years.html.

Smith, Robin L. "The Regeneration Generation: A Conversation With Bob Hariri, Vice-Chairman and Co-Founder of Human Longevity Inc." Huffington Post, November 26, 2014.

Swisher, Kara. "Former Google Ventures CEO Bill Maris Has Decided Not to Go Ahead With a New $230 Million Health Care Fund." Recode, December 9, 2016. recode.net/2016/12/9/13901306/ceo-bill-maris-not-doing-230-million-health-care-fund.

Tchkonia, Tamara, Yi Zhu, Jan Van Deursen, Judith Campisi, and James L. Kirkland. "Cellular Senescence and the Senescent Secretory Phenotype: Therapeutic Opportunities." *The Journal of Clinical Investigation,* March 1, 2013.

Terry, Mark. "New Jersey Startup Celularity Launches With Clinical Assets From Big Name Biotechs." BioSpace, August 22, 2017.

The Scientist Staff. "How We Age: From DNA Damage to Cellular Miscommunication, Aging Is a Mysterious and Multifarious Process." *The Scientist,* March 1, 2015. the-scientist.com/features/how-we-age-35872.

Tullis, Paul. "Are You Rich Enough to Live Forever?" *Town and Country,* March 30, 2017.

Van Meter, Michael, Andrei Seluanov, and Vera Gorbunova. "Wrangling Retrotransposons—These Mobile Genetic Elements Can Wreak Havoc on the Genome." *The Scientist,* March 1, 2015.

Wade, Nicholas. "Scientist's Plan: Map All DNA Within 3 Years." *New York Times,* May 3, 1998.

——. "Craig Venter: A Maverick Making Waves." *New York Times,* July 27, 2000.

White, Mary C., Dawn M. Holman, Jennifer E. Boehm, Lucy A. Peipins, Melissa Grossman, and S. Jane Henley. "Age and Cancer Risk; A Potentially Modifiable Relationship." *The American Journal of Preventative Medicine* 46, no. 3, Suppl. 1 (2014): S7–S15. www.ncbi.nlm.nih.gov/pmc/articles/PMC4544764.

Williams, Ruth. "The Aging and Inflammation Link: A Protein That Keeps the Immune Response in Check Leads a Double Life as an Anti-Aging Factor." *The Scientist,* May 24, 2012.

World Alzheimer Report 2015: The Global Impact of Dementia. Alzheimer's Disease International, January 2016.

INDEX

INDEX

Index

ABOUT THE AUTHOR

Chip Walter is an author, journalist, filmmaker, and former CNN bureau chief. He has published articles in *National Geographic, The Economist,* the *Wall Street Journal,* and *Scientific American,* and he has written four earlier books, most recently *Last Ape Standing: The Seven-Million-Year Story of How and Why We Survived.* He lives in Pittsburgh. You can learn more about him and his writing at www.chipwalter.com and on Facebook or Twitter @chipwalter.